PRAISE FOR *SURVIVORS*

"A very useful book on an important topic. Everyone concerned with downsizings and reorganizations will learn important lessons from it."
William Bridges, Ph.D.
Author of the bestselling *JobShift* and *Transitions*

"*Survivors* outlines the challenges facing businesses in preparation for the next century and charges those responsible to plan for the survivors as well as to engage the survivors in implementing the future organization . . . healthy food for thought and action in corporate America."
Paula W. Carter
District Manager
AT&T

"Organizations that are trying to change are beginning to discover that in addition to changing, they have to help their people develop change capability, or the changes will slowly drift back to the status quo or worse. This book gives absolutely critical advice on how individuals and organizations can develop change capabilities."
Dennis Jaffe, Ph.D.
Professor
Saybrook Institute

"*Survivors* is the missing link needed in the Business section of all bookstores. It presents, quite accurately, every reason why employee 'survivors' elect to leave their companies and provides the 'Why didn't I think of that?' common-sense solutions to stop it. This is a must read!"
Linda Kline
President
Partners in Human Resources International

"*Survivors* addresses one of the most critical issues facing American corporations today. The insights described and actions recommended are excellent. Focusing on these recommendations will make the difference between mere compliance and wholehearted commitment on the part of employees."

Rich Burk
Sales Vice President
Pacific Bell

"Change, reorganization, and continuous improvement are now 'business as usual.' However, most companies are ill equipped to effectively lead and manage their most valuable asset, their people, during such time. *Survivors* provides an excellent framework to analyze the challenge of managing during turbulent times and protecting and preserving your human resources."

James A. Hoffman
Regional President
Key Bank

"Most companies involved in downsizings, consolidations, mergers, or acquisitions pay considerable attention to the employees who are losing their jobs. *Survivors* addresses the equally, if not more, important issue of ensuring the continued motivation and productivity of the employees who remain. Well researched and well written, it provides insights and pragmatic solutions to one of the most overlooked problems in organizational restructuring."

Edward T. McKeon
Vice President, Director of Corporate Relations
California Casualty Management Company

"During this period of corporate downsizing and structural change, executives need to be aware of the effects on employees. In this important new work, the authors find that the reason companies fail to achieve their goals is their employees' resistance to change and go on to tell executives what to do about it. This book fills an essential need for American corporations."

Ben E. Laden, Ph.D.
Economic Consultant
Former President, National Association of Business Economists

Survivors

SURVIVORS

How to Keep
Your Best People on Board
After Downsizing

—

Gayle Caplan and Mary Teese

DAVIES-BLACK PUBLISHING

Palo Alto, California

Published by Davies-Black Publishing, an imprint of Consulting Psychologists Press, Inc., 3803 East Bayshore Road, Palo Alto, CA 94303; 1-800-624-1765.

Special discounts on bulk quantities of Davies-Black books are available to corporations, professional associations, and other organizations. For details, contact the Director of Book Sales at Davies-Black Publishing, an imprint of Consulting Psychologists Press, Inc., 3803 East Bayshore Road, Palo Alto, CA 94303; 415-691-9123; Fax 415-988-0673.

Jacket illustration © John Martin/Stock Illustration Source, Inc.

Jacket photography by Russ Fischella

00 99 98 97   10 9 8 7 6 5 4 3 2 1

Printed in the United States of America

Library of Congress Cataloging-in-Publication Data
Caplan, Gayle
    Survivors : how to keep your best people on board
after downsizing / Gayle Caplan and Mary Teese. —
    1st ed.
       p. cm.
    Includes bibliographical references and index.
    ISBN 0-89106-091-X
    1. Labor turnover—United States. 2. Downsizing of
organizations—United States. 3. Employees—
United States—Attitudes. 4. Employment stabilization—
United States.
    I. Teese, Mary. II. Title.
HF5549.5.T8C36 1997
858.3′14—dc20
                            96-20606
                              CIP

FIRST EDITION
First printing 1997

To my children, Hilary and Andrew, she for her psychological insights, he for his shared gift for the written word. Their support never ceases to amaze me.

GC

To Jim, for his unflagging support and his understanding over the long haul; and to my daughter, Elizabeth, who unerringly had the right words at the right time to keep me going.

MT

CONTENTS

PREFACE

Gayle Caplan (Cap)

On January 6, 1993, I telephoned my friend Rita Green, the president of a search firm in Ohio. I called to wish her a happy new year. And, as I customarily did, I asked Rita how she anticipated her business was going to go in the new year.

"Great!" she said. "The recession's lifting; I've got a number of available positions, but you know what the problem always is: candidates, qualified candidates. Well, I've got plenty—and they're calling me for a change."

"Terrific!" I replied. "I'm not surprised by the candidates, though. With all the downsizing the Midwest has experienced . . . the layoffs. . . ."

"Oh, no," she interrupted, "it's not the ones who have been laid off I'm talking about. It's the people who are still employed—they want new positions. It's happening at other search firms as well, not just here in Ohio. And they're great candidates! Really, the cream of the crop."

I was struck by her comments. The current literature, news reports, everything I had read and heard suggested that people were feeling lucky to have a job. Feeling grateful—and even guilty—that they had been spared.

I called Mary.

Mary Teese

It was ironic. I had just received a call from a colleague. Dave's organization was experiencing downsizing. His job was safe. He was close to being vested. Yet Dave was telling me that he was thinking seriously about leaving.

Two months later, my friend Dave, the star performer, resigned—along with most of his department. None of them had new jobs or even the promise of employment when they gave notice.

Terry, another colleague, reported to us that he'd walked into his boss's office and told her that he had his résumé out and that unless things changed dramatically at the company, he'd be gone by the end of the year.

OUR SEARCH FOR ANSWERS

We were perplexed. Here were people leaving good jobs or looking for new ones in the midst of layoffs and cutbacks; star performers resigning; search firms flooded with résumés from those already employed.

These events aroused both our personal concern and our professional curiosity. As consultants and as managers ourselves, we had been dealing with organizational change for years.

We went first to the literature to find answers. Our search of a national database yielded 1,362 articles on downsizing, but only twenty-two on the people we'd been talking to and about—those employees referred to as survivors.

Even the studies we did find in our initial search yielded only second-hand accounts of survivors' attitudes and motivations. The sources for these accounts were managers, CEOs, and human resources and organization development professionals like us—not the survivors themselves.

So, we hadn't answered the question: Why were survivors leaving? Meanwhile, we were hearing about the same phenomenon at more and more companies.

We decided that if we wanted answers, we needed to take a more direct approach. We decided to interview survivors ourselves. We began by interviewing thirty survivors in the San Francisco Bay Area.

What these first interviewees told us matched what we expected to hear: that survivors, indeed, were feeling guilty that they, not their friends, had been selected to stay and simultaneously grateful that they still had jobs. But it was what these survivors told us above and beyond that—and the pervasiveness and intensity of their messages—that we found startling and perplexing. They were telling us what organizations didn't know—what they (the survivors) were doing and why as well as what actions they were planning to take. We heard about hidden files, customers turned away, interviews with other companies. We learned of covert plans for the future, from saying no to new assignments to resigning when children's orthodontia was done. What survivors were saying—as well as the anger and alienation that accompanied their words—surely represented more than the natural resistance phase accompanying transition.

But did these responses represent survivors generally, or had we uncovered an isolated pocket of hostility and resistance: disenfranchised, angry survivors referring their like-feeling friends?

It is now more than three years since we began our research. *Survivors* is the result. *Survivors* explains why key employees are leaving their organizations literally, or leaving figuratively by retiring on the job.

But *Survivors* does more than that. It also answers the critical question, What can organizations do to stop high performers from going out the door?

Survivors

- Profiles three distinct groups of survivors
- Examines survivors' issues and their impact on the organization and fellow employees
- Presents strategies and methods for dealing with these issues
- Identifies the barriers that may prevent an organization from effectively managing the changes
- Provides examples of organizations' Best Practices—those methods, programs, and tactics that are effective from survivors' points of view
- Lists the actions an organization must take to manage its own transition

Most importantly, it provides insights and strategies that you, the reader, can apply immediately in your organization, whether you are

- A CEO or company president who recognizes the correlation between dealing with the human aspects of restructuring and achieving bottom-line results.
- A line manager or supervisor looking for practical ways to avoid losing key performers and maintain productivity. You have the ultimate responsibility for "getting it done"—motivating, managing, and stopping the survivors from leaving. Many managers and supervisors we interviewed felt ill-prepared to deal with the day-to-day consequences of downsizing or rightsizing.
- A human resources professional, management trainer, or organization development consultant inside the organization. As a representative of management and an ombudsperson for employees, you bring a dual perspective to the development of change management strategy. How can you devise programs that speak to the needs of these two competing constituencies?
- An independent consultant who realizes that survivors now make up the population base of your client companies. Dealing with

survivors' issues and concerns is a part of your work, no matter what the assignment or presenting problem.

- A member of an outplacement firm that increasingly has responsibility for working with survivors as well as those laid off. Some of the studies and professionals quoted in the book come from those organizations.

- A mental health professional, employee assistance program provider, or career counselor who confronts the profound impact of work and the workplace on an individual's identity and sense of worth.

- A survivor who wonders whether other survivors are experiencing similar thoughts and feelings. Survivors have been very interested in our research and results, perhaps because we provide a voice for your unspoken concerns. This book offers reassurance that your thoughts and feelings are not unique or abnormal but echoed in the experiences of others.

- A family member or friend who wants to provide support to a survivor as well as understand, from the survivor's perspective, the behaviors and feelings he or she now brings to the relationship.

We recognize that there are various business books that treat aspects of downsizing or restructuring, including Robert Tomasko's *Downsizing* (1987), William Bridges' *JobShift* (1994), and Michael Hammer and James Champy's *Re-Engineering the Corporation* (1993). Other books address the topic of survivors more directly, including Bridges' *Surviving Corporate Transition* (1988) and *Managing Transitions* (1991) and David Noer's *Healing the Wounds* (1993).

What is different about *Survivors?*

We know of no other work that profiles survivors as distinct groups, each with its own set of issues and concerns. It is not our intent to put labels on people or to fit them into boxes. But addressing survivors as one population with common needs not only negates what they told us but suggests that one set of methods or strategies will address their concerns. Professional practice—and these survivors—have taught us that "one size does *not* fit all."

This is a firsthand account from the survivors; we are merely the narrators of their stories. "Who speaks for the survivors?" we ask in one chapter. We asked the same question when we reviewed the literature and found primarily secondhand accounts. In this book, the survivors speak for themselves.

All books offer recommendations and strategies. We have taken an additional approach. We point out the barriers that get in the way, that over and over prevent organizations from successfully implementing even the most comprehensive and well-considered plans. The same barriers, if unaddressed, will thwart companies' efforts to apply what we propose.

METHODOLOGY

Our research, our analysis, our writing—indeed, our entire approach—spring from our roles as practitioners.

Over the course of the last three years we

- Conducted oral interviews with eighty-seven survivors
- Surveyed seventy-three survivors through written questionnaires
- Solicited information from more than 400 survivors in our transition workshops and consulting assignments

Recognizing that confidentiality would be a concern for survivors, we did *not* call companies directly to find interviewees. Instead, we found them through what we called "dialing for survivors." We told colleagues and friends that we were seeking survivors from companies that had undergone downsizing and restructuring. Colleagues told colleagues. Employees told co-workers. Survivors told other survivors.

Not surprisingly, there was no shortage of potential interviewees. The difficulty was in overcoming people's reluctance to speak freely, despite our promises of anonymity. We held interviews in managers' offices behind closed doors, in after-work rendezvous at coffee shops far from an interviewee's employer, via prearranged phone conversations across time zones. Frequently, meetings were canceled, or someone simply failed to arrive, or voice mail greeted our scheduled call. The odds of a scheduled interview taking place were higher when survivors resided outside the San Francisco Bay Area, perhaps because they felt more secure, recognizing that we were unlikely to be acquainted with their current or former employer.

We also conducted spontaneous interviews, in movie theaters, on dog walks, at airport gates. One of our more memorable interviews began in the lavatory waiting line on a DC-10 and continued during most of the flight, Cap scribbling furiously on the cocktail napkins accompanying the peanuts.

These survivors represented a cross-section of persons still employed by an organization (whom we termed "survivor stayers") and individuals who, like Mary's friend Dave, had left voluntarily ("survivor leavers"). We selected survivors from different types of industries and sizes of companies. They varied in organizational rank and tenure as well as in gender and age. We wanted to see if those factors had any impact on the results.

They didn't.

Survivors came from cities across the U.S., including Boston, Denver, Atlanta, Los Angeles, Washington, D.C., Miami, and Toledo, Ohio. We wanted to know if what we had found in the San Francisco Bay Area could be explained regionally.

It couldn't.

We went to organizations directly to interview those responsible for managing the change—members of management ranging from CEOs to first-level supervisors. We talked with change management experts—human resources and organization development professionals, career counselors, and mental heath and employee assistance program providers. Some were company employees; others were private practitioners or members of consulting firms. We found many of these interviewees through referrals and contacts with professional organizations across the country.

We reviewed more than 300 articles on change, downsizing, and restructuring in the academic literature, professional journals, and the popular press. Our work builds on the research of Joel Brockner, Mitchell Marks, Kit Cameron, The Wyatt Company, Right Management Associates, Lee Hecht Harrison, and the American Management Association. Our analysis also relies on the models developed by William Bridges, Elizabeth Kübler-Ross, Cynthia Scott and Dennis Jaffe, and others.

Woven throughout the text are the comments of survivors. To protect confidentiality, we have changed locales, industries, positions, and survivors' gender. The change management professionals quoted in this book have given permission for the inclusion of their names. Some of their statements have been edited for brevity.

THE AUTHORS

As partners in training and consulting for eight years, we have worked with organizations experiencing all kinds of change. Our assignments have ranged from designing an operational system to team building or training new groups of managers.

One of us before starting a corporate career taught mental health professionals; the other gained an appreciation of company life through work in a variety of corporate environments. We have managed divisions, departments, and teams of employees.

Our formal education in psychology and social work and our experience with employees at all organizational levels aided us not only in evaluating what survivors told us but also in eliciting their stories. Creating "safe" environments in which people can take risks is a skill we both brought to our interviewing.

ORGANIZATION OF THE BOOK

Survivors is presented in an introductory chapter followed by three sections. Though some people skip from section to section when reading a book, we urge you to read this one in order, as each section builds on the previous ones.

The introductory chapter, "The Unexpected Costs of Downsizing," answers the question, Why bother dealing with survivors' issues? The chapter focuses on the unanticipated results and unexpected costs of downsizing and lays out the book's themes and premises.

Section One: "The Survivors" introduces the three distinct survivor groups we found. We profile each survivor group's characteristics, career focus, impact on other survivors, and challenges to the organization.

Section Two: "Keeping the Survivors on Board" examines the four issues—history, communication, change, and transition—that survivors identified as critical to their acceptance of the downsizing and their adaptation to the reorganized company. Each of the chapters in Section Two focuses on one of these issues, describing the issue and its impact from survivors' perspectives. Each chapter then provides organizational strategies and illuminates the barriers that frequently arise.

Section Three: "Keeping the Organization on Course" focuses on the organization's transition, occurring simultaneously with that of the survivors. It explains how managing the organization's transition affects the survivors, suggests the tasks the organization must accomplish in each of its transition phases, and identifies the common barriers that prevent management from completing the tasks.

THE BOTTOM LINE

Perhaps you're thinking, None of what you've said so far applies to our organization. We have not downsized nor merged, our best people are still in place, and we're growing.

Congratulations and good luck! But before you close this book, think about your new employees—the high performers who are carrying you forward to your goals. Where did the search firm tell you they came from? What was the nature of their prior work environment? Are they better acquainted with downsizing than you realize?

If your new employee was another organization's top performer, then certainly that company's loss is your gain. But how do you know whether that top producer is waiting for one indicator that replicates past experience—an indicator that will justify updating the résumé yet again?

How do these employees view you—that is, what kind of filter has past experience with downsizing put in front of their eyes? Do they expect you to lead the organization so it doesn't happen—to them—again?

How will you use that information rather than have it turned against you? These "survivors" may have their antennae out to pick up any signs that the company is in trouble. So they are valuable in ways you probably haven't considered.

Increasingly, organizations are managing survivors, whether they are survivors of their creation or survivors of another company's reorganization. So survivor characteristics, concerns, and behaviors are part of the package a new employee brings and which must be addressed.

These are the issues that survivors bring. If any or all of these apply or are of concern to you or your organization, then the time you devote to this book is well spent.

ACKNOWLEDGMENTS

Our heartfelt thanks and appreciation to:

Rita Green, who started it all, piquing our curiosity and challenging our assumptions with her astute observations.

Ashley Penney and Lee Langhammer Law, who convinced us that there was a book to be written.

Rose Cohan, Anna Ewins, Aubrey Pettaway, and Paula Taylor, whose valuable insights and continuing feedback shaped the work from beginning to end.

Our friends—Dina Burg, Linda Cashdan, Miriam Counts, Susan Laden, Bern Peterson, Roberta Rothman, Joan Sire, Robert Tindall, and, as always, George Schumm—who provided ongoing support and encouragement.

Our colleagues around the country—change managers, human resources professionals, management consultants, researchers, CEOs, executives, and managers—who shared their experience and expertise. While some of you are quoted by name in the book, all of you influenced our thinking over the past three years: Billie Alban, Alexander Auerbach, Anthony Barron, Kim Barnes, Debbie Benami-Rahm, Peter Berkley, Jean Blakely, Pat Bidol, Leona Bodie, Carol Canzoneri, Gayle Carson, Mason Cartmell, Richard Chagnon, James Challenger, John Challenger, Jane Chatterjee, Jeanne Cherbeneau, Karen Valentia Clopton, Gary Cluff, Patricia del Valle, Shari Duron, Tom Fletcher, Patricia Fritts, Jeff Gill, Mark Griffin, Eric Greenberg, Ralle Greenberg, Linda Squires Grohe, Ann Hagan, Ozzie Hager, Katherine Harrington, Virginia Hayes, Tom Isgar, Dennis Jaffe, Marianne Jones, Betsy Kendall, Meredith Kimbell, Peggy Lawless, Drew Lebby, Hilda Logan, Nancy Matthews, Jacqueline McHale, Steve Mirman, Barbara Mitchell, Virginia Nelson, Peter Norlin, Esther Orioli, John Parkington, Roseanne Rohrbacher-Grey, Lina Rusty, Gary Rybak, Houda Samaha, Cynthia Scott, Trish Silber, Michael Smith, Gwen Stern, Joanne Adams Stroud, Kathy Sunshine, Valerie Taylor, Nancy Veazey, Judith Vogel, Jean Wallace, Mardy Wheeler, Joe Willmore, and Kathy Wright.

We are indebted to William Bridges, Joel Brockner, Elizabeth

Kübler-Ross, and Abraham Maslow, whose thinking, research, and practice have not only influenced our perspectives on this topic but provided a foundation for our work as change practitioners.

We are also deeply grateful to our families:

Our mothers, Bernice Foreman and Rose Caplan. Championing the welfare of others, they shaped our values and thereby insured that we would be empathetic to the issues of survivors.

Our late fathers, Dr. Benjamin Caplan and John Foreman, whose convictions about what we could do and aspirations for us have challenged us throughout our careers.

JoAnn Foreman and Bill and Susan Caplan, our best friends as well as siblings. They continually devised creative ways to show their support: allowing us to turn their vacation home into a writers' retreat; acting as surrogate parents to our children, grandchildren, and pets; taking on our filial responsibilities in addition to their own.

Melissa and Mac Caplan and Ruth Pluss; Dave and Sabrina Enlow; Jeff, Linda, Kyle and Cory Teese; and Kevin, Becky, Katie, Brianna, Megan, and Kristina Teese, who tolerated our infrequent visits and postponed celebrations, and who continued to show their love despite our absences.

A special thanks to Laura Ackerman-Shaw, Melinda Adams Merino, Laura Simonds, John Walker, and members of the Davies-Black Publishing team—alumni of the "speak softly and wave a big stick" school of author management. They alternately persuaded and prodded, knowing just which motivational tool to use.

Lee Langhammer Law, Davies-Black's director and our editor and publisher, believed in this book from the beginning. She, more than anyone, is responsible for turning a set of notes for a conference presentation into a book outline and an "intuitive playground" of a draft into a coherent and organized text.

Finally, we thank all those unnamed survivors, whose willingness to let us see behind their masks made this book possible. We are merely the narrators of your stories. "Who speaks for the survivors?" On these pages you speak for yourselves.

1

The Unexpected Costs of Downsizing

"I'm a single parent with two children to support. So I thought a lot about 'What's the worst thing that can happen?' I thought it was losing my house. But I finally realized that wasn't it. The worst thing that could happen was staying at my job."

Survivor Leaver

THE PHENOMENON

Employees are resigning. Top producers are taking leaves of absence. From newspaper headlines like "The Ones Who Got Away," to managers and human resources professionals lamenting the loss of their best people, to employees themselves saying "yes" to severance packages never intended for them, all signs are pointing to a new phenomenon: Survivors of corporate restructurings are voluntarily leaving their organizations.

Downsizing, rightsizing, and restructuring have cut through all industries, regardless of size, product, or region. Experiences in Dallas are replicated in Denver. A major bank with branches across the country cuts ten percent of its workforce, as does a credit union one one-hundredth of its size. Even nonprofit, governmental, and educational organizations have cut back.

Why are the very ones chosen to stay with the company, the survivors, heading for the door?

Layoffs

Layoffs are not a new phenomenon. Indeed, some long-tenured employees may have survived layoffs in the past and remained on the job. So, why are some of them leaving now?

Although not new, these layoffs represent the most dramatic set of changes that our nation's workforce has experienced since the Great Depression.

In a way, it is misleading to characterize these dismissals as layoffs. When we think of layoffs, we think of a transitory state, temporary unemployment followed predictably by a return to employment at the same organization or, at worst, absorption into a similar company. In the auto industry, for example, people laid off from one plant or product line moved to another company's assembly line or to a different product division.

Castoffs

The downsizing and merging going on in businesses today are different. People laid off are not, for the most part, being called back to work. They are being terminated, permanently severed as full-time employees from their organizations. Secretary of Labor Robert Reich (1996) suggests, therefore, that the classification "laid off" be replaced by the more telling "castoff."

In the past, termination occurred primarily for one of two reasons: the employee's failure to perform or the organization's failure to stay in business. Neither of those reasons generally applies to today's terminations. Top performers receive severance notices. Many companies dismissing employees are not gasping their last breath. Indeed, most of those organizations intend to become stronger than ever and are using termination proactively, as part of a strategic plan for the company's future health.

Change Today

The nature of change itself is different than what companies have experienced. Change is no longer an event with fixed beginning and ending points. It is constant. Change is also discontinuous and unpredictable. The paths and patterns are often not clear. Plans must be made with the expectation that they will be changed as a matter of course.

And the scope of change is far-reaching inside companies. There are and will be profound changes in organizational structures and shapes, whether one talks about Charles Handy's "shamrock" or "doughnut" (1992), Jack Welch's "boundaryless company" (Tichy, 1993), or William Bridges' "dejobbed workplace" (1994). And employees must not only survive but adapt and thrive in the midst of all these changes.

The Psychological Contract

For those employees escaping layoffs, for the survivors remaining, workplace life is very different. That termination can occur at any time, to good performers as well as poor, means that the psychological contract (also referred to as the employment contract) between employee and employer—the promise of continued employment in exchange for loyalty and hard work—has been broken, severed.

For most people, what they do and how well they do it defines who they are. In addition to job security, the psychological contract met needs for self-identify, self-esteem, and affiliation. What happens, then, not only to those who no longer work, the downsized, but to those still doing the work, the survivors, whose work is now often ambiguous and excessive?

THE COSTS

Though organizations may not intend to be callous or uncaring, concerns for the welfare of employees must be balanced with business realities. Downsizing, merging, and restructuring are not done on a whim but to achieve certain business objectives and bottom-line results. The actual results of such actions are frequently not as planned.

Unexpected Results of Restructuring

In a landmark study of corporate restructuring practices, the Wyatt Company (1993) surveyed 531 U.S. companies across industries.

Ninety percent of the companies surveyed said that reducing costs was a primary reason to restructure. In terms of results, only sixty-one percent actually achieved that goal. Almost as many, eighty-five percent, cited increasing profitability as a primary reason for the resizing actions they took; fewer than half of this group achieved the objective. And these were the best results. If we examine other reasons companies cited for restructuring, the story gets worse; the level of success is significantly less. For example, in terms of meeting the goal of increasing productivity (a goal of fifty-eight percent of the companies in the study), only a third actually achieved it.

To date, studies on restructuring report on short-term results; they indicate whether the strategy was effective as an immediate business tactic. The truth is, for longer periods, we simply do not know. We do not know whether the story gets better or worse, or whether the results that were achieved are lasting or temporal. In the 1995 survey conducted by the American Management Association (AMA) that tracked five-year trends, fewer than half of the responding organizations reported an increase in operating profits a year or more after downsizing.

Companies participating in the Wyatt study and other surveys seemed equally unable to accomplish their goals via restructuring, regardless of whether the objectives were financial ones or goals that focused on customer satisfaction.

Why were they unsuccessful? Although there were certainly external factors, including the economy and foreign competition, fewer than one in five executives in the Wyatt study felt external forces impaired their ability to succeed. Much more significant for them were internal factors.

In only thirteen percent of the cases was a poor result based on the organization's failure to choose the appropriate business solution. So the pivotal internal factor was not poor strategic planning or lack of financial data. The number one reason for companies' failure to achieve their goal was their employees' resistance to change—resistance manifested in their leaving the organization both literally (walking out the door) and figuratively ("resigning" while staying on the job).

Unanticipated Costs

Survivors' resistance offsets the gains of restructuring with new costs. These include higher turnover, decreased productivity, higher rates of stress-related illness, and employee hostility.

Higher Turnover

The costs of higher turnover result not only from the unexpected departure of top employees but from the additional costs of their taking corporate dollars via severance packages never intended for them.

Even if the number of survivors leaving the organization voluntarily is small, the price of replacing them—the costs of recruitment, selection, and training—is considerable.

As one MIS manager bemoaned,

> The cost of recruiting one MIS professional runs from about $3,000 if someone is referred to us to over $25,000 if we use a search firm to find a top candidate, and that doesn't include the costs of people's time spent looking at résumés, interviewing candidates, the testing, etcetera.

I've lost three good employees recently—and Human Resources tells me that it will very likely cost the company over $90,000 to replace each one.

Obviously, replacement means more than putting a candidate in place. Tom DeMarco (1996), a management consultant, notes that for one of his clients, bringing a new engineer up to speed takes "a bit more than one work year, including all the costs, salary, and overhead." In DeMarco's example, the dollar cost is "$150,000 . . . before the investment begins to pay off."

Decreased Productivity

Another factor causing corporate concern is the failure to achieve productivity gains, a primary reason for the downsizing in many cases. According to the AMA study already cited, only one-third of the companies surveyed experienced increased productivity immediately. And even over the long term (five years), fewer than half of the organizations, forty-one percent, had seen gains.

In many organizations, productivity decreased or leveled off as a consequence of multiple factors, including the knowledge and expertise walking out the door, survivors' failure to keep up with new demands, their resistance to the change, and new employees.

DeMarco points out that lost production attributable to new employees comes from two sources: One is the investment of time and money it takes to bring a new employee up to speed. Lost production also results from the impact that a new employee has on others' productivity. DeMarco gives this example: "Every now and then Ralph (new employee) has a question, so he looks for another team member for help. Ralph's productivity on the first day is not even zero; it is negative. He is keeping other people from working at full capacity."

Ralph may be a bit less of a burden each day, but the consequence is still diminished productivity to some degree for some time for the colleagues who assist him.

Higher Rates of Illness

Another organizational cost of downsizing is the price of increased stress-related illness, ranging from more frequent time off for doctors' visits to worker's compensation claims or higher fees for employee health plans and employee assistance programs (EAPs).

An EAP in the Midwest provided an astonishing report. A client company announced pending layoffs; this marked the start of the organization's second round of downsizing. Immediately employees began to experience panic attacks, according to the account. Some people had symptoms so severe that they could not come to work. Others had to be hospitalized with heart attack–like symptoms.

How is this experience relevant to our discussion of post-downsizing costs? Three-quarters of the employees with these stress-related illnesses were survivors of the initial downsizing. And these same survivors had already been notified that they would *not* be laid off in this second round.

Workplace Hostility

One of the most troubling costs of corporate downsizing is an increase in survivor hostility. By "hostility" we do not necessarily mean workplace violence, for there are no statistics tying survivors to this phenomenon. Nor are we talking about the even more extreme acts of mayhem sometimes seen on the six o'clock news.

We are referring to the increasingly common and covert malicious acts initiated by survivors—acts that incur such costs as having to restore computer programs or customer databases mysteriously erased, having to replace stolen property, and being forced to deal with the consequences of vandalism—for example, the slashed tires of one company's automobiles. Those cars were parked in a supposedly secure garage; as a result the company had to resort to round-the-clock security, a new and unexpected corporate expense.

PREMISE OF THIS BOOK

Our initial premise for this book was that if organizations understood survivors' resistance and concerns, management could help survivors and retain them as productive employees. Unfortunately, this perspective placed the survivor in the role of a patient needing to get well, rather than as one player in situ, in a relationship in flux.

As one of our interviewees, Drew Lebby, Ph.D., an organization consultant, pointed out:

> By definition there's no way (for an organization) to go through transformational change with a minimum of stress ... approaching crisis, a

massive downsizing—from what we know about change, [it is] the very act of going into chaos that produces the transformation.

Our revised premise: Survivors do not go through change and transition in isolation. Survivors go through them within the context of the organization undergoing its own change and transition. And it is how that organization is dealing with its own needs, while simultaneously addressing those of survivors, that determines whether survivors stay or leave.

The Three C's

Competence, connection, commitment—the Three C's—are key aspects of organizational well-being, and they are discussed throughout this book. They are important to both the individual employee and the organization as a whole in multiple contexts.

Competence means know-how, expertise, and the sense of security and control that comes with mastery. Connection refers to the sense of belonging and attachment that emanates for employees through relationships with peers, bosses, and the organization as a whole. Commitment means the employees' and organization's dedication and loyalty to the work and to each other manifested in the psychological contract.

For survivors, the Three C's represent what they value, what they lose during the change, and what they need to regain in order to be productive, effective employees.

Survivors whom we interviewed varied on which of the Three C's was more important to them. Some had a special affinity for competence. For those survivors for whom the work was often an end in itself, being competent meant they were able to be of value to the organization not only for doing the work but for the way in which they performed it. For these survivors the loss of competence, then, devalued their work and, by extension, themselves.

For other survivors, those for whom "the company has been like a family to me," connection was the glue that held them to the organization. Downsizing spelled disconnection; surviving often meant saying good-bye to departing co-workers, moving to a new department, joining a new team, or reporting to a different boss with whom they had no attachment. Sometimes these disconnections were more than survivors could withstand. How well they reconnected was a better predictor of whether they would stay than how they felt about new roles or more work.

The employment contract is the evidence that the organization is re-ciprocating survivors' commitment. For some survivors this was more important than the work they did or how or with whom they did it. For these survivors, commitment meant being responsive to the organization's needs and giving loyalty as an offshoot of that agreement. For them, the breaking of the contract severed the commitment, dissolved the loyalty, and left them stuck in limbo.

Survivors expect the organization to help them regain the Three C's. The survivors we spoke to looked to the company to put in place the struc-tures, leadership, programs, and practices needed. Thus, helping survivors to regain competence, connection, and commitment was, from survivors' perspectives, the organization's charge.

As the organization itself undergoes change, it, too, suffers the loss of competence, connection, and commitment. To transform itself and become the successful organization of its vision, it has to have the Three C's firmly in place.

Competence for the organization means that it has a sense of control and mastery, competent management to lead the organization, and the structures, products, and services to achieve its new goals. And part of the organization's competence is having systems in place to ensure the compe-tence of survivors.

Connection for the organization refers to its relationships and bonds with its industry, customers, processes, and employees. Connection for the organization is also internal—its structures and systems, roles and reward systems, are in alignment with one another. For the organization, commit-ment means the loyalty and dedication to the workforce and the work that the psychological contract demands.

Survivors apply the Three C's in another way. They use them to eval-uate the organization and its management of the change. Does the change plan demonstrate the organization's competence? Will leaders bring the now-requisite knowledge and skills to the restructured company? Has the organization connected the past to the future? Has it provided ways for employees to become connected to each other as well as to that future? Is the organization committed to employees? Does it value their contribu-tions? So the Three C's also are the elements survivors use to measure the organization—and make decisions about their own future.

The theme of the Three C's is woven throughout our examination of survivors and our analysis of their issues. It appears as well in our discussion of the issues facing organizations. Many of our recommendations focus on how to rebuild the Three C's for survivors and the organization separately and in relation to one another.

Barriers

Communicate often and repeat the information. Make managers available to help employees through transition. Select a change manager. These are some of the key actions recommended in this book.

These are not revolutionary ideas. And that is precisely the point. If these ideas are so basic, what prevents companies from putting them in place? What are the obstacles that get in the way?

We found a number of barriers that stand in the way of successful change management. They range from an individual's personal discomfort to the absence of a succession plan. Sometimes barriers emerge only in response to a particular situation; others create problems over and over. Key barriers are discussed in each chapter.

The Survivors

To the survivors we interviewed, we promised confidentiality.
They wanted secrecy.
We sought information.
They told secrets.

My goal is to stay another six months, because then I'm eligible for a paid sabbatical. After the sabbatical, though, I'm out the door.

The countenance survivors presented to their organizations was a facade, masking their fears, their concerns, their plans, masking who they were, and what they had decided to do. For the organization, then, there was more going on than what it perceived.

And that situation has not changed; indeed, quite the opposite. Given the waves of downsizing that so many organizations have gone through since we began interviewing survivors in 1993, many employees who talked to us were second- or third-generation survivors; they had survived two or three rounds of layoffs either in the same organization or in a combination of companies. They told us how their feelings had changed as they became veterans of the ordeal.

These survivors spoke to us of greater feelings of fear and instability. Their emotions did not necessarily translate into a greater willingness to follow the rules and cling to positions; rather, they increased employees' determination to look out for themselves.

A survivor one of us interviewed three months ago telephoned just as we were finishing this manuscript. When we spoke to her initially, she was in the midst of her company's third round of downsizing, and she had a significant role in its implementation. She was completing plans for the development of cross-functional teams, to be set up when the layoffs were done.

What prompted her call? We were not available when the call came in, but we did have her voice-mail message:

> *I thought you'd want to know. . . I resigned last week. You're probably surprised. I thought I could hold out. . . . It's not like I haven't been through this before. . . but it's the never-ending part of it. I couldn't stay anymore. I'd rather risk it somewhere else.*

It is our belief that organizations, by recognizing and dealing with the issues and challenges of survivors, can alter the course of events, retaining those people who might otherwise leave the organization or remain as less-than-productive employees after downsizing.

THE SURVIVORS

We interviewed two groups of survivors: the survivor leavers, those employees who had voluntarily left the organization; and the survivor stayers, those still working in the organization.

We expected that the survivor leavers and the survivor stayers would give us very different kinds of information. We expected that the survivor leavers would tell us what their company had done poorly and what it should have done to keep them. We expected that the survivor stayers would tell us what their company was doing right—why they were staying.

Yet the answers our questions generated often were not very different at all. Many of the survivor stayers sounded just like the leavers.

From a survivor leaver:

They saw us as interchangeable parts—those of us who were senior and the ones who hadn't been in the department and had little understanding of the work.

Next, a survivor stayer:

During the downsizing, management focused on the reorganization— like moving chess pieces on a chess board—but they forgot that the chess pieces are people.

There were distinct differences among our interviewees' perceptions and behaviors, however—differences that appeared clearly in dialogues directly with survivors, in the reports of others, or in our own observations inside companies. These differences were consistent regardless of region or industry.

These patterns formed the profiles of what we came to identify as three survivor groups.

The Foot Out the Doors (FODs): productive, high performers who are one step away from leaving the organization, alternately engrossed in their work and disengaged from the organization.

The Wait and Sees (W&Ss): those employees most visible due to their vocal, often confrontational stance at meetings and in conversation. They are clearly very engaged with the organization.

The Ride It Outs (RIOs): the least visible by choice, the most connected to friends and the past, and the least likely to leave the organization of their own volition.

Note that while we have named only one group as "Foot Out the Door," survivor leavers—and stayers—are represented in all three groups. Some of the RIOs we interviewed told us why they had left the organization voluntarily. Likewise, we talked with FODs who had decided to stay.

These profiles gave us a foundation for understanding the survivor phenomena we encountered. They also gave us a framework for determining how organizations need to address survivors' concerns.

In each of the next three chapters we introduce these survivor groups. We delineate their characteristics and career focus, their impact on other survivors, and the challenges organizations face in motivating, managing, and retaining them.

2

The Foot Out the Doors

"One more year and I'll be vested. I think I can hold on till then. But then, that's it."

Survivor Stayer

PROFILE

The first survivor group, the Foot Out the Doors (FODs), is just that—one step away from leaving the organization. They are not motivated to go elsewhere by concerns about whether they will continue to have a position with the company. Instead, their disquiet lies with longer-term issues.

Future Oriented

The FODs we interviewed might have been fast-trackers—rising stars with bright career paths ahead of them. But now they had determined that the company was not going to make it or, at the very least, would not provide the organizational future that they had envisioned.

"Where am I going?" rather than "Am I staying?" was their quandary. Ever future-oriented, FODs believed that they had lost control of their careers. Now many felt cognitive dissonance between their career goals and where the organization appeared to be going.

Goal Directed

For the FODs, personal goals are not separate from but interwoven with their career plans. The importance of personal goals may have been an issue for the other survivor groups, but it was not articulated to us. In contrast, the FODs were very cognizant of personal goals vis à vis what the organization had to offer them.

As Jean Wallace, a director of human resource development, explained:

> What is happening simultaneously with the downsizing is that these people want to have a personal life or they want to have some kind of a balanced lifestyle where they're not just killing themselves and

working—because you don't just have those employees anymore who are out there to do their job, that's their entire life.

For the FODs especially, the results of downsizing frequently introduce or exacerbate paradoxes around goals.

OK, I'm making a lot of money, but so what! How can I have a balanced life when I'm now doing three people's jobs?

Independent

Some of the FODs we encountered were self-described mavericks. Though ardent about their work, they were not necessarily going to follow the rules, color inside the lines, or stay within the set parameters. Whether because they had found a work environment that welcomed independence or because they were high performers, these FODs found their autonomous style valued by management.

One FOD described her rationale for leaving her company:

Going back to my own personal philosophy, I said to myself it was time to move on. "Let's not stay in this negative environment." I took a lesser position and a salary cut as well. It wasn't something I wanted to do forever, because I'm very ambitious.

Upon first hearing this survivor, one may conclude that FODs are self-centered or selfish. But that is not, in fact, an attribute of this survivor group. FODs are at heart survivors. Their focus on attaining their goals makes them more independent than other survivor groups.

Compared to W&Ss and RIOs, FODs are less likely to remain with the organization out of a sense of commitment or loyalty. But the FODs do not perceive themselves as disloyal. Indeed, they are personally vested in the organization's success. As one FOD explained to us, disloyalty would have meant

doing less than what was expected or badmouthing the company or even sabotaging a project.

Proactive

The FODs, of all the survivor groups, appear most able to step back and detach in order to dispassionately evaluate the situation.

People who I talked to said, "Well, your niche here is well needed, and you should probably feel pretty comfortable knowing that." And I really liked the work. But I try to be proactive in anything that I do, and I had read that it takes six months to find a position that you really want, and I had six months, so I said to myself, Well, I'll see what's really out there.

One of the identifying characteristics of this group is how proactive and in control they sound. What FODs recognize is that they, not the organization, have to create their own destiny. Evaluating the downsizing events and corporate messages, FODs told us that they needed to take care of themselves.

My goal is to stay another six months, because then I'm eligible for a paid sabbatical. After the sabbatical, though, I'm out the door.

Many FODs were event driven, deciding to stay until they had attained a specific milestone with the organization—becoming vested or taking a promised sabbatical. We even heard of FODs who stayed until they completed covered dental work.

Others were actively looking for new positions.

Career Focus: Professional Growth

Productive, high performers, the FODs hold career objectives focused on growth and expansion—as the FODs define those terms.

They not only froze our salaries, cut our benefits, but they stopped allowing us to go to conferences. That's my life blood. I stopped growing.

What are the FODs' career goals? It became clear to us that for many FODs, a career plan does not necessarily mean becoming an executive of the company.

For many FOD interviewees, having work that was progressively more interesting and challenging was their primary career goal—an end in itself rather than the means to another position or move up the ranks.

When asked about her career objectives, one FOD at the headquarters of a national retailer reported four moves in five years with the company.

I moved mostly because I requested them. . . . I'm very systems-oriented, so as departments needed to be automated or to be improved, they moved me around. And I asked for it! . . . Once I got a department into shape, I would go and say, "I'm bored; whenever something more challenging comes up, move me."

Three of the moves were lateral. Yet she saw all as integral to her career goals rather than as deviations or "time-outs."

For the FODs we interviewed, the work not only had to be interesting and challenging but had to have a recognized value for the company.

Why did I take another job? I could have stayed in quality control at [the company]. In the past we were recognized as quality leaders in the industry. But with the reorganization, they cut the department in half and reduced the standards. Their memos started to reflect a real emphasis on numbers; quantity, not quality, was the direction. I couldn't stay.

Doing work valued by the company is of such critical importance to FODs that even when the rationale for restructuring makes sense, these survivors struggle. As one FOD put it:

I hate the thought of anybody thinking, or even myself thinking, that I may have had an unnecessary job.

What's more, FODs need to feel valued themselves as the producers of that work. Here is where many of them felt the organization had failed them. To this FOD, the way in which the company had handled the downsizing sent a direct message about her value:

The way they cut really good people—it makes you wonder, Well, how valuable am I, and should I put in that extra ten percent, knowing that it may not matter?

Value: Competence

FODs need to know that the organization has a rationale for the actions it has taken or is about to take and that the rationale is tied to a well-conceived plan for the future. As importantly, the rationale and the plan have to make sense to the FODs.

Unlike some other survivors, the FODs do not need fine details about the future; indeed, part of the challenge for them is determining those specifics. But they need to know that the plan is sound, provides options and contingencies, and offers some avenues for employee involvement in the process as well as in the outcomes. For the FODs personally, the future needs to provide challenging opportunities and growth—hardly surprising, for these are the people who were attracted to the organization by these very qualities rather than by a title in the table of organization.

> *The company has always had a unique position in the industry. Our marketing approach has enabled us to avoid some of the pitfalls other companies encountered. Management has taken some very creative approaches to business problems. Now all of a sudden they announce this layoff as the only solution. I guess I don't buy it. What other alternatives did they consider?*

What turns off the FODs and pushes them closer to the door are not the organization's mistakes in themselves. Many FODs we talked to had stayed through one round of downsizing, even if that meant accepting management's contributions to the situations that caused it. For the FODs, the "fatal flaw" is the organization's failing to learn from the mistake and, instead of correcting it and steering a new course, repeating the same actions.

So although the FODs appear less threatened by change and chaos than other survivor groups—they are, after all, change initiators themselves—if a second round of downsizing results from failure to correct the mistakes that led to the first one, FODs have little willingness to stay put again. They lose confidence in management. They lose patience with what they perceive as the organization's faulty analysis and circular motion.

Thus, multiple rounds led many of the FODs out the door. In some cases, even event-driven FODs crossed the threshold. We heard of FODs who gave up vesting, took lowered retirement packages, even pushed up surgery dates. Again, what struck us was their proactive stance.

> *I don't need to sit around and watch people become demoralized; I need to maintain some sense of movement and optimism.*

It was not the downsizing itself that drove out those FODs but either the rationale provided or the way in which management handled the process.

IMPACT ON OTHER SURVIVORS

What is this survivor group's relationship with and impact on others?

■   IMPACT ON OTHER FODs

FODs use other FODs as barometers. Thus, they talked openly among themselves about their concerns for the future.

When Sam left, I knew there was no future here. He's not an impulsive kind of guy. And it just confirmed that if you were good, the jobs were there.

An FOD's leaving frequently creates a "domino effect" involving other FODs. For some, it is confirmation that the organization does not have the wherewithal to direct its future or that the work is not going to match their career goals. For others, the issue is more direct: The team that did the work, that made the work interesting, that created the synergy, is no longer there.

The best people in my department left within two months of each other. It really had an impact on me. I stepped up my interviewing.

FODs seem to be held in high regard—well respected among other employees. They told us that others frequently sought their advice.

People tell me I'm their best resource for getting a new job inside the company. I do seem to have the pulse of many departments. And I'm apparently a good sounding board.

■   IMPACT ON W&Ss

At the same time, we sensed a lot of tension between the FODs and other survivor groups, particularly the W&Ss. As one FOD who was about to leave his company told us:

I really have to be careful what I say around Joe. He already has the sense that I know more that I'm not telling him. I really don't, and I've made my decision based on what we both know. But he has so many questions he needs answers to. He can't believe anyone would leave without knowing more. It's created a really difficult situation.

This was not the only instance of tension we heard about. From the FODs' perspective, it sometimes seemed that W&Ss believed that FODs had inside information, bad news, which is why FODs were getting out. This may have fed the W&Ss' anger, giving them fuel for challenging the organization. An FOD's leaving confirmed to W&Ss that the organization had let them down, and it made W&Ss feel as if they were on the outside looking in.

■ IMPACT ON RIOs

The proactive actions of the FODs, from asking questions in meetings to actually going out the door, are very unnerving to those who are trying to stay in denial. Thus, although some of the RIOs may have believed that the FODs had information, they were almost afraid to ask. Finding out—indeed, even asking questions—forced them to confront reality.

ORGANIZATIONAL CHALLENGE

As productive, effective employees, FODs often provide little evidence of their concerns and potential leave taking in their outward behavior and interactions. What may look like committed employees—arriving on time, performing responsibly and responsively—masks their internal stance. Where others are argumentative, FODs may calmly ask about the organization's plan or next steps.

If the organization is not able to provide satisfactory answers or if the speaker does not have credibility, the FODs are not going to stop performing or slow the pace. Indeed, they will continue to do the job—as they simultaneously make plans to leave.

Though FODs may still enjoy the work, they become turned off to the organization. The first of the survivors to disengage psychologically, they are ready to move on.

Feeling cognitive dissonance, FODs may or may not be pursuing new job opportunities.

I know I should probably be putting energy into my new responsibilities. Don't get me wrong—I'm doing my job all right. But, frankly, I'm putting that energy into me and my future, sending out résumés and activating my network.

Be clear: The FODs do not abandon their jobs. Many we talked to were attracted by and attached to their work. However, they perceived that the company had devalued their work, them, or both.

I feel there's no future for me here. The things I felt I contributed are no longer valued.

In our interviews, what emerged over and over was the FODs' perception that they and/or their work were expendable.

Of all the survivor groups, the FODs are the most likely to be misperceived. FODs speak and behave as productive, interested employees. Their actions and emotions are appropriate, not exaggerated. Only those who knew them very well and/or were privy to their thoughts were aware that FODs' countenance and behavior did not match their plans.

A lot of people, especially my boss, were shocked when I resigned. I was surprised at their surprise. I had always been known for my energy and enthusiasm, and the last six months, it wasn't there. The change was so obvious to my friends—I couldn't believe management hadn't picked up on it.

So, particularly in the case of FODs, looks and behavior can be deceiving. One of the challenges that organizations face with respect to this group is not taking FODs' productivity as an indicator of their satisfaction or intent to stay.

The primary organizational challenge with the FODs, therefore, is determining how to reengage them, how to recommit them to the organization, and how to do so long before they walk out the door.

THE FODs

GROUP ISSUES
Profile   Future oriented, goal driven, independent, and proactive
Career Focus   Professional growth
Value   Competence

ORGANIZATIONAL CHALLENGE
FODs are most likely to be disengaged. Management must find ways to reengage the FODs and recommit them to the organization.

Lack of engagement and commitment is not the issue—indeed, quite the opposite—for our next survivor group.

3

The Wait and Sees

"They told me there could be opportunities for advancement. They were asking me to commit a lot in exchange for some very vague assurances."
Survivor Leaver

PROFILE

Of all the survivor groups, the Wait and Sees (W&Ss) appeared to us the most focused on the here and now. W&Ss are not uncaring about what will happen in the future, but what concerns them most is the impact of change on their lives right now.

Present Centered

W&Ss focus their concerns about the present on the organization's structure. The current structure not only provides parameters for doing tasks but gives W&Ss role clarity and creates boundaries for their career pathing. Structure also provides a system of checks and balances and measurement tools to ensure fairness, a primary concern heightened during a period of change.

When the current structure is threatened, when it appears about to be modified or dissolved and replaced, these survivors fall into crisis. In our opinion, the W&Ss' outward anger and displays of hostility mask their anxiety and their fear of being out of control, cast adrift without a structure to anchor them. They have to have new anchors to regain control of their lives. Not surprisingly, they wanted these bulwarks now, even if they are quick fixes.

Goal Directed

Like the FODs, the W&Ss we interviewed were goal directed, and some were clearly fast trackers. But one difference struck us right away: In contrast to the FODs' plans for the future, the W&Ss' visions were embedded in the organization's structure; W&Ss developed their career goals in accord with the company's hierarchy.

I expected to be at a level four by the end of this year, which would put me on track for a lead position. The reorganization has left me with no place to go now, and I won't go back down.

Reactive

Compared to the other survivors, W&Ss have a much more reactive stance, responding to events and others' behavior rather than initiating them. Daily work life for W&Ss seems to be a series of others' actions and their reactions. It came across vividly in the interviews: No matter what question they were asked, W&Ss began their response by telling us what their managers or other employees had done followed by how they had responded.

She [the manager] said she'd make time at the staff meeting for questions. Well, we got close to the end, and I called her on it. . . . You bet I had questions.

Within the organization, W&Ss' reactive behavior frequently comes across as challenges to information, criticism of plans, and seemingly endless questioning of details.

At a meeting to reveal plans for relocating some employees to East Coast sites, we observed one survivor dominating the discussion. Every time there was a lull, this employee was ready:

Will their phone system work with my headset? I need this headset. . . . We're going to be in much closer quarters. . . . You know how distracting sounds are. . . . We have to deal with so many people in an hour. . . . And what about the phone consoles?. . . We're not going to have to learn a whole new system.

The headset issue was raised in a very volatile fashion—the employee's eyes flashing, hands banging on the table. All this occurred, intentionally or not, in the presence of a visiting executive from the East Coast location.

Although this behavior might be seen by some as assertive risk-taking, it struck us as uncalculated and unplanned, a spur of the moment reaction, characteristic of behavior we came to recognize in other W&Ss. So "wait and see" is somewhat of a misnomer, as this survivor group often comes across as impatient, short-fused, demanding, and argumentative.

The W&Ss' incessant quest for and challenge of information is often more than off-putting to management; it can be threatening, particularly when the recipient of the barrage does not have all the answers. Thus, the short-term impact is to negate the credibility or merit of the issues, as bosses become defensive or walk away, putting off meetings and avoiding discussions. To W&Ss, the effect of management's "no-response" response is to discount both W&Ss' issues and, by association, the W&Ss themselves. This response triggers more demands and challenges by the W&Ss, followed by more avoidance. The result is a stalemate.

One RIO, caught in the middle of such a situation, reported,

It's really upsetting the way Sally and our boss are in a real standoff. Sally challenges nonstop, so our boss doesn't volunteer information anymore. The rest of us are afraid to ask questions, because we don't want to set Sally off, and we sure don't want the manager to think we've taken Sally's side. I just hate being in the office with the two of them.

As a result of their reactiveness, W&Ss cannot seem to take charge of their lives; they are unable to take control and work through the changes. They are on hold, stuck, waiting to see what the company will do, waiting to see if the company will make it or can meet their needs.

I suppose I have to give them a chance to prove they can turn things around. But, I've got to say, they haven't impressed me so far. I hate to dump twenty good years in the toilet.

This survivor's skepticism was echoed by many of the W&Ss we interviewed, as they doubted that the organization would rise to the occasion.

For some W&Ss, their response to feeling threatened and not in control is to become guarded. They become protective of their own interests, literally guarding workspaces, files, and information.

We have these Monday morning product development meetings. He [the manager] wants everyone to come up with ideas. This is the same guy who still has not given us much information on the reorganization . . . how it affects us. But he wants us to give to him. Are you kidding? My ideas are worth something. I'm not giving them away.

Given the reactions to downsizing described so far, imagine the W&Ss' response to multiple rounds of reorganization or downsizing. For some W&Ss, losing any remaining anchors results in escalating displays of anger. For others, the organization's failure to respond to their questions satisfactorily causes them to pose even longer lists of concerns. Most importantly, their behavior seems to spiral even more out of control in direct proportion to their increasing fear and anxiety.

One survivor told us about his former boss, Bob, whom he called an "on the fencer." His description fit our profile of a W&S. Bob kept getting reassigned through each downsizing. Though almost all the moves were lateral, Bob "became very bitter, convinced that the company was out to get him, to trip him up." What were the cues and clues as to this "on the fencer's" fears? Our interviewee continued,

> Bob really became a control freak. He started asking all of his subordinates to write detailed monthly reports. Everything had to be documented. I think he wanted to convince the world he was doing something. But, you know, he really created his own death spiral.

Analytical

We do not want to imply that W&Ss raise only frivolous or extraneous issues. They very often pose pertinent questions that display thoughtful analysis. Their analysis is thorough, detailed, and focuses less on how things will work in the future and more on what actions to make the plan work in the present.

More immediately, the W&Ss serve as barometers. Despite the noise, they often reveal the truth. It is the W&Ss' questions that will tell management whether the organizational plan has substance and whether it is unclear, contradictory, or incomplete.

Career Focus: Hierarchical Movement

One W&S we interviewed became a survivor leaver despite the fact that the organization took deliberate steps to retain him. According to Jack, each time he questioned his role in the restructured organization, management responded by increasing his salary and benefits and creating new job titles and responsibilities for him. While the work was challenging and even interesting to Jack, he kept questioning his boss and his boss's boss:

> Where does this lead? What is it connected to? Where am I headed, career-wise?

The organization's response, once again, was to up the ante—as it misperceived what he was asking for.

In fact, Jack was neither dissatisfied with his position nor seeking a new one; what he was looking for was a road map, a well-marked path up the organizational chart. Ironically, having a newly created position, no matter what the perks, was antithetical to his aims if it did not have a clearly delineated place within the hierarchical structure.

For W&Ss, the question "Will I have a job?" is asked within the context of where that job fits. The real question is, "Will I (or won't I) have a place in the organizational structure?"

Two W&Ss we interviewed who did leave their organizations returned within a year. In both instances they told us they left their new employers because "they didn't keep their promises of promotional opportunities." What these employees expected vis à vis the organization's structure did not become reality. As one of the W&Ss recounted:

They were centralizing the marketing function. The corporate department was now responsible for the midwestern region. My position was supposed to be the second rung of a new career ladder with five tiers in all. This was supposed to be in place within a year. Based on my performance, of course, I would be a candidate for promotion within that time.

Last month they announced that they were flattening the organization—a far cry from the career plan they offered to me!

For the W&Ss, the "employment contract" between them and the company represents mobility and the path for movement and promotion.

Value: Commitment

The W&Ss hold certain values central to their work life. One is that loyalty is a given and loyalty is two-way. The employment contract symbolized that exchange of loyalties.

W&Ss also believe that loyalty begets a commitment. The employment contract also speaks to mutual commitment—the exchange of hard work and loyalty for promises of job security—and career opportunities.

For W&Ss their commitment is a mandate; thus, these survivors perform even when assignments are not challenging or when they disagree about the value of the work or the way it is to be done. W&Ss may voice their feelings, but they still complete the work—and with the same high standards for performance they ordinarily bring to their roles.

So, loyal and committed to the organization, the W&Ss we spoke to now often felt betrayed by the company. Their apprehensions were coupled with disbelief that the organization could disregard its commitment to them, given their years of loyalty and commitment to the company.

IMPACT ON OTHER SURVIVORS

We were intimately aware of this survivor group's impact on others, as we experienced a friend's reactions during a six-month period of downsizing at his organization. This individual was not one to pound his fists or shout at meetings, and he did not do so during this time. Instead, he did a lot of complaining one-on-one and "around the water cooler." People who knew him outside of the company were equally aware of his displeasure and the details of what was happening to him. Telling his story almost became his mission, perhaps as a way of coping with his fears and/or assuring support.

■ IMPACT ON OTHER W&Ss

W&Ss alternately support and one-up one another. In the same relocation meeting described earlier in this chapter, another survivor jumped in, echoing the W&S's complaints.

> Joe is absolutely right. The company is going to have one hell of a problem if they don't address this headset issue now—before we get there!

This second W&S acted as a cheering section, agitating his colleague and keeping his momentum going. We could almost feel their blood pressures rising. By contrast, we heard about other W&Ss who engaged in shouting matches—not *at* but *with* each other, in concert, competing for airtime in meetings.

W&Ss we interviewed frequently developed a group of followers among their co-workers. Because the W&Ss voiced so many concerns and were willing to vocalize others' issues, they often became folk heroes to these individuals initially. Over the long term, W&Ss often find themselves unsupported by FODs and RIOs.

■   IMPACT ON FODs

Although they may recognize the legitimacy of the issues the W&Ss raise, the FODs are frequently turned off by the W&Ss' presentation style and hostility. And, turned off by the W&Ss' reactive stance, FODs will not take on the role of leading them.

There are a few folks on my team who come across as malcontents; no matter what is announced, they find fault. You can't count on them to have a thoughtful discussion. They're like loose cannons—waiting to go off.

If the FODs do not want to lead the W&Ss, they do not want to follow them, either. As we have described, the FODs have their own issues and agendas during the reorganization, and those certainly do not include taking on others' causes or joining forces with reactive people. On the contrary, the FODs look to management to deal with these employees. In fact, to the FODs, the W&Ss' unchecked behavior is a red flag, an indicator of an out-of-control process and of an organization not doing its job.

Our group meetings are a disaster. Ed gets started with his issues; then Rick jumps in with his, and before long, it's disintegrated to a free-for-all. I don't know why management continues to insist on this useless exercise, because our boss can't handle the group. You'd think they could see how unproductive these meetings are.

■   IMPACT ON RIOs

The "water cooler" behavior of the W&Ss poses a dilemma for the RIOs. The W&Ss' highly vocal rallying cry makes them sound as if they know what to do, so it is tempting for the RIOs to turn to them as leaders who will take care of them. At the same time, the RIOs are threatened by the very same volume and noise, the *Sturm und Drang*, that make everyone conspicuous, bringing an end to the anonymity to which the RIOs desperately cling. In their opinion, no good can come of this attention.

I wish he'd leave well enough alone. His continual haggling over our assignments only makes things worse, I know. He's raising issues management probably hasn't even thought of.

The RIOs' dilemma is moot, however, because the W&Ss are not going to lead. They are, after all, reactive rather than proactive; responders, not initiators. Those water cooler discussions are not only a call to join but a cry for help.

ORGANIZATIONAL CHALLENGE

W&Ss need answers to their questions, to their concerns as to where they and their organization are going.

And W&Ss need an arena in which to present these questions. W&Ss look to the organization to provide a structured way to hear from them— to provide a venue for the voicing of W&Ss' concerns and analysis. So the organization's merely making announcements and providing one-way communication has the effect of creating a tenor of antagonism surrounding W&Ss' responses. W&Ss' questions become challenges; instead of thoughtful, focused queries, they appear as a barrage of complaints.

W&Ss' commitment—rather than detachment—is positive from the standpoint of the organization. It is easy to understand why management may conclude that W&Ss can be counted on for the long haul. After all, W&Ss are not FODs. But again, as the FODs demonstrated, looks can be deceiving.

The W&Ss do not stay on hold forever. Some leave. Our friend did. Indeed, we interviewed a number of survivor leavers whom we would classify as W&Ss.

We hope we have made it clear that W&Ss have very strong skills— skills that make them attractive to other companies. If W&Ss feel strongly enough that they are not being heard and that their concerns are not being addressed, they tend to heed recruiters' calls.

At the same time, some W&Ss seem to leave as a reactive, spur-of-the-moment decision rather than as the result of planned-out action.

After the meeting I walked into Ron's office and said, "OK, I quit!"
I surprised myself. But it was the last straw. I packed up that day.

Often, a W&S's leaving is a surprise to the organization. On one hand, that is puzzling, given how verbal this survivor group is about its unhappiness. At the same time, we understand an organization's dismissing those complaints as another example of "Bill's crying wolf," particularly if "you know Bill; he always complains." Bill, after all, is also an "always can be counted on" type of employee. But as it turns out, the organization's "betrayal" is just too much for him to handle.

The actions of W&S stayers take a variety of forms. Some previously top performers become "job adherers," strictly adhering to work hours and job descriptions—doing what is required but no more.

You want to know about productivity and how the work is getting done? Well, there are at least thirty files that have been sitting around for the past month, and they need follow-up calls. Everyone's supposed to take a few when they can. (Chuckling) Those files have been sitting right there—untouched—for weeks, 'cause no one's volunteering.... Not in your job description, doesn't get done.

For others, complaining may initially be a way of letting off steam. But they take action when, in their opinion, the organization fails to do so. One W&S told us that she had gone to see her attorney a month after the downsizing announcement but before the actual layoffs took place:

He told me what to start watching for—how to, in his words, "scan the environment." He told me what to document and how to keep records. So that's what I've been doing the past two months.

We also heard a lot from W&Ss about back problems, high blood pressure, and recurrent illnesses—the result, we believe, of their internal turmoil.

Perhaps our description of W&Ss makes them sound like unappealing employees. Their behavior under the stress of downsizing may be unpleasant or difficult to address, but they are productive and able to meet goals. Whether or not their current performance is exceptional, they have demonstrated their ability to excel through past successes and their movement up the organizational structure. Remember: W&Ss have followed career paths. Coupled with their loyalty and commitment, this survivor group has many positive qualities that the organization needs, particularly as it undergoes change.

If W&Ss speak, the organization should listen. W&Ss present the real call to action for management and provide the first measure of employees' emotional response. Although they are not the only ones feeling this anxiety, they may be the most vocal.

From this description it is obvious that the W&Ss, unlike the FODs, are not disengaged. In fact, quite the opposite. The problem is that W&Ss are *misengaged*—locked into a rigid perception of their place within the organizational structure.

From an organizational perspective, the task is to redirect W&Ss' engagement, not toward their role in the old company but toward the new organization and their role in it.

THE W&Ss

GROUP ISSUES

Profile	Present centered, goal directed, reactive, and analytical
Career Focus	Hierarchical movement within the organization
Value	Commitment

ORGANIZATIONAL CHALLENGE

W&Ss are "on hold," stuck, waiting to see what the organization will do. The organizational challenge is to move them off "hold" and redirect their engagement toward the new organization and their role within it.

The third survivor group, RIOs, need to be redirected as well but for quite different reasons.

4

The Ride It Outs

PROFILE

We found our third survivor group, the Ride It Outs (RIOs), difficult to pin down. It was a challenge for us to get them to commit to a meeting time or place or even to agree to be interviewed at all. Appointments were canceled and phone calls not returned. Even when we were able to arrange a meeting, the RIOs were opaque and elusive.

Past Oriented

For the RIOs, the present brings unresolved conflicts; the future, uncontrollable danger. The past, by contrast or default, represents security and safety. The past is where, prior to the downsizing, these survivors found comfort in jobs with friends in an environment that fostered tradition and provided them security. A part of coping with the changes is acting as if the past is still happening. Hence, the RIOs deal via denial, reflecting on and often acting on what they perceive as "the good old days."

There is a price for all this denial and emotional upheaval: They keep trying to do the job as they've done it before. If you look in their file drawers, you may find now-obsolete forms, records that are no longer relevant, and copies of old files—all symbols of their holding on to the past.

We heard about one sales organization that discovered its processing department employees had been entering data in the new computer system

31

while simultaneously maintaining the same information, albeit surreptitiously, in inventory binders kept at their desks—as they'd done in the past.

We ourselves worked with RIOs at one company office who were handing out old business cards with obsolete titles—a year after the change.

Their denial extended beyond the office. One RIO confided to us that he had not yet told his family about his upcoming transfer to another branch out of state, though he had known about it for three weeks.

My wife really likes her job. . . . My son just made the varsity team at school. . . . Life is just starting to go really well . . . now this. . . . I keep waiting for my boss to tell me that I won't be transferred after all.

When living in the past and denial are not possible, RIOs turn to avoidance and escape. They flee from new realities literally and/or figuratively, withdrawing into themselves when actual retreat is not an option.

Cautious

The RIOs we interviewed held their concerns and emotions most closely in check. They often gave information almost grudgingly and in a generally hedging, vacillating manner. They were so cautious in their statements that they appeared very indecisive and passive. Answers to questions were usually variations of "Everything's fine," and qualified "yes, but's."

Sure it's been rough. We're down three people. In a department of seven, that's a lot, but I guess we'll get used to it. It means a lot of overtime, but that's about all you can do.

It was hard to go beyond their words, to get a sense of their thoughts or feelings. Interviewing survivors separately, we experienced this phenomenon independently.

Well, the work is harder and we're down three people, but everything's basically OK. And I know it will get easier.

In another case a division manager began,

I was the senior guy and most credible in—

He froze in mid-sentence, apparently determining he had said too much, and pulled himself back. He quickly began to talk about a different topic.

Not all RIOs avoided or disappeared. But one way even those survivors managed to keep us at arm's length was by smothering us with extraneous information. An introductory query, "Tell me a little bit about the company," brought a litany of facts and figures about products, acquisitions, stock prices—even debt ratios.

When we observed and listened to them more intently, we realized that the RIOs are not without feelings or opinions. What appeared as passivity was in fact their caution and concern that any action they took would upset the status quo even more.

The more vocal people just leave. It's very secretive.

They do not want to be seen or heard, because of what being visible may bring. As one RIO put it,

It doesn't seem too smart to be making scenes or complaining. That's a sure way to get the wrong kind of notice.

Their desire for anonymity, their need to maintain a low profile and not to stand out, means they avoid giving opinions, asking questions, or expressing dissatisfaction or concern.

Risk Averse

Within the context of downsizing and change, RIOs' caution plays itself out in aversion to risk. We heard about it and saw it in action.

We have a lot of work these days, and I really need all my time at my desk to do it. I know some people like to get together and share ideas, but I don't feel comfortable giving an opinion. I always keep thinking of the work that needs to be done.

We coached one manager whose new team was composed primarily of RIOs. Jim was in the midst of training them on new procedures. His problem was determining if the team had "gotten it," since no one asked questions or gave any feedback. And he wanted to find out in a way that did not add to their anxiety. Not surprisingly, Jim was very frustrated.

We heard from another manager, Sue, about her efforts even to keep her direct report in sight:

If I didn't have structured meetings with built-in participation, and if I didn't go after him, I'd never see him.

Likewise, Jim, the manager training his new team, lamented to us:

How will this team ever meet the new goals if they won't take any risks?

"Risk averse" takes on multiple meanings and dimensions for this survivor group. They shrink from trying new tasks not only because of the fear of failing but because of what they perceive the ultimate consequences will be: termination.

Taking risks means acknowledging the past is over, letting down their defenses, and shedding their denial system.

RIOs' avoiding risks occurs not only on the employee level. We worked with one department in which members complained about the cutback in staff meetings that had previously been regular Wednesday morning occurrences. The company was in the midst of reorganization, and the quest for information was particularly keen. The department manager explained the cancellations in terms of his increased work load. Notwithstanding the work load, we surmised that the manager's actions were equally explained by his fear that in meetings the staff would challenge him to take an action that would have him "rocking the boat." Hence, this RIO restricted opportunities for such communications.

We observed this same quest for safety elsewhere. A vice president in another organization was torn between wanting to know what was going on with his division and fearing that he would learn of his employees expressing opinions that might generate unwanted attention and increased visibility for them and ultimately him.

We were teaching a leadership course for a group of high-potential managers at a financial services institution. Their performance in the course was being evaluated. They were cognizant of this and knew the results would be used as part of a succession planning program. The organization was preparing for downsizing, so assessment would have significant impact not only on decisions about promotions but possibly demotions or even layoffs.

When we discussed our concerns about one participant, Sam, with the succession project manager, he replied, "I know what you're talking about, but Sam is very highly thought of by the organization. People will question why he was rated so low." When we reiterated our concerns, this RIO manager was obviously distressed. While he did not question our assessment, we presumed he believed that others' doubts about the rating would be dropped at his door. His solution was to remove himself from the process of reporting the observations—to disassociate himself from the evaluation.

Career Focus: Safety First

Avoiding risks and using caution do not appear only under crisis. For RIOs, safety is an operating principle of their work life.

Jobs are jobs. You hang on if you need it. . . . You don't give up something unless you have something to go to.

When asked "How do you get perceived as an asset in your company?" one RIO replied,

Luck, timing, who you are, who you know; then what you do or how well you do it.

This fatalistic attitude was typical of many RIOs we encountered. Their belief that much of their work life was beyond their control may also have explained their desire to play it safe and their willingness to "hang on."

Given their perception that much of organizational well-being and their future is beyond their control, RIOs turn to relationships to shelter them and make work life safe.

One RIO we interviewed told us that her goal had been to become a branch sales manager when she joined the company. A high-performing sales representative, she had actually been promoted to the new position three months before a downsizing took place. She had not been certain of what would happen to her position for "six tense weeks." Then her boss broke the news that three sales manager positions were being eliminated and, regretfully, he had to redeploy her to her previous position, as she was the newest manager. Our interviewee told us that her overwhelming feeling was relief that she finally knew what would happen, and she accepted the demotion.

A week before our interview, the same boss called her to tell her that a sales manager position had opened up and he wanted her back in that spot.

I did think about it for a few days. But, frankly, I just wasn't willing to put myself out there again. I decided to stay as a sales rep. I'm just not one for taking risks.

Many of the RIOs we met were not without ambition, though they appeared to lack the strong sense of empowerment we heard in other survivors. Given that many were in management roles, how had they pursued their ambitions? We found that they tended to identify and affiliate with mentors and champions. RIOs were political, in the true sense of the word.

The RIOs we interviewed, like the W&Ss, looked to the organization for a long-term relationship.

When I started working here, I didn't think, "I'll work here for a few years and move on." And I wasn't alone. My boss—at fifty-one—had thirty years.

Value: Connection

From the RIO perspective, bosses, friends, the CEO, and social networks all define the job. A key value expressed by RIOs is the importance of feeling connected to the organization and people in it.

This company has been my family. I mean, I've worked with those people for twelve years. We're a team. I don't know what I'd do if we weren't together.

The RIOs struggle because of their conflicting attachments. They are torn between loyalty to the leadership and loyalty to their co-worker friends. Dual loyalties, which are their strength, become their undoing during downsizing. How can they support both management and their colleagues? How can they declare their loyalty to the organization when it is causing such grief for their friends? How can they publicly support their friends who are angry at what the organization is doing?

Larry and I have been friends for years. We're always having coffee together. But since the layoff, he's so angry. I know he feels betrayed and anxious about his future, but I never know when he's going to sound off, what he's going to say, or who he's going to blast. I've gotten to coming in earlier and having coffee at my desk.

Though RIOs may believe that management's actions are unfair, they will not challenge leadership with their perceptions of inequity. On another level they are averse to making any statements or taking any actions that may alienate their friends or cause leadership to perceive them as disloyal.

Some RIOs we encountered came up with ingenious, though obviously painful, methods for dealing with their dilemma. One RIO at a high-tech company told us that when the organization posted the reorganized positions, she had not applied for the senior manager job, though she was certainly qualified and even the logical choice. She hadn't applied, she said, because she did not want to seem disloyal to her good friend and colleague, who had been demoted one level. When her boss approached her about the position, she still did not campaign for it but did agree to allow her name to be put on the list. When she was selected, she accepted the position, saying that she felt better about it since it had come to her and she had gotten it really by default.

RIOs' denial is compounded by their misperception that "the organization (or people within it) will take care of me," as they believe it has done in the past. Whereas W&Ss may anticipate that the organization will make good on its commitment in exchange for W&Ss' hard work and loyalty, RIOs believed that leaders or specific individuals will champion their welfare. So great is their need to believe this that they misread communication, do not ask questions, and fail to hear the organization's message that things are going to be different. Thus, they are incredulous when situations change or champions leave.

We concluded that RIOs are hit harder than any other survivor group when downsizing occurs in waves. They tend to burrow more into their denial, to put their masks on even tighter. Because they tend to go into hiding after the first round of downsizing, it is hard for them to make new friendships, to forge the alliances that are so important to them. Without support systems, subsequent rounds of layoffs become progressively more painful and frightening.

IMPACT ON OTHER SURVIVORS

In good times relationships are a source of strength and support for RIOs. In bad times, that may not be the case. If these relationships threaten their safety, as, for example, W&Ss' confrontation of management may do, then connections with other survivors become dangerous, threats to be avoided.

■ IMPACT ON OTHER RIOs

Given RIOs' reticence to speak, it is difficult to determine their impact on one another.

We did interview two RIOs from the same department—co-workers who sounded like friends. Although they both expressed the same "things will be fine" philosophy, it was not only hard, as we've said, to determine what feelings lay behind the denial but also difficult to know how much they had shared with one another. Were they each thinking, "If I don't talk about it, it isn't happening," thus reinforcing each other's denial? Or were their statements part of a collaborative front?

On the other hand, we knew two managers at another company, a pharmaceutical firm. These colleagues shared interests outside the office in addition to collaborating on management issues during the workday. When the changes came and a new structure—with its uncertainties—was put in place, the phone calls became fewer and the collaboration stopped, as if by mutual consent. As one of the two confided to us, "I just don't know who to trust these days."

RIOs are generally uncomfortable working with or hearing the FODs or, even worse, the highly vocal W&Ss.

■ IMPACT ON W&Ss

RIOs' avoidance and silence are particularly frustrating to W&Ss. Looking for support, W&Ss find instead colleagues who will not back them up, will not respond, and, indeed, sometimes cannot even be found.

What a wimp. He acts like nothing's happening. I always thought he was pretty sharp. He sits during meetings like a lump. They'll walk all over him.

We have said that the W&Ss are not going to lead. But if they are looking to the RIOs to champion or even support their cause, they certainly will be disappointed. RIOs do not want to rock the boat, will not make plans, and avoid taking any actions that require visibility.

■ IMPACT ON FODs

Often FODs are initially concerned about RIOs. Their concern turns to frustration, as FODs recognize that RIOs' denial sets them up to be hurt.

How could Sam not think he'll have to make a decision about taking the demotion they offered him?

FODs are particularly concerned when the RIO is in a management position.

How can any manager think that avoidance, not taking action, will not have an impact on their staff?

FODs see RIOs' reticence as one more reason the restructuring will not work.

ORGANIZATIONAL CHALLENGE

While the RIOs often frustrate their bosses because of their avoidance, they also fool management—temporarily. Seeing them working diligently at their desks and arriving early and leaving late, management believes they are keeping up. But the RIOs we talked to were struggling; they were running to maintain the pace and their productivity. But the situation was temporary. Many could not keep up with the changes and demands of the new organization—and they did not want to be found out. So some of the survivors we interviewed had dropped back to lower positions. Others were clearly experiencing stress and burnout, with increasing rates of absenteeism and illness.

Though their loyalty to management is an asset, RIOs' loyalty comes at a price. By hiding out, by failing to ask questions and take risks, RIOs actually lessen their chances of acquiring the requisite new skills and achieving the necessary productivity. Their failure to speak up also means that the organization does not get the benefit of their ideas or gain an awareness of their concerns.

Not surprisingly, they are the least likely of survivor groups to become survivor leavers—to leave of their own volition. But, ironically, they are probably the most likely to be asked to go in second and third waves of layoffs as their inability to maintain productivity and their stress become clear.

Some RIOs do leave, but usually in a follower mode, saying yes to a "Follow me" offer from a departing colleague or boss. Some have departed upon the insistence of family or the instigation of a persistent headhunter.

Why bother saving the RIOs? Although the organization can be misled by the loyalty, management can count on it. RIOs, who are so willing to put in the time and try harder, have many of the qualities organizations need and that are likely to be in short supply in a changing environment. Thus, this survivor group presents a paradox: a workforce that will stay with you but won't necessarily give you what you want—and not for lack of knowledge, skills, or desire.

With the RIOs, the organizational task is to help them disengage and then reengage—disengage not only from past work tasks and structures but from dependent relationships that may be the result of RIOs' quest for safety. The organization has to help RIOs become personally empowered so that they begin to rely on themselves rather than on relationships that will be increasingly in flux. Management has to foster an environment in which RIOs can feel safe—safe to take risks, make mistakes, and share disagreements and concerns. Taking these actions will enable RIOs to reengage as productive, self-confident employees working in the here and now of the changing organization.

THE RIOs

GROUP ISSUES

Profile   Past oriented, cautious, and risk averse

Career Focus Safety first, relying on mentors and champions

Value   Connection

ORGANIZATIONAL CHALLENGE

The organization has to cut through RIOs' denial, to disengage them from reliance on the past and dependent relationships and to help them become self-reliant, empowered employees.

KEEPING
THE SURVIVORS
ON BOARD

History, communication, change, and transition: For Foot Out the Doors, Wait and Sees, and Ride It Outs alike, these four issues are the most influential in determining whether to jump ship or stay on board.

None of these issues stands alone. History influences not only the organization's development and management of change but also survivors' acceptance of change plans. The success of these plans hinges in turn on the organization's management of employees' transition. Communication— whether in the form of an executive communiqué or one-on-one interaction between a manager and a direct report—permeates all the other issues. Conversely, communication is affected by history, change, and transition.

Survivors defined an organization's history as the company's demonstrated ability (or demonstrated inability) to run the business and to keep promises and treat employees fairly. Survivors used history as a filter to interpret management's words and behavior and to evaluate management's motives. They also used history to predict the future, anticipating management's actions based on past experience.

Survivors used history as well to decide how they would respond, and what roles, if any, they would be willing to take in the company's future.

For survivors, the quantity and quality of organizational communication formed a continual theme, cutting across all survivor groups. Communication is not limited to an organization's message but encompasses the messenger, media, and methods as well. Rumor, myth, muffled conversations at the water cooler, shrugged shoulders, resignations, leaks, disloyalty—these were frequent fallouts if the organization's communication was problematic.

For the purposes of this book, we define change as the events involved in going from one state to another, whether converting from manufacturing munitions to making bicycles, expanding from a local operation to a global market, or shifting from a department of sixteen to sixty or six.

Transition is the psychological process that people experience *in response to* a change. Although models vary, most authors concur that transition includes saying good-bye to the past; passing through a middle state or states of limbo; and embracing the future.

Some experts suggest that problems of productivity and morale result from the organization's failure to manage transition. We certainly found that to be true. But, in addition, many survivors emphasized the impact poor change management had on productivity and morale. Hence, we address both topics.

In each of the chapters we define the issue, discuss the pertinent factors, present the concerns and impacts on each of the survivor groups, provide organizational strategies and key actions, and illuminate the barriers that frequently impede the organization's ability to manage the issue successfully.

5

History of the Organization

INTERPRETING THE PAST

For survivors, the adage that past behavior is predictive of future performance has a special twist, for it is the company's past behavior or history that survivors use not only in predicting how the organization will perform but also in interpreting and reinterpreting actions and events.

An organization's history or, more accurately, survivors' perceptions of that history, has a profound impact on survivors, from their interpretation of a CEO's communiqué to their acceptance or rejection of a step down in position during difficult times.

Survivors use the organization's history to create a filter, positive or negative, through which they perceive management's current behavior and predict the company's future actions. Thus, some expect that management will make sound decisions; conversely, others doubt management's ability to lead in the post-downsizing times.

What do we mean by history? Based on our conversations with survivors, we are defining history as the company's demonstrated ability (or its demonstrated inability) to run the business and to keep promises and treat employees fairly. For the survivors we interviewed, the term *company* was synonymous with management. Like the survivors, we have used the terms interchangeably, intermixing *organization* as well.

A preliminary note: History reflects the period of time from the inception of the organization to the present. An individual's history can start and end at any point within that continuum. One employee's "good old days" may consist of the past two months, while someone else's encompasses thirty years. We cannot assume that because someone has been with a company only three months that that employee has no historical perspective or perceptions. However, we found evidence that long-term history really sticks, as the historical perspective becomes more grounded; hence, expectations and interpretations are harder to change.

RUNNING THE BUSINESS

Our definition of history leads immediately to the question, What do we mean by running the business?

Solid Foundation

Running the business is defined most succinctly as competence, measured by survivors in part through evaluation of elements that make up the organization's foundation, for example, the strategic plan, fiscal soundness, capital management, and marketing plans. Therefore, assessing how well a company has run the business means not only determining whether these elements are in place but answering such questions as, Are they realistic? In line with current developments in the market and industry? Appropriate to the organization's present size and scope? Do these elements together help to provide a foundation for successful operation of the business? Or are they faulty or lacking?

> *I've been with this company twenty-two years. Sure there's been some rough times, but the company's done OK. Even at the worst of times we held onto our market share. The industry has some problems, but I know the reorganization will position us to stay competitive.*

Successful Implementation

For survivors we interviewed, running the business meant execution as well as design. A strategic plan might be brilliant on paper, but having the practices in place to operationalize that plan was equally, if not more, important. How effective was the organization at implementing policies? Were business and financial resources used appropriately? These were key questions asked by survivors.

Handling the Bad Times

Another historical measure for survivors has to do with company actions during periods of crisis. What has been management's behavior in the bad times as well as in the good? Does the company still make solid decisions and demonstrate fair treatment, or does management collapse?

They just could never get themselves back on track after deregulation took effect. It was like working for a different company.

Running the business encompasses not only the actions management puts in place to make the company run smoothly and profitably but also the steps the organization takes to get back on track when the company is in trouble.

In the past, had management's actions reflected an ability to maintain the focus, identify problems, and make mid-course corrections if necessary? Had management shown an ability to ride out and overcome industry and business problems? More immediately, did management employ appropriate strategies to try to avert the downsizing? Did management use layoffs as a last or a first resort?

Planning for the Future

Survivors measure the company's success at running the business not only by how well the organization has done in the past but by the way that success has come about. How well planned has it been? Has the organization had a focus—a clear vision for the future? From the survivors' perspectives, has the company used good business sense?

Formal Benchmarks

Survivors referred us to those formal and informal benchmarks they used to measure the organization's ability to run the business. The formal benchmarks that interviewees referenced most frequently included the organization's industry ranking, its track record of profitability, and the company's record of growth.

When I graduated, we were all competing for positions [here]. . . . I mean, everybody knew which companies were one, two, three. When the new ratings came out, it was like tracking baseball statistics— everyone could recite not only the numbers but which organizations had moved up, which ones had slipped.

Survivors are, for the most part, very cognizant of industry ranking systems and how their company fares on them. Those survivors with a longer tenure are able to chronicle how the company's ratings have changed over the years.

Of the survivors we interviewed, many were quite knowledgeable about the company's profitability. Survivors who had stock options were keenly aware of how the organization had done vis à vis hitting sales goals and achieving bottom-line results. Employees also tracked sales and how they related to the organization's market share.

> *When I joined the company twelve years ago, I was given a great stock option plan. It was a real incentive for my deciding to join, even though I had to uproot my family and move across the country. The stock's done very well. Gave me a lot of confidence in the company. Even when the market was down, they have maintained themselves well.*

Informal Benchmarks

How effectively the company can run the business is determined by informal benchmarks as well.

One informal benchmark survivors monitor is "the word on the street"—in other words, how the non-business community perceives the organization. At issue for survivors is the organization's reputation—is the organization perceived as being on the leading edge in the industry, innovative, providing quality products or services?

> *The real acid test is how quickly you tell the name of your company at a cocktail party—or do you leave it at "I'm in finance"?*

Employees affiliated with professional organizations reference the industry scuttlebutt. Within their profession's ranks, is their company reputed to be a good place to work? Is the organization seen as a leader in its field?

> *It didn't matter what the salary was; everybody wanted to work in [the company's] lab. They were the top researchers, and the opportunities were incredible!*

The most significant informal benchmarks are comprised of personal events experienced by survivors or their co-workers.

> *I had the highest regard for management until they brought in the new VP. Unfortunately, she became my boss . . . and I have to say, she*

really couldn't manage. She sure didn't live up to the press they were touting when they hired her. It made me start to have serious questions about leadership.

KEEPING PROMISES AND TREATING EMPLOYEES FAIRLY

The second historical factor that our survivors mentioned again and again was the organization's demonstrated ability—or demonstrated inability—to keep promises and treat employees fairly.

Policies and Practices

This second factor, like the first, is reflected in policies and practices. Areas of concern encompass the typical conditions of employment: Is the salary structure equitable? The benefit program appropriate in scope? Are there adequate grievance policies? Are policies in place to ensure that employees are treated fairly—for example, that reward and promotion systems are tied to performance? Do policies reflect prevailing standards?

What about the application of policies, that is, employee practices? Are they administered fairly? In a timely manner? Are practices current? Are managers trained to administer them?

Often, the issues of promises and fairness converge in survivors' experiences:

I haven't had a performance evaluation in eighteen months. Why would I trust their promises about the future if they couldn't even follow common personnel practices?

Keeping Promises

In addition to fulfilling explicit promises—supplying a regular paycheck, paying promised amounts, providing benefits, granting time off for holidays, adhering to the conditions stated in hire letters—the organization needs to demonstrate its ability to carry out implicit promises: provide competent bosses, an environment in which one can be productive and successful, and training and coaching, to name the more common ones.

Promises, by definition, are commitments to be met. So survivors have a simple measure: Promises have been kept or they have not. And an organization's repeatedly failing to keep promises, whether they are explicit or implicit, sets a pattern.

Sometimes the issue is not only whether the promise is kept but the very conditions and/or terms of the promise:

They promised me that if I covered Al's desk I'd get recognition and it would be sure to be noted at performance review time. What did they mean? Was I going to get Al's perks for doing his job? Was Al going to be paid less for not performing? Fair, huh?

Fairness

Fairness, whether attached to a promise or not, is also an issue.

Since the last downsizing two years ago, sometimes we work as much as two full shifts a week at a time. And there doesn't appear to be any letup planned.

This survivor told us that the issue was not the overtime policy—everyone had to do it, and the pay was appropriate—but rather the fairness of requiring overtime as if it were part of standard working conditions. He added that he knew most of the people in his department were looking for jobs.

The issues that survivors spoke to most frequently when discussing the organization's fairness were salary equity, adequacy of benefits, performance management, and what we have called "fairness to me."

Salary Equity

Newspapers have reported that employees at many companies have had their salaries frozen or been asked to take cuts. At the same time these employees have seen salary increases for executives.

Now my salary's frozen for the next two years, and the CEO's just gotten a six percent increase. And I don't want to even tell you about the bonus on top of that. They created this mess, and now it seems like they're getting rewarded for it!

Historically, if executives profit in good times while employees receive only minimal rewards, employees are more resentful when asked to give up anything during downturns. They are much more skeptical about management's sacrifices, no matter how substantial or well intentioned.

On the other hand, some of the survivors we interviewed described their management as being particularly sensitive to the issue of salary equity. One interviewee reported,

> The last time employees had a wage freeze, the executives agreed to a salary freeze and substantial reduction in their bonuses. We all felt that they really meant to turn this around.

This employee went on to tell us how this action on management's part had served more than anything else to draw management and employees together as a team.

Adequacy of Benefits

The second fairness issue, the adequacy of the benefits program, comes to light when survivors use it as a measure of their salaries. Though employees may not take issue with salaries initially, when benefits are called into question, employees take another look and often find their salaries more and more unpalatable in view of their decreased benefits.

> Our union in the past has only had to deal with salary disputes. During the last two bargaining sessions they've had to fight to maintain benefits—and I mean, not to increase benefits, just to maintain what we've got.

We heard most about medical and retirement benefits. Employees across the country and across industries are being asked to take on a larger share of the premium costs, previously paid in full or substantial part by the organization. It is not surprising that this change generates discussion about salaries, particularly by those employees who have had their salaries frozen or have been asked to take a cut as well.

> Management always seemed to take actions that I could understand. This last year, though, they have repeatedly told us our salaries were on hold and at the same time told us our benefits were being reduced. Now, the president has always been fair in the past, but I don't know, this seems like a different company.

Changes in benefits, though important in themselves, also impact survivors' perceptions. For some W&Ss, benefits are a company commitment; thus, a change equals a breach of promise and prompts a "what's the next way you're going to desert us?" stance. Many RIOs are devastated by a benefits change, as it offers tangible confirmation of their worst fear, that the organization "will not take care of me."

Performance Management

Performance management—and especially what happens or does not happen to poor performers—is the third issue survivors talked about frequently in their focus on the company's fairness.

> *Mary has been hanging on for years. We're always being asked to redo her work or finish an assignment. And what's happened to her at review time? Nothing! She gets the same increase as everyone else. And, eventually, she'll get the same retirement package, too—because they'll sure never fire her.*

Consequences abound for a company's historical practice of not addressing employees' poor performance. Even if employees with exceptional performance are rewarded, failure to address others' poor performance signals inequitable standards. Maintaining "deadwood" becomes a critical historical issue when companies engage in downsizing, as it prompts employees to question the criteria that will be or have been used to determine who will be laid off. What extraordinary measures will management take to protect poor performers? After so long, do they even recognize them?

> *I try to go around Sara when I need to get work done. She hasn't been able to deal with the complexity of the work for years. If anybody else made the mistakes she's made, they'd have been out the door or at least demoted. But she came here with the vice president, and it's hands off. Talk about protected status. . . . They've been covering for her so many years . . . after sixteen years, they probably couldn't do anything to her if they wanted.*

If protection of poor performers is frustrating to employees, imagine the reactions when survivors perceive the organization does not even have adequate standards for measuring performance.

For FODs, if management cannot or will not distinguish good performance from poor performance, they are unlikely to do so in the future. Since employee performance is integral to running the business, FODs infer that the company may not be capable of managing the people part of the equation.

> *If they can't even agree on what showing up [attendance] means or how to deal with employees who are usually late, how will they come up with a fair way to judge our performance in the future?*

"Fairness to Me"

Fairness is more than a general measure applied across the board. "Fairness to me" is at the center of an employee's personal standards for the organization's fairness. Employees may generalize about fairness, but in the end they base their final judgment largely on how they feel they have been personally treated by management over the years, along two lines. One is recognition for performance:

> *Even when the budget was tight, he always found a way to reward my performance. It wasn't just a good review—he backed up the words with money as much as he could.*

The second is how the organization responds to extraordinary circumstances or conditions employees encounter. We heard several times from survivors about how the organization helped them through difficult personal challenges. As one employee, who had a catastrophic illness, related:

> *They stuck by me ... kept my job open. ... My sick leave ran out. ... My boss said not to worry ... kept temps in my job until I could come back. That's what I mean by how great this company is!*

SURVIVORS' ASSESSMENTS OF COMPANY HISTORY

FODs, W&Ss, and RIOs reveal different priorities in evaluating the organization's history.

How the Groups Differ

To put this most succinctly, we conclude that FODs weight most heavily the organization's track record for running the business. Keeping promises counts most for the W&Ss and "taking care of me" for the RIOs. These historical elements become the primary factors guiding each group's evaluation of the organization's subsequent actions as well.

 FODs' ASSESSMENTS

"Can do" is the marker by which FODs evaluate the organization's history and thus their own future. For the FODs, the critical measure is competence. Management's track record, based on the capability of its leaders and their history of planning, implementation, and results, is a crucial element in the FODs' beliefs about the future.

> *The very people who got us into this are still there. Why would anyone think they could get us out?*

Indeed, the FODs' assessment of historical (and thus future) competence in running the business is often a predictor of this survivor group's decision to leave or to stay and be a part of that future.

Given their concern with their career future and their orientation toward planning, FODs assess the organization's actions less in terms of immediate impact than in terms of long-term consequences—for example, management's keeping the business afloat so there will be a future for the organization. No business in the future equals "no future for me."

FODs recognize that managing change and managing the future often call for new kinds of leadership. They assess the organization's leadership potential and management's own assessment of its talent. Which people are assigned key roles? Which executives are put in charge? Are people placed in change management roles because of capability rather than availability?

> *It was apparent that the president recognized the criticality of the change, because he moved John, the director of finance, into the leadership position. Everyone was surprised he was willing to shift John to this role, since he was a key player in a critical division already. That really spoke volumes to us about the company's commitment to making this restructuring plan a success.*

■   W&Ss' ASSESSMENTS

Where competence is the focal point for FODs, a record of keeping promises and "treating me fairly" is the critical issue for the W&Ss. For this survivor group, "treating me fairly" reflects the organization's commitment to employees.

W&Ss are always alert to issues of fairness, no matter the scope, but primarily those focusing on them. Whether their concern is about their career path or keeping their phone extension, they are carefully measuring the justice and equity in how the decisions are being made.

> *We have people who've given ten, fifteen-plus years of hard work to the organization. Some of these people are going to be out on the streets. And I could be one of them. And why? Because the company can't manage. They always said, "hard work pays off." For who?*

When W&Ss critique the integrity and competence of organizations, they do so with the principle of equity—"how fair is it?"—in the forefront. They are truly concerned about equity for colleagues, often championing their case. Further, W&Ss tend to personalize issues; their actions are sometimes colored by the idea that "if they'll do it to Joe, they'll do it to me."

Thus, their refrain, "How fair is it?" often means, "How fair is it to me?" Likewise, some W&Ss interpret unethical and unfair actions as intentional acts, sometimes aimed at them.

Some W&Ss expressed a certain skepticism in evaluating the organization's history. Yet, given the W&Ss' reactive posture, history provides them with an important tool. While laying out a carefully considered analysis, W&Ss occasionally cite historical examples when they need ammunition to support a current stance. They may talk at length with no mention of history, until an incident triggers their selective recall. At that point they begin referring to historical events that support their doubts about either the integrity or competence of the organization. If, for example, W&Ss are uncomfortable with the organization's failure to spell out details of the reorganization, the W&Ss may point to past events to justify their conclusion that the organization lacks competent leadership to run the business in the future.

W&Ss are not ambivalent about the issue of competence. It emerges from their laundry list when they are feeling particularly stressed or threatened about their future. So, again, they evaluate the issue from its impact on them personally.

Before the downsizing, our department consisted of seven engineers . . . all well educated . . . some truly brilliant people. We'd won international recognition for their work. The company paid good money for them. Three of my colleagues are laid off primarily because the organization didn't know how to utilize their talents. . . . What happened to them could happen to me. I do what I'm told, work on the projects I'm assigned, even though I don't necessarily think it's the best use of my expertise.

■ RIOs' ASSESSMENTS

For RIOs, in contrast to the W&Ss, history is critical because it provides essential grounding. History offers answers to the questions, "What can I count on?" "What can I expect?" RIOs find comfort in tradition, stability, sameness, constancy, and consistency. Thus, RIOs anchor themselves to the past as a means of providing security for the present and direction for the future. While the W&Ss bring out history selectively and wave it like a banner, the RIOs depend on it.

Consistency is the glue that holds the world together for the RIOs. When it comes to history, consistency has to link elements of integrity, stability, and fairness into a pattern that says to this survivor group, "The organization has taken care of me in the past, and it will continue to take care of me in the future." RIOs are less interested in how this is done or the competency with which it is accomplished. That it will continue to happen, that it can be counted on, is their primary benchmark.

Integrity is an essential element for this third survivor group. Often overwhelmed, confused, and fearful of the changes taking place, RIOs look to the organization's history to find an ethical rationale for what is happening to them. The organization's integrity is paramount as well in explaining what may otherwise be perceived as unfair acts, from their friends being laid off to their bosses retreating.

While the W&Ss sometimes use history to substantiate their challenges of organizational actions, the RIOs, in the worst case, use history in the opposite way—to avoid questioning these same actions.

> *[The organization] has always tried to be fair with employees. Those*
> · *people [disgruntled employees] are just trying to cause trouble. They'll*
> *push the company too far, and we'll all suffer. I don't want to be a part*
> *of it. If they'd just leave well enough alone...*

TRUST

Why have we put running the business and keeping promises and treating employees fairly in "history"? How do these seemingly disparate factors relate?

Employees who found the organization's running the business quite successful, survivors who perceived employees are treated fairly, and all those who held the opposite perceptions had one important element in common: their trust or lack of trust in the organization. As one manager told us:

> Trust is probably—if you are to talk to the people who work here, the
> workforce in general—trust is the number one issue. I think that's
> what has suffered the most.

Competence and Integrity

Drew Lebby, an organization consultant, defines *trust* as the assessment employees make about the probability of management's keeping future commitments. Lebby suggests that trust is composed of two parts: the organization's competence to keep future commitments and the organization's integrity in keeping future commitments. To tie this definition to our hypothesis: Survivors' judgments about the future vis à vis trust are based on their assessment of the organization's track record for running the business (competence) and keeping promises and treating employees fairly (integrity).

Lebby further contends that if employees perceive the organization as lacking integrity, then competence will have greatly diminished weight. We found this generally to be true; all of the survivors we interviewed rated integrity as critical. Lebby continues that if employees assess that the organization has integrity, they will be less likely to criticize the organization for lacking competence. We found this statement holding true for some but not all of the survivor groups.

Pat del Valle, Human Resources Director, Vice President at Bank of North America, adds,

> I don't think you can gain employees' trust quickly if you haven't demonstrated it in prior situations. [Our president was able to do that so well] because he has always been open with people; there was a trust there initially due to his focus on relationship building and forthrightness.

Judith Vogel, an organization development consultant in Maryland, referencing her work with downsizing companies, noted,

> Layoffs deeply stress whatever trust there is. . . . The organization may in fact not be able to sustain itself if not enough "credit" has been accumulated beforehand.

Consistency

Ozzie Hager, a leader of a human resources consultant team at Honeywell, brings up another critical issue in the development of trust:

> People like things that are consistent, that they can count on. They don't have to be great things. They don't have to be things that make them happy. But they have to see some consistency to it. And they'll start believing. That way, when you say, "We have to turn ninety degrees," they'll turn ninety degrees.

Consistency cuts across all areas, and from an historical perspective, it is not difficult to track. Has the company consistently met organizational goals? Has management dealt with employees in a fair and equitable way? The issue is not whether the organization did it once or twice but whether it does it consistently over time. So, in terms of running the business, even if the company had spectacular results in one year or two, that is not what survivors look at in determining trust. What they want to measure is dependability; that is, what the pattern has been over a decade. In the same vein, consistency in treating employees equitably is not the company's method of paying bonuses, no matter how fair or generous in 1993. Is it an ongoing practice or was the 1993 bonus a fluke, albeit a pleasant one?

Consequences of Assessments

Whether their trust level comes from their perception that the organization can be relied on to run the business or from a positive view of the company's track record for treating employees fairly, survivors who trust tend to accept the company's decisions and believe the company's rationale. Relying on their positive assessment of the organization's history, survivors told us they were willing to give management the benefit of the doubt, which meant that they overlooked mistakes and tolerated more ambiguity and vagaries.

Conversely, if survivors' experiences were the opposite, if their assessment was poor, then survivors mistrusted leadership. Overtly or covertly, they questioned announcements and discounted management decisions. They challenged management's policies and mistrusted management's promises and plans.

The survivor groups display varying reactions.

■ FODs' REACTIONS

FODs put their historical assessment of the organization's track record and leadership to immediate use. Given their proactive nature, FODs identify projects and leaders that have the greatest likelihood of being successful and impacting the organization's future. They set out to align themselves with these individuals and the work.

I had opportunities to work on two similar projects developing new operational systems. Even though one had a higher profile in the organization, I wasn't convinced the project leader could pull it off. So I opted to go with the other, a smaller, less visible endeavor, but with a leadership team that had a reputation for successfully completing projects.... I made the right choice.

When their trust level is not high, FODs' first recourse is to try to influence the course of events. This might mean pointing out problems and suggesting alternatives: "I see some pitfalls." "I think this will be problematic." "How about . . . ?" If they feel they cannot make headway, FODs begin the process of disengaging and focus instead on creating their own future elsewhere.

It doesn't occur to me to spend any more time trying to get them to modify . . . I've made as many recommendations as I'm going to make. When they just die, it's not a productive use of my time to keep hammering away, so I go do something else.

■   W&Ss' REACTIONS

For the W&Ss, if the history is negative, the result is mistrust—mistrust particularly of promises and future plans.

Now they're talking about everyone being in a self-managed work team. Sounds good on paper, but they'll find a way to screw this one up, too.

W&Ss are then less willing to tolerate ambiguity and more likely to question management's statements and actions. If they cannot see it or hear it—in other words, if they do not have tangible evidence—the message is not credible. These survivors are not going to rely on words. Past experience is the criterion. They challenge the message, and they are not above (figuratively speaking) killing the messenger.

We saw the impact firsthand when we were consulting with a W&S manager and her direct report, who was also, in our assessment, a W&S. When the manager laid out a consolidation plan, the employee went on an attack, challenging the equity of the plan on everything from new offices to job assignments. The manager mounted a counterattack, arguing for the fairness of the proposed items. There were rationales and elements of truth on both sides, but they were expressed dogmatically, as absolutes rather than subjective perceptions. Both parties became so aggressive that they seemed oblivious to our presence and unaware of the impact on other staff members. When the manager left for a few minutes to take a phone call, the W&S raged to co-workers, "Did you see how unfair she is? She cut me right off, attacked all my ideas."

The employee was clearly trying to rally the troops to her cause. But the group's response was a non-response, neither supporting the speaker nor defending the absent manager. We saw a few individuals rolling their eyes and making nonverbal contact, while the rest shuffled papers or busied themselves with work.

In another case, a W&S, losing patience with what he perceived as mistakes or inequities, had taken to drafting inquiry memos each time a communiqué came forth from the president. In his memos he cited historical precedents for his challenges to the president's actions.

■   RIOs' REACTIONS

If the history is poor from the RIOs' perspective, they go further and further into avoidance, hiding out even more. "If you can't find me, you can't hurt me, and given what you've done in the past, I can't trust you not to hurt me." This was somewhat paradoxical since in the case of a positive history, RIOs are reassured by the notion that the organization will take care of them. For RIOs there is no middle ground: They are either very safe or in imminent danger—and history, rather than current promises or threats, is the determinant.

When RIOs feel that they have not been taken care of in the past or that friends have been let down (Remember those people who had to take lateral moves?), it diminishes the trust account they are carefully monitoring. The past is one side of a ledger against which current events are debited. If too little is in the bank or too much withdrawn, then RIOs distrust to the point that they wonder how much loyalty they can continue to give. And, from their perspective, the greatest thing these survivors can give the company is their loyalty.

Whereas in negative situations the W&Ss look to rally people and the FODs opt to move on, the RIOs, even from their bunker positions, scout for caretakers. They may go back to old bosses or to peers who have been protective in the past.

> I knew going to my former boss wasn't the correct thing to do, but I felt like I didn't have a choice. I was sure the end was coming at any moment, and I couldn't trust any of them.

Their need to be protected means they engage in misalliances and even become victims of those with other ends.

LEADERSHIP

Whether they focus on the soundness of the organization's foundation, the effectiveness of everyday implementation, or the company's track record for keeping promises, survivors see management as an integral part. So, in assessing the organization's history, survivors measure not only the policies and practices but the people behind them—the executives and managers. Have senior executives, in survivors' perceptions, demonstrated the business acumen to develop strategic plans and create visions? Have middle managers displayed the ability to translate visions and plans into practices?

> *I had very little faith in whatever decision they were going to make. The history of [the company] has been that way. They have reorganized in the past.... Whatever decision they make, it turns around and they change it in two years; they decide it didn't work.*

Assessing Individual Leaders

Survivors referred to management in general but more frequently spoke of specific individuals.

> *My boss had welcomed me with open arms and told me how much he supported my department. Then he told me I had to cut my budget by a third. That meant, of course, that I had to downsize. There was nothing else to cut. He suggested that everyone in the division was going through this.... I believed him. Then I talked to my colleagues. I was the one really getting hit this bad. It was very blatant—to everyone but me.*

Survivors may never have had personal contact with the organization's senior executives. Nonetheless, survivors have very clear perceptions of management's performance; they know what roles the executives play beyond those that are listed on the organizational chart. They know which ones are the movers and shakers, the rainmakers and deal makers, the creative forces and the financial wizards. They also know which executives are ineffectual or inept, no matter what the hierarchy. They glean this information either from personal experience or from colleagues' narratives.

> *John's a really nice man; he's friendly; he's dedicated to the company and the employees. But I don't think he has the ability to pull us out*

this time. And he certainly hasn't surrounded himself with a strong executive team. I think they're out of their league.

Leaders' Roles: Champions, Caretakers, and Hatchets

Survivors also know the additional roles individuals have played historically and by which they are known to employees.

I wish I worked in his department. He always goes to bat for his people, no matter who he has to take on.

We heard frequently about these "champions." They came from a variety of positions and managerial levels. Distinguishing characteristics were their awareness of colleagues' issues and perspectives and their advocacy of these concerns.

Survivors also referenced certain managers as "good guys." They did not mean "goody two-shoes," and they were not talking about people who gave in, were soft touches for raises, or even necessarily took their sides. "Good guys," male or female, were defined as such by their fairness; their actions, popular or unpopular, reflected that they were not arbitrary but reasoned and unbiased in their judgments, whether or not the result was favorable to management or to employees.

The "messengers" were those sources employees counted on to give them information. Messengers can clarify vague memos, interpret obscure actions, and turn the gray into black and white. They were the managers noted not for telling it like it is but for actually telling what the "it" is. Like the good guys, they presented an unbiased rendering of the facts.

Interviewees also identified "caretakers" in their organizations. These individuals were known for looking out for their employees. Caretakers wanted to protect their people by ensuring that they were moved into safe positions.

I will not go along with that realignment because some of my people would have to compete for their positions.

Caretakers, unlike champions who would stand up for issues and rights of groups, tended to push for the needs of select people. Caretaking had an edge of manipulation; often caretakers exacted loyalty or gratitude from their employees as payment. While employees might align themselves with a champion's cause, individuals ingratiated themselves to caretakers as a way of gaining favor.

Ironically, people in many organizations described at least one person in upper management as having a Machiavellian bent. Employees neither gave these people information nor necessarily believed what they said, since these individuals were likely to communicate in a self-serving way. They were often powerful and independent, forming and disbanding alliances to suit their needs. Employees saw their actions as based on self-interest and self-promotion—all of which made them suspect and lacking in credibility.

Employees also defined the "hatchets," the individuals seemingly put in place to do the organization's dirty work.

Sam was known as a good manager but someone who couldn't fire people. I think John [the president] replaced Sam with Tom now because John knew we were going to go through downsizing. Tom has a reputation as a hard-liner who's had no problem letting people go.

Not surprisingly, survivors attempted to stay clear of the hatchets and mistrusted any messages of reassurance from them. In fact, even the movement of a hatchet to a key role or task force was enough to send employees scurrying for champions or caretakers.

CREDIBILITY AUDIT

Generally speaking, how can an organization build on a good history to strengthen survivors' perceptions and ensure their positive reactions to the current reality? How can management reinforce a positive filter and strengthen employees' willingness to adapt and perform even in the midst of turmoil?

What can an organization do to neutralize a poor history, to adjust the filters to change survivors' perceptions of current reality? How can it modify survivors' responses to current activities and the measures they will use to evaluate future actions? How does it position or reposition itself for credibility?

To begin with, the organization needs to know where it stands. Management needs to identify the employees' perceptions of the organization. Conducting what we have titled a Credibility Audit is one way to get the information. A Credibility Audit provides insight into three areas: (1) how employees themselves reacted to past events, which should be predictive of how they will react in similar situations in the future; (2) how employees evaluated or judged past events and the organization or people responsible for managing them; and (3) how employees are currently feeling about the organization—that is, their level of trust—with historical clues as to the reasons. This historical perspective explains the what and the how of the filters survivors employ. Consider a W&S whose vocal reaction seems out of proportion to the organization's announcement that it is considering an acquisition. Knowing that he perceives he has been treated unfairly in a past reorganization offers some explanation for his current response.

Predicting Performance via Perceptions

From a prognostic point of view, a Credibility Audit suggests past behavior as predictive of future performance in a particular way: Employees' perception of the organization's past behavior serves as a predictor of how much employees trust the company's ability and willingness to perform in the future. So in answering "Can the CEO manage the change?" employees are not just considering "Hmm . . . let's see, how did he do on a similar task in the past?" but "How do I perceive that the CEO did?" Do employees believe that the company will take the right course of action? How much do they trust that the company's downsizing selection process will be fair? What are their assumptions about whether the organization will handle downsizing or merging in ways that indicate managing the business and treating employees fairly?

Therefore, employees are in readiness; they have a certain lens on, and when the company starts to act, its actions get filtered through that lens, emerging as perceptions, which may or may not match the company's behavior. The Credibility Audit, then, suggests employees' expectations/anticipation of the company's future behavior.

Clarifying Expectations

A Credibility Audit clarifies expectations—what employees expect of the organization, and what the organization can expect from them in terms of reactions and actions as the company undergoes change and transition.

That's why the Credibility Audit is so important. When employees' assessments of the company are negative, even if the company has improved dramatically, changing employees' perceptions is still a significant issue for the company to deal with in order to make change successful. How can the perceptions be changed? How can trust and believability be increased?

The Credibility Audit's Content

The Credibility Audit probes those general areas that survivors have defined as the historical basis for trust and that we have presented throughout this chapter: the organization's demonstrated ability to run the business and to keep promises and treat employees fairly.

A Credibility Audit offers an historical perspective not only on day-to-day practices—for example, whether managers do performance reviews on time—but, as importantly, on how the organization has dealt with change, reorganization, or similar large-scale events. With regard to the latter, a Credibility Audit reveals the level of trust and credibility that emerged as a result of employees' perceptions of how those events were managed.

There is no "one size fits all" Credibility Audit. Although there are general categories to be audited, the specific questions drafted will be based on actions and events emanating from the organization's own history.

Designing the Credibility Audit

We recommend that the audit assess employees' *awareness* of organizational elements (such as strategic planning and fiscal soundness) and events.

The second level of inquiry extends to employees' *analysis* of the same elements, issues, and events and, therefore, calls for qualitative responses. Here the Credibility Audit might probe survivors' opinions as to how realistic the strategic plan is and its appropriateness in terms of the organization and industry.

Table 1 outlines recommended areas for focus and offers an overview of the kinds of inquiry issues the organization might address. It is not a sample questionnaire but a tool to help generate a Credibility Audit that will address the organization's history in a comprehensive way.

Customarily, people will answer Credibility Audit questions looking at the organization as a whole. If management believes that a specific division, department, or site warrants a review, the same model can be utilized in developing a specialized audit.

Introducing and Drafting the Credibility Audit

We recommend that the organization communicate clearly and at length as to how the Credibility Audit will be developed, administered, and used. To prepare for creating the Credibility Audit, we suggest that management hold focus groups simultaneously in different areas of the

Table 1 **AREAS OF FOCUS FOR A CREDIBILITY AUDIT**

Areas	Inquiry
Organizational Goals/Vision	Are goals and a vision communicated?
	Are they realistic?
	Are they appropriate to the organization and industry?
Leadership	Is leadership competent? (check all levels—executive to first-level management)
	How effectively has leadership performed during prior change or crises?
Roles	Are roles clearly stated?
	Are processes in place to ensure employees are competent to perform roles (e.g., training and coaching)?
	Are the promotion criteria explicit? Perceived as fair?
Reward Systems	Are reward systems fair and equitable?
	Are reward systems administered fairly?
	Do the systems support organizational goals and vision?
	How effectively have these systems been maintained and administered during times of change or crisis?
Benefits	Are benefits fair and equitable?
	Are benefits fairly administered?
	Have benefits been modified in recent years?
	Have the modifications improved the compensation package?

organization. The results should be incorporated into the audit's design. The initial focus groups should review the audit draft and provide feedback for fine-tuning the questionnaire.

Administering the Credibility Audit

Establish a specific and limited time frame for administering the audit and collating the results. Develop and communicate the schedule for administering and analyzing the audit and reporting the results.

We anticipate that our suggestions for announcing and administering the Credibility Audit have not met with surprise. Indeed, we assume that they reiterate what readers already know are good basic practices for organizational surveys.

Table 1 **AREAS OF FOCUS FOR A CREDIBILITY AUDIT** (continued)

Areas	Inquiry
Communication	Are organizational communication systems in place?
	Is information communicated in a timely manner?
	Is information communicated consistently to employees?
	Is information provided complete and relevant?
	Is communication effective during change or crisis?
Planning	Does the organization have a strategic plan?
	Are plans appropriate and comprehensive?
	Does the organization effectively carry out plans?
	Does the organization develop contingency plans?
	Does the organization implement contingency plans?
	Does the organization modify or alter plans as needed?
	How effective was the organization's planning during prior change or crisis?
	How effectively was the plan carried out during prior change or crisis?
Resources	Does the organization use outside resources?
	Are these resources competent?
	Does the organization effectively utilize these resources?

Why then, as our survivors reported, have surveys often been problematic, if they have been carried out at all? What are the primary barriers that have gotten in the way?

B/A/R/R/I/E/R
Inexperience

Recommending a survey of the scope of the Credibility Audit assumes that management currently has some process for assessing how well it is doing. So one barrier exists from the onset when companies are not accustomed to reviewing organizational procedures and structures. Unfortunately, this is too often the case. As the Wyatt Company (1991) determined in its first survey, "Only four in ten companies initiated a process to question basic business assumptions, despite losses they sustained in profitability, share price, market share, and other indices."

An organization may see little value in analysis of past events. Or, unaccustomed to seeking others'—specifically employees'—feedback when assessing events, management may be reluctant to introduce the process during a time of major change.

B/A/R/R/I/E/R
Past Practices

Another potential barrier, ironically, has to do with history: What has been employees' experience with company surveys in the past? Has the company used surveys positively? Has management acted on the results? Or, as survivors often reported, has the exercise died?

While the Wyatt study (1993) revealed a limited number of organizations doing organizational assessments, at the other extreme, some survivors reported companies with a history of engaging in excessive analysis and/or mismanaging the assessment process. For example, one interviewee told of her organization repeatedly bringing in outside consultants to administer surveys, then never doing anything with the results.

> They've had consultants in three times in the past seven years. We've filled out surveys and gone to focus groups. And we've never heard what happened or what the results were. I don't know of any changes that came from our efforts—I doubt there were. Seems like a waste of time and money. Those consultants aren't free.

In the past, have the surveys been managed by people who have credibility? Or have hatchets or untrustworthy others used surveys as vehicles to set employees up?

> They asked employees to be honest.... We were... we told them what was working and what wasn't.... They weren't happy with the results. ...I guess they didn't hear what they wanted to.... We told them the promotional system wasn't always fair ... employees lacked opportunities for advancement.... The last half-dozen key hires have come from the outside.... It's like they're retaliating for what we said.

Based on past experience, will employees welcome the Credibility Audit or resent it? Will they trust that anonymity and confidentiality will be preserved? When issues are organizational hot buttons and/or the company's track record for administering or using surveys is poor, employees will naturally resist. And if employees are likewise leery as to whether confidentiality will be maintained, the results will be skewed.

Communicating the Results

When communicating the results of the Credibility Audit, be clear as to the next steps—how the results will be incorporated into the future plan(s). Where specific concerns cannot be addressed or systems changed as suggested, acknowledge the request and clarify the organization's position. That clarification may include future options for revisiting the issues. But don't promise modifications if management cannot follow through. And clarification does not include an iteration of excuses.

Addressing the Results: The Credibility Audit As Prescriptive

The Credibility Audit is diagnostic. It will tell companies where survivors' concerns lie, what the underlying issues are, whether the malady is chronic or acute.

The Credibility Audit is also prescriptive. It will tell the organization what it needs to do, which medication should be used, when it should be started, and in what dosages it should be administered.

If the Credibility Audit reveals, for example, that survivors mistrust the company's vision, believing the organization's approach is shotgun, a reaction rather than a well-thought-out plan, then one of the first things the organization has to do is to determine what steps to take to institute a vision that provides the missing framework. So the plan to address the audit's results might call for a process to engage the company in defining a clear statement of vision, prefaced by the acknowledgment that there has been a problem, or at least recognition that the vision is not clear.

Suppose the audit uncovers employees' concerns about management practices, and in the audit employees specifically identify problematic leaders—for example, an individual perceived as inept. Subsequently putting that person in any key role probably will not work. The assignment is unlikely to change the leader's persona. And survivors will still distrust the skills or intent of the person and will further perceive the organization as indifferent to their concerns.

When the Credibility Audit identifies problematic leaders, the best thing for the organization to do is to neutralize their effect by inviting them to join the change team but refraining from placing them in key leadership roles.

Does the audit reveal the organization's failure to involve employees? If so, it's not easy to build in employee involvement this time. The organization needs to ask, Who are the employee leaders? Which survivors have high credibility? Put those people on task forces and on communication, change, and transition teams. Include them in correspondence, with their names listed on change management letterhead. Changing employees' perceptions can begin even with determining who will distribute and review the Credibility Audit.

Should the audit suggest that communication is the problematic area, the Credibility Audit will tell you what your options are; that is, whether the believability quotient is such that the organization can address the situation on its own using internal resources, or whether you need to call on an outside neutral source—in other words, whether the organization needs to change the message, the messenger, or both.

For example, if the organization wants to communicate information, will the company's best strategy be for the CEO to make an announcement, for a transition committee to send out a memo, or for a neutral outsider to facilitate an open meeting?

The organization will need to act immediately to address the deficit area revealed by the audit. It will have immediate opportunities: reporting on the audit itself as well as presenting the resulting plans.

As important as the messenger and the message selected by the organization is the way it decides to apply the information. The answers to this will be in the Credibility Audit as well. For example, if the audit reveals that in the past, outside resources have either been less than competent or used inappropriately (such as to deliver bad news), the organization will need to consider whether or not, and to what degree, consultants will implement a part of the plan. The organization will need to communicate to employees its decision as well as carefully monitor the process.

Just Say No!

If a consultant engaged to facilitate the changes comes in with a template plan, we would be highly suspect. To the degree that the individual wants to make the organization's situation generic, just say no. Designing the Credibility Audit and implementing the results are instances in which "This is our program to address X" will not do. We are not challenging off-the-shelf programs. However, employees know what's healthy and what hurts and even what prescription is needed.

B/A/R/R/I/E/R
Here We Go Again!

If the organization has a poor track record for follow-through, whether on surveys, projects, or plans, it can be a significant barrier to implementation. Employees will naturally think, "Here we go again," disbelieving management's statements and/or discounting the organization's plans.

If the leadership has made poor decisions or exercised faulty judgments in the past, employees may not be willing to "go down the path" behind the leader this time.

The fact is that the company may do all the right things the next time around, but if employees anticipate that the company will not, then what management does will be interpreted negatively. If the organization does not fit employees with different pairs of glasses, then "doing it right" will not be enough.

How to address this barrier? One action may be to acknowledge past poor performance, to acknowledge that "we've made mistakes in the past" or that the process or results "did not meet our expectations." And in addition, the company may need to overexplain the rationale for the plan, communicating how it has assessed the current issues and arrived at decisions differently than in past times.

Admitting past mistakes does not mean management has to "eat a lot of crow," nor does it suggest management include excuses. But officially acknowledging errors does mean that the organization has to be very realistic about what did and did not work before, because employees know, or at least they perceive they know, what did and did not work.

Additionally, although management can look to outside resources for help in keeping the plan on track, only the organization's actions (versus consultants') will reverse employees' perceptions.

The organization's interpretation of the Credibility Audit is as important as its determination of what questions to pose. To have the Credibility Audit be truly meaningful, the company needs to have some awareness of how management perceives the past, of how the organization would measure its track record.

We talked with a variety of organizations and consultants about this very issue. One consultant told us of an assignment to determine the company's (management's and employees') assessment of the organization's performance. She surveyed the executive team and upper management. Then she asked employees the same questions. The results were surprising to all, and gave food for thought. Where management thought the company had done well—for example, in communicating plans—few employees agreed. Conversely, where the executives felt they managed part of the business poorly, employees gave management higher marks, even though the organization's actions had resulted in a budget freeze.

In this case, management used the information to reassess the company's experience and modify the plan. In other cases, such conflicts of perceptions have been the source of another barrier.

B/A/R/R/I/E/R
Disparate Perceptions

When management and employees hold disparate perceptions and assessments of history, that becomes a barrier if the organization discounts the results of the survey, dismissing employees' perceptions because management disagrees with the results or believes survivors' perceptions do not match the facts.

When organizational behavior is contradictory to what is stated or expected, it not only becomes a barrier to implementing the current change(s) but also becomes an historical issue that will have to be dealt with at some time in the future. Every organizational decision, every action that is taken in the present, whether good or bad, effective or ineffective, becomes a part of the organization's history that survivors reference again and again.

The Good News

Thus far, we have focused on the bad news. But the Credibility Audit will identify the good news, the positives, as well. If the audit reveals that something has worked well in the past, replicate it as appropriate. Who has credibility with both management and employees? Put that individual in the change management forefront. Comb the past for what worked. How can you adapt it to the present situation?

▶ *BEST PRACTICE*

During a major change at one company in the Northeast, executives were assigned as resource people (sponsors) for various departments. The departments could direct questions to their sponsoring executive as well as through regular channels. The program served as a way for executives to team up, support each other, and listen to other departments. And it gave employees input from another source.

NO PROMISES

In our interviews it became clear that an organization with a poor history cannot make promises for the future or delay rewards. As this survivor said,

They said I might be up for a promotion in six months if I proved myself. Prove myself? What do they think I've been doing the past five years?

The organization has to ensure that promotions and monetary increases for merit or increased work load not be put off. The company's message to managers must be: Provide rewards and promotions now.

A caution: Managers, concerned about increased work loads and depleting ranks, may be tempted to make promises the company cannot keep. The organization has to keep close tabs, and discourage bosses from making promises of future payoffs. Leaders need to remind them of the legal ramifications of making such statements.

B/A/R/R/I/E/R
Outstanding Debts

If the organization has outstanding promises (debts) to a group, for example, that the department will be expanded or equipment updated, or promises to an individual of developmental opportunities or future assignments, these unfulfilled promises can become a barrier because there is unfinished business from the past, an historical issue unresolved. Management needs to take several steps. First, the organization needs to pay these debts and honor commitments. Otherwise management has to acknowledge that a promise cannot be met due to the changes and examine alternative ways of addressing the debt. Second, the company has to weed out any "carrot" promises that might not be deliverable. In this regard, identify promises that are person-dependent—linked with a boss, for example—because that individual may not be there when the reward is due.

KEY POINTS

Survivors define history as the organization's demonstrated ability (or its demonstrated inability) to run the business and to keep promises and treat employees fairly. Leadership is a critical component. Survivors use their perception of history as the basis for trust, as a filter for perceiving current actions, and as a predictor of the organization's future.

GROUP ISSUES

FODs	Management's competence
W&Ss	The organization's fairness
RIOs	Security; continuity

STRATEGIES

Develop and administer a Credibility Audit to assess employee perceptions of the organization's past behavior. Use the audit results to identify historical barriers and develop strategies for implementing current changes.

As we have stated, a significant issue that the Credibility Audit addresses is the organization's communication. This is also an issue that survivors across all three groups identified as a major concern. We found what they had to say about communication surprising. We turn to this topic next.

6

Communication

"'Well, we're not ready to communicate yet because we're not sure,' they said. 'But you're doing things to people,' I said. 'But we don't know everything that we need to know.' After the meeting one manager stopped and said, 'You know, when you're in the middle of it, you always think it's not time yet. But when you're on the outside of it, you're always thinking, Why aren't they telling us? Why aren't they telling us?'"

Joanne Adams Stroud, Ph.D.

THE MOST POWERFUL PIPELINE

Of all the issues we explored, we expected that communication would be the one that organizations would have mastered or done best. Organizations certainly have had time to develop their skills—after all, they have been communicating as long as they've been in existence. And should they need assistance, the business world is replete with communication books, seminars, programs, and consultants. Hence, we found it puzzling that communication was the issue mentioned most consistently as problematic by survivors at companies that seemed otherwise to do an excellent job of managing change as well as by interviewees at organizations where communication was but one more item on survivors' laundry list of mismanagement.

We also found it puzzling because we expected that organizations would be aware of the criticality of communication in the day-to-day business environment. After all, communication permeates their every transaction and interaction. Communication connects all other elements; it is the vehicle through which history is translated, organizations implement change, and departments, teams, and employees impact each other.

And the impact can be of great magnitude: If communication is effective, it can clarify history and strengthen trust, facilitate transition, or support management. If ineffective, it can supplant history with myth and undermine credibility; foster animosities between those same departments, teams, and employees; impede change; and keep people from moving through transition.

So, from survivors' perspectives, what is important for effective communication? And to reiterate a theme: Some of what we are about to present sounds somewhat basic. But do not be fooled. If these ideas are so basic, why are they not always implemented? What prevents some companies from putting them in place?

THE AUDIENCE

All too often, in survivors' opinions, the focus of communication is that of presenting the corporate philosophy to the outside customer, the shareholders, or the press.

> We got this memo from corporate communications telling us what we were supposed to say to the customers about the merger . . . so they wouldn't get upset. . . . I can't believe they thought they could sell us with the same message.

Survivors could understand that customers needed to get information. At the same time, they felt strongly that management needed to recognize them as a legitimate audience with unique communication needs.

To be sure, we did find excellent examples of communications addressed to employees.

▶ *BEST PRACTICE*

One financial institution effectively applied what it learned from its first downsizing experience.

The organization had a pretty good reputation for truth telling—until the first downsizing took place with almost no written communication. Rumors flew and credibility sank.

The second wave of downsizing was preceded by a four-color fold-out report distributed to all employees. It stated the company's strategy, policies, and problems. It named departments to be affected and provided numbers. It also gave a step-by-step plan, including dates. As an HR manager told us:

> When the rumors started this time, it was not uncommon for employees to respond, "But that's not what the Bible says," as they had named the report. They also felt free to approach management with stories that seemed to conflict with what was stated there.

▶ **BEST PRACTICE**

One high-tech company sent employees a copy of a pending shareholder letter with a cover memo explaining how this communiqué would be used and letting them know that management recognized that they had concerns and questions.

Some survivors suggested, however, that when there was communication directed at employees, it most often focused on those to be downsized. Again, we did not encounter a single interviewee who negated the needs of those individuals for information. At the same time, survivors wanted to hear information that was directed at them and, moreover, communication that reflected some connection to them, some acknowledgment of the impact of the words, some recognition that survivors were a distinct audience with their own set of concerns.

B/A/R/R/I/E/R
Communication As Usual

One barrier to successful communication is treating the communication of change to employees as a functional responsibility rather than a task requiring special attention.

As one consultant pointed out:

> In the planning stages for large-scale organizational change, organizations tend to look in the organization for whatever function is responsible for internal communication and hand it over. They look at it as functional responsibility. They're not paying attention to how different this communication is. They're not seeing it as an integral part of transition that you need to plan for specifically.

B/A/R/R/I/E/R
Lack of Awareness

Another barrier is lack of understanding of survivors as a separate constituency with its own issues and concerns. Based on interviewees' statements and our direct experience with clients, we think that failure to consider the survivors as a distinct audience is an oversight rather than an intentional act.

In summary, the issue is not simply what is said, who says it, and how, but whether the communication that results meets the needs of the listeners.

In our opinion, there are tools to address this issue. To be sure, a Credibility Audit, as outlined in chapter 5, will provide many answers. In addition, understanding the survivor groups and their needs and concerns—and applying that learning as the organization considers the message, messenger, media, and methods of its communication plan—will certainly alter the outcome.

THE MESSAGE

Survivors raised a number of issues related to the message itself. They focused primarily on the content and consistency of the message.

Content

We heard of organizations that did a very satisfactory job of communicating facts—dates, times, places, and the who, what, and how. Many survivors described leaving meetings satisfied with what had been said. They did not equate satisfaction with feeling reassured or freed of anxiety but rather with feeling they had gotten the information they wanted to know.

It was initially somewhat surprising, then, to hear other survivors from the same organizations recall what were clearly the same meetings and describe very different reactions of confusion and dissatisfaction.

So, again, the content has to address the needs of the audience, and FODs, W&Ss, and RIOs express their requirements in quite different terms.

■   FODs' CONTENT NEEDS

One FOD offered the following appraisal of the announcement meetings he had attended:

A lot of the information they told us was really basic understandings: One was that they were going to downsize the organization; second, they need to do this because they need to reduce costs; third is that everyone will be treated fairly . . . which all are really just givens. . . . If this is going to happen, someone's going to say this. . . . There wasn't a lot of value in it.

"What would have been valuable to you?" we asked him.

Where was the organization headed? What was the direction? What were their ideas? I didn't know any more about that when I walked out than when I walked in.

His response typified what we heard from other FODs. This survivor group wants to hear about visions, goals, ideas, opportunities—the future. What is the after-downsizing plan? FODs need to know something about that plan, even in the initial announcement, as reassurance that the organization knows where it is headed, that management has undertaken restructuring proactively rather than as a reactive attempt "to cut costs."

We are not suggesting that the communication exclude what the FOD quoted above dismissed as "basic understandings." Indeed, we are pleased that he had to listen to it—not for himself, but because it is exactly the kind of communication the W&Ss and RIOs, in the same meetings, need to hear.

■   W&Ss' CONTENT NEEDS

Like the FODs, W&Ss want to know that the organization has a plan, but their concerns lie as much with the details as with the overall strategy. If the organization is relocating, what is the move plan? How will termination decisions be carried out?

This reorganization is the biggest thing the company has done in the last twenty-five years. We'll need a step-by-step plan to carry it out. If the details haven't been thought out. . .

W&Ss' motivation for having this information is based in large part on their concern about their place within the organization. These are the survivors, remember, who are attached to their roles within the organizational structure. So they need to know the whos, whats, and whens as to their role at each stage of the change.

■ RIOs' CONTENT NEEDS

RIOs want to know that everyone will be taken care of; they need to be reassured that people will be treated fairly.

They talked about closing plants, retooling the equipment, focusing on new market strategies, but I didn't hear anything about people.

Their loyalty to the organization as well as their sense of security derives from these sorts of values. With their world about to be turned upside down and their stability diminished, RIOs need to know that the foundation is still in place, that the organization for all the impending changes is still the organization they have counted on.

Consistency

Given that organizations communicate to a variety of audiences, consistency of information is a critical issue for survivors generally. Organizations need to be alert to the consistency of (1) messages to external and internal audiences, (2) information coming from different sources, and (3) communication coming from the same source over time.

I have some friends in other divisions. And they have gotten essentially the same information from their management that we got from ours. It may not be good news all the time, but at least they're not sending different messages across the organization.

Contrast that survivor's experience with that of this interviewee from a company across the country:

Every time we have a staff meeting, our manager has a different line. Is he even aware of it?

Inconsistency is particularly damaging the higher up the chain of command. As one survivor told us,

Our president sent out a memo with the plans for the downsizing. Three days later our division head sent out a memo which was supposed to add details but seemed to contradict what the president had said. Talk about confusing!

Certainly even carefully worded messages may have a limited life span. Situations can change, and there generally is an acceptable reason. What seemed to be missing in what people told us was *why* the message is different—the rationale for the change. And this omission served to exacerbate survivors' reactions to what they perceived as inconsistencies.

We encountered one telecommunications company in which employees had been notified that they would be relocating to new office sites on specific dates. There were significant construction problems causing the schedule to be pushed back. Employees received notices of revised relocation dates, with no clear explanation of why. These dates were subsequently changed three more times. Survivors learned the details about what had happened via word of mouth, after spending valuable work time seeking answers.

Yet another issue of consistency/inconsistency is the familiar one of matching words and actions.

> *They kept asking our head of manufacturing, "Are you going to outsource manufacturing?" And he kept saying no. The feedback I got was that they didn't believe him. . . . Why didn't they believe him? Because for about the past year and a half, about every four months or so, the company came out with another announcement about another manufacturing piece that we were outsourcing from the organization.*

All of the survivor groups were alert to inconsistencies; their reactions were different.

■ FODs' REACTIONS TO INCONSISTENCIES

For the FODs, whether there were inconsistencies between speakers or over time, it spoke to them of the organization's not being in control of the situation.

> *It was the old issue of "Does the left hand know what the right one's doing?" It sure didn't sound like it. And people kept trying to discover who did know.*

■ W&Ss' REACTIONS TO INCONSISTENCIES

W&Ss translated inconsistencies into beliefs that the organization had hidden agendas or was withholding information.

You listen to management and they can't get their stories straight. . . . You go to one meeting and they say one thing . . . then the vice president sends out a memo saying something else. . . . I know they're not telling us everything.

■   RIOs' REACTIONS TO INCONSISTENCIES

Inconsistencies supported this survivor group's denial of change, as RIOs might use inconsistencies in the organization's communications as a means to discount information. Thus, consistency can be a tool for management to use to get RIOs through that denial.

Consistency of communication was also particularly important when bosses asked RIOs to take action or try something new, since inconsistency brought RIOs not only confusion but sometimes immobilization.

This is the fifth time they have changed our assignments. First they want it one way and then before we can finish it someone else comes in with a different set of directions. I can't keep up. Frankly, I've stopped trying.

Rumors

Every survivor we interviewed was hungry for communication. Not one felt sated with the quantity or quality of information the organization provided. How had survivors dealt with the scarcity of information?

If the organization wasn't communicating or wasn't communicating enough or wasn't communicating clearly, employees made it up—or listened to and believed what their co-workers made up. Rumors flowed over the phones, across e-mail systems. One survivor told us that his department circulated its own underground rumor sheet.

Rumors tended to be negative, doom-and-gloom messages, giving the worst scenarios as if they were foregone conclusions.

Address the rumors! We have not found any way to eliminate rumors, but the organization can minimize their negative effects by attending to them—which means acknowledging rumors as a legitimate form of communication.

► *BEST PRACTICE*

One company had a Rumor Bulletin. Survivors attested to its effectiveness.

I knew the company knew what employees were thinking just by the way they addressed the rumor mill. All I had to do was check the Bulletin. I felt they were on top of it. That was very reassuring.

Rumors became a critical issue for W&Ss. Remember, they had all the questions for which they needed answers; they found the limbo resulting from lack of information too anxiety-provoking. So if they could not get satisfactory responses from management, they queried their co-workers, whether knowledgeable or not. Several non-W&S interviewees admitted that, as one survivor put it, "I might make something up just to get rid of her."

She's always after me for what do I know about this or that. I'll say, "Yeah, I really don't know, but it seems logical to me that—" and then I'll tell her what I think it should be. . . . Afterward, I'll regret it. . . . I know I shouldn't have said that . . . but she just wears me down.

If W&Ss cannot find anyone to answer their questions, they, too, might "make it up." Taking that action put them back in control.

What are the barriers that prevent organizations from communicating clear, consistent messages?

B/A/R/R/I/E/R
Beliefs Versus Facts

One survivor reported that her organization, in an attempt to bolster morale and improve productivity following a downsizing, announced, "OK, we're done; this is it; you're the survivors." Six months later the organization announced Round Two.

Another interviewee described the opposite scenario:

They told people that after three months, they weren't going to have a job . . . but that didn't happen, because management realized that they couldn't do without them. Of all the departments that I know of that were supposed to be closed, they're all still open. . . . It's been over a year.

Although both messages may have been well intended, what happened is that the organization's beliefs about the situation—that there would or wouldn't be downsizings—were presented as facts.

The impact? In the first case, said one survivor, "When the next downsizing took place, no one ever believed anything they said again." In the second situation, a similar skepticism was fostered. In both situations, employees discounted subsequent messages of any kind, treating even well-documented facts as "maybe, maybe nots."

Drew Lebby, organization consultant, suggests that organizations tend to confuse assessments, statements of opinion ("It looks like it's going to rain") with assertions, statements of fact ("It's raining"). How much better for the outcomes in the examples above if the organizations had not canceled the messages but begun with a positioning statement: "Based on projected outcomes . . . Given what we know at this time . . . Given what we believe . . ." By using these positioning statements, companies will allow themselves to present what is factual at a moment in time but acknowledge the possibility of change because of conditions beyond their control. This will mean, of course, that management has to be willing to admit that it has neither the answers nor a crystal ball.

Adding positioning statements will also preclude employees' allegations that "management is not being honest," a charge sure to arise at a later date if the situation changes. How different the outcome would have been for the organization that had announced, "OK, we're done; no more downsizing."

■   FODs' RESPONSE TO UNQUALIFIED ASSERTIONS

FODs thought all "this is the last" types of statements were suspect. They were uncomfortable when organizations made that kind of blanket promise; they assessed the organization's naiveté and/or unrealistic sense of its power to exert that kind of control over the future. "How do you feel confident enough that you can make that kind of statement?" was one FOD's questions to management in a company meeting.

■   W&Ss' RESPONSE TO UNQUALIFIED ASSERTIONS

Presenting beliefs not only as facts but as absolutes, as in the first situation, was likely to later result in W&Ss vociferously challenging any change in position and seeking support from others.

But prefacing information with positioning statements was also not without peril. W&Ss in particular found this "indefiniteness" unsettling; they were likely to press for clarification ("But what do you mean?" "Do you expect some change?" "What aren't you telling us?") or badger management to provide guarantees.

As a counter to this challenge, our advice to management has been that the organization stick to its guns, reiterating, "Given everything we have . . . we don't think so . . . but we can't guarantee. "

■ RIOs' RESPONSE TO UNQUALIFIED ASSERTIONS

The RIOs appeared to prefer absolute promises at the time because they offered security, even if short lived. In truth, RIOs were still always so hopeful that there would not be more change that they might try to ignore any positioning statement, denying to themselves that it had been added. In fact, it was just these sorts of reality checks that the RIOs need.

B/A/R/R/I/E/R
Language

Sometimes the communication barrier is the language itself: Is it appropriate to the audience, to the criticality of the topic? In the course of interviewing survivors of mergers, we heard frequently about communications using the language and jargon of one organization, not both. In one case survivors kept hearing about "closing offices." Our interviewee was sure that the organization was talking about more downsizing, since in his company, "offices" meant sites. In fact, the organization was speaking about offices literally; it was "closing offices" by knocking down walls and removing doors, as part of conversion to an open-space plan. We imagine that the communication had been reviewed extensively for content by legal and HR departments. How much anxiety—and probably lost productivity—could have been avoided had the message been reviewed for language by members of both organizations?

This example reflects survivors' need for definitions of the new terms, whether they are positive or negative. In addition, communication needs to take into account the multicultural, multi-language issues of a diverse workforce.

Perhaps, as well, there needs to be a list of hot-button words that the organization should avoid. As a number of books and newspaper articles have pointed out, current word usage related to downsizing includes terms associated with death, destruction, and mayhem (Noer, 1993). Additionally, each organization has its own list of red-flag words—words that have the power to stir people up and that often have historically negative connotations.

THE MESSENGER

Survivors reported getting information from multiple sources: executives, supervisors, peers, newspapers, television—even the repair person.

One of our favorite stories concerns an organization that was moving one corporate division from the East Coast to the West. The company had not yet announced the new location. Tension was high. As reported to us, two employees were talking about the scuttlebutt they'd heard, that the organization had pared the list down to two sites. One employee asked her colleague, "They promised they'd make an announcement next week. Do you think they'll actually have a decision by then?" Up popped a telephone service man who had been repairing a cable under the desks. "Don't worry, guys," he said. "It's going to be Portland. We got the service order last week."

When it comes to the official messengers, those people designated by the organization to deliver the news, we heard some outstanding stories.

▶ **BEST PRACTICE**

The head of a strategic business unit whose operations were dispersed around the world spent a whole month flying from country to country to talk to each location about what was happening. As our interviewee surmised, "A lot of executives wouldn't have done that. Maybe send out a nice memo; might put themselves on videotape. But he physically did it." According to our source, it was important to this director to communicate in a way that allowed him to say what he needed to and that permitted employees to get everything off their chests.

Messengers' Attributes

According to survivors, critical issues need to be communicated by authority figures. All of the groups, whatever their individual needs, were influenced by the status of the person presenting the message. The communication carried so much more weight if the CEO was the messenger. The

CEO as bearer of the news ratcheted up the volume—alerting employees that the message was important.

All of the studies we read confirmed the importance of upper management as active participants in communication. According to Wyatt (1993), "Increased senior management visibility" was rated as a "very effective" communication tactic by over half of the companies that employed it.

We are not suggesting that executives be the messengers of all information. But whoever the messenger, that individual has to possess certain attributes, which vary according to the survivor groups.

■ FODs' PREFERENCES

For the FODs, the messenger has to have the proper business credentials—that is, has to be in a high position of authority and thus have the ability to make decisions (on the spot if necessary) as well as report them. The messenger has to have the business savvy that they respect. Depending on the import of the message, the messenger in many cases has to be someone who is not simply repeating the vision and strategy but is the generator of same—one of the originators of the plan.

I don't want her interpretation of the big picture; let's face it, mine is as good as hers. I want it from someone who has pulled the vision together.

And for the messenger to have credibility, FODs have to believe that this person will be in the organization of the future, that she or he is planning to go with them, to take the same risks, to be a player rather than a spokesperson.

■ W&Ss' PREFERENCES

For W&Ss, communication equals a dialogue, a verbal give and take. So they need a messenger who is not only an authority but also a skilled communicator—someone who can engage the W&Ss in discourse. And to make the plan tangible for them, the messenger also has to be well versed in the facts and details. Thus, the project manager and the MIS engineer have potential messenger credibility with the W&Ss.

He just came on and gave the overview and it was really sketchy. . . . We next had a meeting with the company controller, and he went into a lot of detail. . . . I've got to say, he knew what he was talking about . . . and he wasn't afraid to answer questions.

■   RIOs' PREFERENCES

RIOs, as we've said, sometimes try to deny the message. This survivor group, though respectful of authority, often feels intimidated by messengers at the top of the organization who, by their position, reinforce the communiqué. RIOs are more apt to sit silently, unlikely to ask questions.

Again, messengers at the top play an important role for RIOs in helping to cut through their denial. But in terms of ongoing communication, RIOs need messengers who can act as caregivers—who can listen and respond to their concerns. Thus RIOs want messengers with whom they have a relationship. Frequently, RIOs look to their immediate bosses.

RIOs need their bosses as messengers as well because they need constancy—the daily visibility and proximity that bosses can bring. RIOs need to be able to peek out and see a messenger. For RIOs, "out of sight is *not* out of mind." If the messenger is not visible or accessible, some RIOs take that as an environmental marker, a communication that something is wrong, that more change is coming.

Our interviewees revealed a number of messenger-related barriers.

B/A/R/R/I/E/R
Out of the Loop

Survivors, consultants, and managers voiced a common concern: managers discounted as messengers because they were perceived as being outside the organization's communication channels, outside the communication loop. As Jacqueline McHale, a senior management consultant at the Hay Group, stated:

> What I find interesting is that most people will not go to their immediate supervisor and ask. People want it from the top because they don't trust what anyone else knows. They want it from the horse's mouth. And for them to be happy, they have to be able to ask and hear it from that person.

"So, many employees do not see their boss as representing the horse's mouth?" we inquired of McHale. "Why not?"

> People don't trust lines of communication. They don't think that the executive team lets information out or lets enough of it out.

McHale drew attention to a problem that we heard about many times from survivors: People questioned the truth of the message and therefore were skeptical that their manager was "in the know," or people were unconvinced of their boss's authority and thus questioned the validity of the message.

We got feedback from first- and middle-level managers as well that they themselves did not feel that they were in the communication loop, in the know. Survivors, whether FODs, W&Ss, or RIOs, picked up on that:

> *It doesn't do any good to ask him about the new organization, because he's as out of the loop as we are.*

Many interviewees, then, unless it is an unusual situation, tended to discount the boss's messages—and the boss as well.

> *Over lunch one day, my manager said, "You shouldn't feel stressed out about this. . . . Be thankful there is a need for your function here. . . . I feel you should be safe."*

> *So while that was comforting, it was still kind of alarming also because most of the cuts that were announced that were going to be made were really upper-management type. And my manager was one of the people who was going to be targeted first before other people.*

One of the organization's communication responsibilities is to restructure bosses' roles as messengers, to empower them with information and to charge them with the task. We suggest one method for accomplishing this is to pair executives and managers/supervisors as presenters in an information meeting—and with the latter having a significant speaking part, so it is very apparent to the audience that supervisors and managers are in the loop and in the know.

B/A/R/R/I/E/R
Information As Power

Some organizational cultures hold the belief that information is power. If the company has this belief, it may keep information close to the vest and withhold it from employees, carefully controlling the quantity of information, the timing of messages, and the receiving audience. And leaders may redefine the purpose of conveying information as bestowing power on, or withholding it from, others.

If the organizational norm is that information equals power, employees will use information in the same way—withholding knowledge, questions, and responses. Management will certainly be impotent to anticipate problems if employees will not communicate with them. Employees will also create information—that is, rumors—for power motives.

To deflate these misuses of communication, Joanne Adams Stroud, Ph.D., Regional Practice Director, Hay Management Consultants, recommends:

> Give lots of information and make it a free commodity so that it can't become a source of "personal" power for individuals throughout the organization.

Over and over survivors reported frustrations because of the messenger's failure to communicate. What are the barriers that cause such omissions?

B /A/R/R/I/E/R
Messengers' Discomfort

Stroud offers this explanation of some messengers' failure to communicate:

> Probably the number one reason is that leaders are used to having all of the answers. And they just don't know how to communicate uncertainty. They feel very uncomfortable doing it—half answers, projections, speculations. And they really think that it's going to be upsetting to the people hearing it rather than comforting. And we spent a lot of time just telling them how comforting it is to hear, "I don't know anything right now, but let's keep the *vision* in mind." That is a comforting statement.

Although they voiced their frustration, the survivors we spoke to concurred with her explanation.

For some companies, management's often necessary orientation toward the bottom line, toward decisions and outcomes rather than the process or path along the way, means that leaders are silent until they have resolved problems and made final decisions.

Management's concerns about the impact of the communication exacerbate their discomfort. Some leaders worry that the information will disrupt productivity and upset the status quo. They may rationalize their decision not to communicate as "If you don't tell them, they won't worry (and they'll keep doing what they're doing)."

We must admit that we were struck by the naiveté of this view; the very change that the organization plans is so major that from the first announcement, business as usual is no more. If the status quo is already negated, why try to maintain it? Indeed, withholding information in an attempt to maintain "business as usual" has the opposite effect: The dissonance fosters the very disruption that the organization is trying to avoid.

Sometimes management withholds communication for very benevolent reasons, not wanting to upset employees. This is not uncommon in those organizations that have a somewhat paternalistic leadership style.

Sometimes the leaders' fears about the impact of communication center around management's feeling ill equipped to deal with the fallout, whether it is survivors' anger or distress.

B/A/R/R/I/E/R
Messengers' Assumptions

Adding to their discomfort with vagaries and process, messengers sometimes hold assumptions that act as barriers to communication.

One assumption is that employees have a greater need for detailed answers than is often true. (We are not contradicting our previous statements about W&Ss' quest for details. In a choice between no information and that which lacked all the specifics, W&Ss would certainly have selected the latter.)

Given their assumption, messengers feel stymied by what they do not have answers to—and by what they do. "We can't tell them about it because so much is confidential," confided one manager. "What *can* you tell them?" we countered. "And why not begin with, 'This is a status report. Negotiations are continuing. Much of it is confidential, but here is what we can tell you'?"

Another assumption we heard about is expressed as "Nothing's changed. I don't have anything new to tell them, so what would I say?" So the assumption that "no change" equals "no need to communicate" is another barrier.

"Tell them that—that there's nothing new," we continually reiterate, to the astonishment of some of our clients. Indeed, for people bombarded with change, what can be more welcoming and refreshing than hearing that nothing is new? For example, the RIOs most of all need an anchor, and the status quo—even in the form of communicating no changes, the same news as last week—will provide that stability. The RIOs want to see change as a continuum between the old and new rather than a series of sudden stops and starts.

"No changes" offers all groups a respite, breathing time, and more. For the FODs, it communicates that management is thinking things through, not jumping too hastily while in a reactive mode.

We heard several variations of the "nothing's new" rationale—assumptions that the news is too insignificant or too minuscule to warrant communication. "It's a waste of paper to send out a half-page statement," one senior manager in charge of managing the change, told us, his coaches.

"So, if it isn't worth three pages, don't say anything at all?" we jokingly retorted. We went on to point out the negative response which long statements generally receive.

The assumption that "the best people will leave" if they have the information is the ultimate fear of leaders and it acts as a communication barrier. As a human relations consultant in Florida explains:

> Some of the best people will jump ship. But you know, what about the notion that the best people tend to have an investment in the success of the company, and they're smart enough to know that sharing information and soliciting employee opinions, create opportunities to make decisions with integrity... for themselves and the corporation they support. From the organization's standpoint, all the people ought to be the "best people" or they need to be out of there.

This barrier is particularly problematic for the FODs:

> *Every time the vice president comes in to department meetings, he talks all around the issue ... may be fine in the boardroom, but sure doesn't do anything for us.... Why didn't they just start with, "We're losing money and we have to take some actions to deal with it?"*

B/A/R/R/I/E/R
Messengers' Inexperience

For many organizations, change and transition are new. Thus, communicating in these situations represents an unfamiliar challenge. So it is understandable that messengers often lack the specialized knowledge and skills needed.

B/A/R/R/I/E/R
Undesignated Messengers

In most organizations there are also undesignated messengers—the informal leaders or office pals. Sometimes, as we've noted, survivors assume messenger roles for their own ends.

However, even when they are motivated by concern about their colleagues, informal leaders find this role problematic. If the designated messengers are not communicating enough and employees turn to informal leaders for information, these "default" messengers may or may not have information to give, relying instead on hearsay or their own perceptions.

I feel like I'm letting them down when they look to me for answers... I'm cautious, because it's only my interpretation.

At their worst, misguided attempts to provide information become the basis for the rumor mill.

Communications Coach

Leaders and other designated communicators may need ongoing help as messengers. We recommend a communications coach. This person can be an internal employee or an external consultant. In either case, communications coach must possess specific qualities and skills beyond mastery of verbal and written communication. The coach must understand the organizational culture and employees' issues and be well versed in change and transition processes. Human resources professionals may be the ideal candidates.

The tasks of a communications coach are to help messengers (1) communicate information in a timely manner, (2) address employees as disparate audiences, (3) avoid language that is unclear or inflammatory, and (4) stay on top of rumors. The coach also needs to act as a trainer, developing the messenger's listening and facilitation skills.

The coach must understand that the messenger communicates within the context of barriers. If the coach does not deal with those barriers, then the coaching will be of limited use.

The communications coach must also provide support for the messenger. The messenger role is enervating for even the most seasoned communicator. The coach can help messengers to maintain perspective and replenish energy over an extended period of time. At the same time, the coach must motivate these company representatives to stay in front of employee groups and to maintain constant communication.

Thus far we have talked about the message and the messenger. Survivors also spoke about the vehicles used—the communication methods and media.

MEDIA AND METHODS

No matter how complete the message content or how authoritative the messenger, the organization has to communicate important information through appropriate media using the right methods.

How is the message delivered? By what means? Is the announcement made via memo, e-mail, or video? Is there a meeting? If so, is it company-wide? Held in each department?

As soon as they told us we had to schedule time for an announcement and that everybody had to attend, we knew this was a message we should pay attention to.

This survivor came from an organization that used interoffice memos to provide information about organizational changes. This break with customary communication practices alerted employees to the magnitude of the message.

In the change situations we studied, using customary methods was often problematic because "the usual" method or medium did not convey the criticality of the communication.

As one survivor indicated, companies may invite criticism or misunderstanding when using ordinary media for extraordinary messages:

I can't believe they used the newsletter to announce plans for the merger. It really made it sound like an ordinary event. I would have thought they would have given it more importance than that.

The Wyatt study (1993) results reference the efficacy of written communication media. Of the organizations surveyed, eighty-three percent used letters and memoranda (what we assume were normal communication methods) to convey information about the changes, yet only twenty-eight percent rated them as "very effective." Noting that the results supported those of the previous study, Wyatt suggests that "though written correspondence may be necessary, it is insufficient to communicate effectively on the subject." The study's authors then questioned why executives continued to send out these missives even when they themselves rated them as not very effective communication strategies.

Like the researchers, we are not proposing that companies refrain from sending memos or publishing newsletters. We are stating that companies may need to find alternative communication vehicles to speak to the significance of change.

Small-Group Meetings

A number of studies have demonstrated the efficacy of small-group meetings as a communication method. For example, according to the Wyatt study, executives cited small-group meetings and managerial briefings as having the best results, with over fifty percent of company leaders rating those methods as "very effective."

We're not recommending small-group meetings as "the solution" but as an alternative way to communicate. While written correspondence may be fast, its drawback is that it is one-way. Written communication provides no opportunity for dialogue. The need for two-way communication is discussed in greater detail later in this chapter.

One benefit of small-group meetings is that listening to the group sets the stage for management going to the next level: one-on-one meetings with individual employees.

Like other communication venues, small-group meetings need to be structured. Tossing open the agenda, leading a session in a laissez-faire way, may result in receiving only partial feedback—hearing primarily from the most vocal and extroverted participants, which is not necessarily synonymous with hearing from those who are most concerned. An unstructured meeting also invites random attacks from those who may be angry.

Managerial Briefings

A second communication method is to hold briefings for managers on a regular basis, even if there is no "new news" to report. The Wyatt study reported managerial briefings as highly ranked for effectiveness.

In moments of crisis and/or change, it is natural for senior management to look for the expedient way to communicate with managers: "We'll send them a voice mail," or "We'll tell them along with their department." While these options may be expeditious, they fail to satisfy the managers' need for information. Neither allows the manager or supervisor to ask questions or clarify issues before they must interact with employees.

One-on-One Dialogues

No matter how effective small-group meetings, one-on-one dialogues are essential communication vehicles for survivor groups. Within the context of providing information, one-on-one dialogues initiate FODs' involvement, contain W&Ss' anxieties, and assuage the unspoken fears of RIOs.

Communicating one-on-one also provides real opportunities to see behind survivors' masks. And because dialogues are two-way by definition, organizations may get valuable input that might otherwise go unsaid.

■ DIALOGUES WITH FODs

If the company is going to reengage FODs, it has to enlist this survivor group; it has to get FODs involved. For FODs, taking an active role leads to engagement. Talking—and listening—one-on-one with FODs will enable management to find opportunities for engagement. Even hearing FODs' responses to such requests and listening "between the lines" will help companies determine how detached and how near the doorstep FODs already are—serving as a wake-up call for taking immediate action.

■ DIALOGUES WITH W&Ss

This survivor group tends to react so much that it is probably best to meet with W&Ss one-on-one before holding any small-group meetings. Two goals for the meeting should be to diffuse the W&S's anxiety and to identify any misperceptions that the W&S holds. If these goals are not met, the W&S's subsequent actions in the small group—challenging and questioning—can be off-putting and distracting to other members.

If the company is going to redirect W&Ss' engagement, one-on-one meetings provide opportunities to focus W&Ss' attention on the issues at hand, capitalizing on their analytical skills and engaging them as resources for problem solving. So asking for a W&S's input within the one-on-one environment not only validates the importance of the W&S's analysis but by association validates the W&S. Through this process, the organization displays its commitment to these survivors—a message W&Ss want to hear. And, of course, the content of the analysis is not lost.

■ DIALOGUES WITH RIOs

Given this survivor group's discomfort with change and its anchoring in the past, a one-on-one dialogue can start the process of disengagement in a way that is less threatening. It provides an opportunity to give support, to listen, to break through RIOs' mask of denial.

As a group, the RIOs are very uncomfortable going public with their concerns, for fear of being seen as both unable to cope and disloyal to the organization. Hence they are unlikely to voice any opinions in group meetings, whatever the size. A one-on-one meeting, while not eliminating all risk, certainly reduces it—especially if the messenger, most likely the boss, is caring and supportive. Even if the RIO says little about concerns in the initial one-on-one meeting, it is still an opportunity to assuage fears and lay the groundwork for future dialogue.

COMMUNICATION INVENTORY

Because they have multiple audiences, organizations need to employ communication vehicles strategically. This requires understanding the impact of communication methods and media as well as that of the message and messenger.

In order to do that, the organization needs to carry out a strategic inventory of its communication methods and media. That means reviewing each communication medium and method the organization uses to determine (1) whether employees will hear it or read it, (2) whether they will pay attention to it, and (3) whether they will believe it.

The organization needs to address the following questions in the Communication Inventory:

Historically, how has this communication vehicle been used?

Has the communication method been utilized to communicate crises, or is it the monthly communiqué that announces the company's annual picnic, reports on the employee stock option plan, and summarizes the shareholders' meeting?

Newsletters often fall into this latter category, providing a cacophony of "nice to know" information bits, sometimes interspersed with "need to know" news bites. Whether people will pay attention to it depends on the vehicle's reputation and past content.

Has the organizational use of the vehicle changed over time?

One East Coast health care organization initiated a company bulletin to announce that extraordinary events were taking place. Gradually, over a ten-year period, the bulletin became a catch-all, reporting on everything from promotions to holiday schedules. A once-viable medium for gaining employees' immediate attention, the bulletin became so diluted in value that employees relegated it to the "when I have time" pile. The bulletin had become a rather ordinary communication vehicle, now inappropriate for sending information during an extraordinary time.

Is the medium or method a credible source?

The communication vehicle has to have universal credibility throughout the organization. Will the vehicle, and hence the message, be greeted as credible? Or will it be perceived as cloaked with bias or slant? Or merely a marketing piece with a new layout?

Does this vehicle appeal to each of the survivor groups?

The communication vehicle has to address the varied needs and preferences of FODs, W&Ss, and RIOs. A video announcement from the president may be effective in meeting the FODs' needs for an overview from a person in charge. It may also be effective for RIOs in communicating a "we care" message. But the same video presentation may leave W&Ss dissatisfied, unless it is shown within the context of a facilitated meeting that provides the more detailed information this survivor group wants. A written communiqué providing specifics and accompanying the video will also appeal to W&Ss. The communication medium has to address the disparate needs of the survivor groups or be one of several media used concurrently to meet them.

Is the vehicle effective for those with different communication preferences and styles?

A single vehicle is unlikely to address auditory, visual, and kinesthetic preferences. So the organization has to determine which style(s) the vehicle appeals to in order to maximize its use. For example, a video will appeal to both auditory and visual preferences. Can the organization's existing repertoire address visual preferences with written messages or videos while concurrently appealing to those with auditory needs via audiotape or speakers, and communicating to those with kinesthetic preferences via hands-on activity such as completing a written form?

Even if management believes that it can answer these Communication Inventory questions, we still advise that an organization verify its (management's) perceptions. The company can convene focus groups, send out a survey, or ask about communication more rigorously in the Credibility Audit.

As to the results of the Communication Inventory, if a vehicle "flunks" the test because it lacks credibility or has lost its viability, then the organization needs to determine what to use in its stead. With what, for example, will the company replace the office memo?

If the organization determines that the vehicle is still viable but has been used less than optimally, then the task is not to replace it but to rethink the medium or method's use. The office memo, for example, may be ineffective for announcing changes but very appropriate for providing updates or schedule revisions.

When augmenting the communication repertoire, considering the nature of the message and the makeup of the audience can help the organization decide what to add.

Does it seem that we have gone overboard in proposing this Communication Inventory, given the investment of time and energy that organizations will have to expend? Does the cost-benefit ratio really justify it?

Obviously, we think it does. But we do because we are positioning the Communication Inventory as part of the broader strategy of an Employee Communication Plan.

EMPLOYEE COMMUNICATION PLAN

An Employee Communication Plan addresses such issues as: What is the objective of the communication? What is the best way to meet that objective? Who is the most credible to get the message across? What medium should be used for big-ticket items? To keep people posted? How will the organization get feedback? Gather information? Follow up? Most importantly, each of these questions must be answered for each specific audience.

To communicate effectively, the organization needs to integrate the message, messenger, methods, and media with the needs of the audience. The model shown in figure 1 provides a way to do that.

Let's work with this model. Imagine that the organization has decided to consolidate two divisions within the next two years. The implementation schedule and details have yet to be worked out, but the company wants to communicate proactively. It wants to make an announcement to the workforce rather than have the press break the news or have rumors develop.

FIGURE 1 **EMPLOYEE COMMUNICATION PLAN: BASIC MODEL**

Issue:

Audience	Message	Messenger	Media/Methods	Time/Frequency
Senior Executives				
Middle Management				
First-Level Managers/ Supervisors				
Employees				

Issue	The communication topic(s).
Audience	To whom is the communication directed? What are the group's needs?
Message	The content to be delivered. What does the content mean to the audience? What does the group especially need to know?
Messenger	Who is (are) the appropriate person(s) to deliver the message, given the audience and the content?
Media/Methods*	How can the message best be conveyed by the messenger? And what vehicles will be most effective for delivering the content and getting feedback from the audience?
Time/Frequency	When and how often should the message be communicated? How will the organization follow up?

*Note: We have used the plural forms because we expect that each audience will require more than one medium and/or method.

Various levels of the organization will differ in their communication needs. For example, first-level supervisors need to have details in order to respond to their direct reports' queries; they may, in fact, need to know whether and how they are to answer questions. This is in addition to their personal need for information. Middle management, which has contact with customers, will need to know how much and what to say.

Our focus is on survivors, so let's add some information to our example. The organization has within the past year completed a restructuring that involved two rounds of downsizing. As a result, the primary audience

FIGURE 2 **EMPLOYEE COMMUNICATION PLAN: EXPANDED MODEL**

Issue:

Audience	Message	Messenger	Media/Methods	Time/Frequency
Senior Executives • FODs • W&Ss • RIOs				
Middle Management • FODs • W&Ss • RIOs				
First-Level Managers/ Supervisors • FODs • W&Ss • RIOs				
Employees • FODs • W&Ss • RIOs				

consists of survivor employees. Therefore, the survivor dimension needs to be added to the Audience column, as shown in figure 2.

An important point: At the risk of redundancy, we remind you that survivors, and hence their concerns and needs, are not limited to line employees. Members of senior management, for example, also are survivors. Therefore, communication has to address the audiences' needs based on their role in the organization and their survivor group profile. For example, Joe, as a middle manager, wants to know what to tell his direct reports. And, Joe, as a W&S, wants that information to be detailed.

At no point in this chapter do we recommend that the organization attempt to identify survivors as FODs, W&Ss, and RIOs so that they can be divided into three groups to receive separate communications. We assume readers can list the reasons why. But considering each of the groups separately while completing the plan will be very useful in ensuring that the resulting communication addresses them all.

Communicating Changes

Many survivors reported that their organizations carefully planned their communication of major change events, from the initial announcement of the restructuring or merger to information about the schedule and the plans. At the same time it appeared that companies had not given as much consideration to communicating about changes occurring along the way. Did organizations as proactively plan the means and methods they would use to communicate the "*when . . . then's*," for example, when the relocation was not ready, when the new system was not up, when more employees were leaving than anticipated?

In all of our conversations with survivors, managers, and company executives, we found in every instance implementation of change necessitated mid-course correction and last-minute adjustments to the change management plan. The Employee Communication Plan requires a strategy to deal with those adjustments to the change management plan.

The Communication Update Model we provide in figure 3 addresses this communication issue by requiring the organization to answer the following in advance: When X occurs, what will be said? How will the information be communicated most effectively? And by whom?

PRINCIPLES

There are several principles to which the organization must adhere in its daily communication as well as in its development of the Employee Communication Plan. They include communicating early, communicating so that everyone hears the news, and ensuring adequate communication "volume."

FIGURE 3 **COMMUNICATION UPDATE MODEL**

Problem	Message (Response)	Media/Methods	Messenger
System is not up			
Building is not ready for occupancy			
More people are leaving than anticipated			
Schedule is pushed back			

Communicate Early

There's only one source first with the news, and it has to be the organization. The timeliness of that message is key.

▶ *BEST PRACTICE*

One company received unanimous high marks for communication timing from the survivors we interviewed. This organization told employees well in advance that there were problems—a whole year before the final action, and thus well before the strategy was worked out.

To quote the president: "We are not entirely sure of the extent of the problem and what our strategies will be . . . but we wanted to make sure that you heard about the changes from us."

Some organizations allowed other sources to be first with company news. In those cases in which information was gleaned from the news media before the company, employees treated those news reports and acted on them as if they were reality. The organization's credibility with the public and industry was weakened considerably as well. Even when a company makes statements to the contrary, the first report, the first source of information, has the edge.

The newspaper reported the layoffs three months before they occurred. The company kept denying it. I think they were stalling to give themselves time because they didn't have a plan.

Organizations varied not only in the timing of announcements but in their reactions when they were not the first to present information. One survivor told us of at least three separate media notices regarding his company's financial problems and the impending downsizing; the organization's "response" each time was silence. This survivor spoke of the organization "acting as if employees weren't aware . . . as if nothing had been said, because the organization wasn't the speaker." But "something" had happened, of course. The result was that anytime something came out in the press, employees and the public took it as a given, no matter whether it was true or false—and no matter whether the organization responded or not.

Each of the survivor groups gave evidence of experiencing a different reaction when the organization's position was that of reacting to rather than initiating the news.

■ FODs' REACTIONS TO DELAYED COMMUNICATION

Having control and having a plan were the organizational hallmarks for the FODs. Thus, if the company was not first with the information, FODs were as concerned with the process as with the content of the communication. Their concerns were twofold: First, what was missing in the organization's communication strategy? Why had the organization missed out? Second, why didn't the organization have more control? With regard to the latter, this survivor group expects newspapers to make conjectures about the industry or even individual organizations. What is unacceptable is for the news media to report specific problems about the company via undisclosed sources. For those outside to gain information from insiders suggests internal leaks—yet another example of lack of control.

■ W&Ss' REACTIONS TO DELAYED COMMUNICATION

For the W&Ss, outside reports or speculation opened a Pandora's box. They were frustrated because the organization was not communicating or not communicating enough. They were perplexed as to why the organization would let someone else speak first, since that meant the organization taking a second-place or backseat position. Some W&Ss even perceived communication as a contest, with the winner being the first one to speak. But even more than that, W&Ss felt one down themselves because they had not been privy to the information. It feels like a personal betrayal: Doesn't the organization owe them the courtesy of providing information before the media or public has it?

■ RIOs' REACTIONS TO DELAYED COMMUNICATION

Given RIOs' steadfastness and loyalty, they believe the organization over any outside source. For RIOs, the organization's silence in response to outside speculation might actually be comforting, since it suggests a "no news is good news" communiqué. But if the organization then takes an action like downsizing, this survivor group is devastated, having previously come to the conclusion that "everything's fine."

Communicate Simultaneously So That Everyone Hears the News

Communicating information to the workforce can be especially problematic when there are multiple job sites and/or employees whose work has them traveling much of the time. We did hear over and over of situations in which survivors heard the news piecemeal or secondhand. In chapter 7, we provide a vivid example of a manager on the road with no access to the downsizing communiqué and the impact of the organization's failure to communicate with her or her peers and direct reports. It is crucial that organizations ensure that all employees receive important messages simultaneously.

▶ *BEST PRACTICE*

Another company had the same problem of communicating an important change when employees were away from their worksites. In this case, the sales force from four regions were gathered at corporate headquarters for a seminar. They were in the morning session while an announcement was being placed on employees' desks throughout the company. The seminar leaders had been sent copies of the announcement to be distributed to participants. The organization also arranged for the manager of personnel to come into the session to answer questions.

▶ **BEST PRACTICE**

"How do you 'communicate simultaneously'?" we asked the CEO of a company with a reputation for excellent communication. He replied,

Our goal has always been: Wherever you are, whether you are at your own office or on business at another site, that's where you see and hear the news.

So when the CEO was announcing the news of a merger via video, a series of showings were scheduled concurrently at all sites across the country. All employees attended.

The organization smartly recognized that some employees would still miss out, whether due to illness, vacation, or some other reason. It dealt with this contingency as part of the initial plan, scheduling viewings regularly throughout the next two weeks. Management required that supervisors and managers not only verify that all of their direct reports had attended but make sure that someone in management was present to answer questions each time the video was shown.

The notion of simultaneous videos has relevance to the next guideline.

Turn Up the Volume

People can't hear, much less remember, when they are in the throes of transition. Much of the information communicated at normal "decibel" levels can't get through the filters that shock and bring denial. And the information that does get through is frequently forgotten or distorted.

While it would be inappropriate to shout at people, using a corporate megaphone, or to adjust the tone on survivors' phones, it is important to turn up the volume—organizations need to communicate often and repeat the information.

What is the relationship of the previous video example to this principle? Repeated showings over a period of time allowed "instant replay," giving employees the opportunity to see and hear the message again and again. Providing the information via video and encouraging people to see it more than once not only allows survivors to increase retention but legitimizes forgetfulness and/or discomfort with the message. And having messengers present during some of the showings encourages and legitimizes questions.

What are the barriers that get in the way of applying the principles of communicating early, simultaneously, and at sufficient "volume"?

B/A/R/R/I/E/R
Messenger's Discomfort

We have discussed the messenger's discomfort and assumptions. They foster a reluctance to communicate, leading to failure to communicate early, if at all.

B/A/R/R/I/E/R
Internal System

Another barrier comes from problems in the internal communication system.

The director of communication at an aerospace company expressed her concern that she had let employees down because they were not getting information in a timely fashion. She was frustrated by the many management layers that had to sign off on press releases or internal communication. Even when the internal communication process worked fine in normal times, it was cumbersome and too slow for dealing with extraordinary situations.

It was not good before, but with the downsizing it's become a lose-lose situation.

B/A/R/R/I/E/R
"Play It Again, Sam!"

Management often has lived with the information that it must now communicate for the first time to employees. Familiarity with the information sometimes prevents messengers from taking into account the impact that hearing the news initially has on the audience.

One interviewee told us that the manager he had been coaching agreed that he needed to communicate with employees, and he sent out a memo.

Then the manager came back and said, "There, I told them we were going to change. Isn't that enough?" "Well, no," I said. "It's something you have to do and reinforce over and over again. It's a function of time."

You know, the people running the organizations for the most part are highly intelligent, highly perceptive people. Doesn't take a lot for them to get a message on something. But they're also to a large degree living in their own environment.

B/A/R/R/I/E/R
Underestimating the Magnitude of the Message

Management must recognize that while a singular piece of information may on its own seem relatively inconsequential, for the survivor this information, when taken in the context of multiple bits of information, will be greatly magnified.

The interviewee quoted above continued:

> I don't think they [management] realize the magnitude of the change that the workforce has to go through and what the accumulation of bits of information does to people.

The principles we have iterated about effective employee communication provide guidelines to messengers in presenting information—in "telling" the news. In that sense they address one-way communication. That, however, is only half of the equation.

TWO-WAY COMMUNICATION

To tell a tale on ourselves, several times we stated to interviewees something we had heard from other survivors and then asked whether that matched their experience as well. When they replied in the affirmative, we couldn't determine from their response whether they were confirming our earlier reports or giving a "yes" answer to be compliant interviewees or to keep their "masks" in place.

To come to the point, our best information was what survivors volunteered. Of course, you may say, that was the goal: to find out what survivors thought. Well, isn't that one communication goal of organizations as well— to find out what survivors think and what they need to hear as well as to communicate the organization's message?

Listening

Remember the director of the strategic business unit who traveled from country to country to communicate? His actions speak to a key point. He wanted direct access to his employees not only because it helped him send a message but because it enabled him to "receive back." For him, the communication had to be two-way. He wanted to hear what his employees had to say.

Listening may be as important a skill as presenting information. Listening within the context of organizational change often means listening to a response the manager may not want to hear but still listening in a way that enables the receiver to help survivors move forward rather than become entrenched.

If survivors' perception of managers and supervisors as being "out of the loop" is an issue, then managers' listening, properly structured, can be as potent a role as telling, as managers are perceived as the conduits of information.

▶ **BEST PRACTICE**

At one midwestern company, the chairman holds "listening luncheons" with survivors. The primary purpose is not to tell them anything but to listen to their concerns. The company sends out transcripts afterward to all employees. Reportedly, the sessions have been oversubscribed.

A communication plan needs to build in mechanics to ensure that two-way communication occurs, so the organization is addressing survivors' needs not only for getting information but also for giving it.

We do not mean to suggest that the organizations we studied did not provide for two-way communication. Survivors confirmed there was seldom an announcement meeting that did not include a time for questions. Companies asked for feedback in a number of ways. Yet it was clear that the survivors we interviewed were still unsatisfied.

So what are the barriers that get in the way of organizations' maximizing two-way communication?

B/A/R/R/I/E/R
Selling the Message

Some messengers seem to convey an impression of trying to convince the audience of management's position and the rightness of the decision. Preoccupied by their "mission," these messengers ask for feedback but appear not to hear what is said.

These messengers seem to have the misperception that if people hear the message often enough, they will understand the rationale for the change and be convinced of the soundness of the company's position. They appear to not understand that change, whether positive or negative, brings with it predictable resistance.

B/A/R/R/I/E/R
Communication Assumptions

We have already addressed messengers' assumptions earlier in this chapter. But communication assumptions are not only the province of messengers—or management. Our interviewees confirmed that survivors brought assumptions as well. And it is management's and employees' assumptions taken together that wreaked havoc even on those organizations with the best intentions.

The following communication assumptions are the most prevalent that we encountered:

COMMUNICATION ASSUMPTIONS

Management assumes	Employees assume
They'll ask	They'll tell
They'll understand	They'll clarify
They'll hear	They'll tell me again

Communication assumptions persuade messengers that messages not only have been heard but have been understood. Assumptions assure CEOs that employees will remember and assure employees that management will provide more and more information.

Although assumptions between speakers and receivers may be unavoidable, they are dangerous because they become the rationale for action or inaction, the basis of solutions and strategies. Thus, as we have already suggested, a president may fail to communicate "no changes—yet," assuming that employees only want to hear "new news."

Message Checks

Because communication assumptions are generally unstated, they are difficult to pin down, let alone address. So one way for organizations to ensure that they do not act on the basis of assumptions is to build what we term "Message Checks" into the Employee Communication Plan. Message

Checks are written or oral queries to confirm the audience's understanding of the information presented. Message Checks recognize that there are organizational assumptions operating and address the barriers those assumptions impose.

Message Checks clarify employees' understanding, not their response. Explaining the purpose of Message Checks may not be an easy task when done in the midst of a major change where all communication may be suspect and arouse strong feelings. The organization needs to make sure that employees understand that the purpose of Message Checks is not to test employees' knowledge but to check what is heard. "We need to confirm the key points that were heard. We may not have been clear." Note the wording: not that the receiver failed to receive but that the sender may not have sent.

B/A/R/R/I/E/R
Employees' Immediate Reactions

As we said earlier, organizations customarily built in time for employees' questions when communicating information. Sometimes they were surprised by what they got back. As one manager stated:

> We told them that the relocation site had been selected and the move date determined. And do you know what they asked? "Will we have an employee cafeteria?" I couldn't believe it! Here this big change, and they want to know about eating lunch.

Other interviewees in the management ranks reported being similarly taken aback by employees' initial queries following a major announcement of change.

We certainly understand why this manager had been dumbfounded. What he interpreted as a superficial response is, indeed, a less important query. But, in our analysis, it is anything but shallow.

Depending upon the organization's credibility and climate, survivors sometimes throw out lightweight questions as a way of testing the waters, checking to see "if it's OK to ask questions." After all, which is a safer initial query, "Where will we eat lunch?" or "Am I going to have a job?"

Other reasons for tame inquiries: Employees may not know their real questions or questions may not come easily because they are in shock. Or questions may be absent because of employees' communication assumptions.

Unfortunately, when situations such as the "lunchroom retort" occur, it is not unusual for messengers to interpret the response erroneously, concluding that employees "didn't get it." So employees' questions pose numerous opportunities for miscommunication and misunderstanding.

Obviously, an organization should not refrain from asking for questions when giving information, but management should do so knowing that this is more a polite invitation and will neither yield substantive results nor substitute for a "real" time for queries later.

As one survivor advised:

People can't communicate in old terms, old ways. It used to be, "It's announced." That doesn't do it. People need time now to react . . . they need to be allowed to get into a place where they feel is a safe harbor and they can say, "Damn it, I don't understand this. Why is this happening?"

Questions Session

Like the chairman who held a "Listening Luncheon," organizations need to separate telling from asking, scheduling a separate time for listening to employees' questions.

A Questions Session means just that: a time for eliciting questions, for listening to employees, and that's it. It is not a time for answering. So when we suggest that management hold a Questions Session, we advise that an announcement setting out the purpose and structure go out well in advance.

An example announcement: "We want to hear your questions, issues, and concerns. We don't want to set up a situation in which we frustrate and confuse communication by making off-the-cuff responses or giving incomplete answers now. We will answer your questions at a meeting on [date]."

Allowing people to vent and ask questions is particularly useful when survivors are in the resistance phase of transition, because they need to clarify the sources of that resistance. The organization's asking for questions and encouraging expression helps employees to acknowledge "what I am fearful or angry about."

Letting employees hear everyone else's questions aloud as well as ask their own gives the issues integrity. Thus, Questions Sessions provide legitimate ways for survivors to be heard so they don't have to go underground with their thoughts.

A caution: If the organization hasn't communicated often enough or has an historically poor track record for communication, then survivors will regard this event as one more avoidance attempt.

A Listening Luncheon or Questions Session tells the organization what survivors really want to know and what they're concerned about. So, like the Credibility Audit, a Questions Session is prescriptive—it tells the organization what to address in its change and transition management planning as well as in its press memos, change updates, and other communiqués.

In our experience coaching managers, we caution that holding a Questions Session is not without risk. It requires careful facilitation as well as discipline on several counts. Facilitation needs to be directive, to help people move from griping and complaining to asking focused questions. Leaders needs to listen. If they are preoccupied with "how will I answer?" they sometimes jump the gun: They either start to respond or, afraid to probe, they move on without getting to the essence of the concern. They may then leave the event without achieving the goal, which is to emerge with clear questions to be addressed at a later time.

B/A/R/R/I/E/R
Mixing Asking and Answering

Questions Sessions sometimes fail because the answers aren't put off until later. Bosses erroneously believe that they have to provide answers on the spot. And some managers avoid asking for feedback and querying employees because they feel ill equipped to respond.

When asking and answering are combined in one event, either deliberately or by happenstance, we find that the organization seldom satisfies itself or the survivors. Either because they give an "on the spot" response or because they do not understand the needs, the organization often has to "reanswer" later via clarifying memos and augmenting statements.

Anonymity

No matter how effective Listening Luncheons or Questions Sessions, some survivors will be silent, afraid to unmask their concerns. So the organization must provide some two-way communication vehicles that ensure anonymity. Offering opportunities for survivors to submit questions in writing, via e-mail, or through suggestion boxes are some methods organizations use.

▶ **BEST PRACTICE**

To encourage questions, a company might set up a question hot line. We heard about a number of hot lines in our interviews; the ones that got high marks provided both information and the opportunity to ask questions anonymously.

Offering anonymity is critical if the organizational history is poor, the changes are of staggering magnitude, and/or the survivors are particularly masked.

KEY POINTS

The quantity, quality, and timing of communication are all critical issues for survivors. Survivors concur that they need more information. They also need to be recognized as a unique audience with specific concerns. Each of the survivor groups has special concerns and preferences relating to the message and the messenger.

GROUP ISSUES

FODs	For the FODs, the message needs to address the organization's vision and to reflect the sound, well-planned nature of the change. FODs want the messenger to be one of the architects of the plan—a person committed to its implementation.
W&Ss	For the W&Ss, the message needs to address the specifics of how the change will be implemented. This survivor group wants the messenger to be versed in all aspects of the plan and capable of answering their questions.
RIOs	For the RIOs, the message needs to focus on how people would be cared for during and after the change. They require a messenger who can articulate caring and concern while communicating the facts.

STRATEGIES

Prior to the change, do a Communication Inventory to determine the appropriate content focus, messenger attributes, and media/methods options. Based on the inventory, develop an Employee Communication Plan focusing on the survivor audience.

Whether through a Credibility Audit, Questions Sessions, anonymous hot lines, or a combination of these and more, the organization acquires an abundance of information to utilize in planning and managing the change. So it is appropriate that we now turn to the topic of change.

7

"Ultimately, if you are not
managing change, in
today's climate, you are
not managing."
Kenneth Marbler
(*CMA,* 1994)

Change

POINT A TO POINT B

Survivors spoke of being in the throes of it, they told of the impact it had on their lives, and they related their experiences in dealing with it. The "it" they referred to was change—specifically, organizational change. It is the predominant theme, the main challenge, and the prevailing characteristic of organizational life in business today.

Change, for the purposes of this book, refers to the events involved in going from one state to another, whether converting from manufacturing munitions to making bicycles, expanding from a local operation to global markets, or shifting from a department of sixteen to sixty or six. And experts agree that whether the change is one of expansion and growth or contraction, change involves loss—loss of the old ways of working and being, and, in some cases, loss of the workers themselves.

Likewise, as we said in the section opener, we are at variance with experts who suggest that the problems are solely attributable to transition management.

One of our interviewees was a member of a training department of a utility company undergoing downsizing and relocation. This employee went to the new site, which, a week before, he had been told was in move-in condition and ready for his class.

When I walked into the new classroom, no one was there, and my training supplies were nowhere in sight. A half-hour later two employees wandered in; they were still searching for keys for their new offices. When I finally started the class, two hours late, I had a hard time maintaining people's attention. When I turned around to investigate a loud humming noise, I found a service man, visible to the class, drilling holes for the doorknob behind me.

This survivor added that he left at the end of the day recognizing this situation had been poorly orchestrated, wondering what the fallout would be, and questioning how these employees could be expected to learn in that environment. And they had two more weeks scheduled in that room!

He paused, then continued:

> *I had to repeat the class the following month, because people were not able to do the work.*

In this case the fallout was substantial: lost productivity and the expense of retraining. Those were the tangibles. There were intangible losses as well: employees' feelings of incompetence, lowered morale, resentment, and mistrust of and resistance to the subsequent training.

From our perspective, the case in point does not speak to poor transition management but primarily reflects faulty change management and incomplete change plans.

We are not going to spell out all of the elements of change management or change management planning in this chapter. Nor is our intent to present a new model for designing a change plan; there are many excellent models and programs already in use. Instead, we are focusing on those change management issues that appeared to have been of most importance to survivors.

What were survivors' preeminent concerns? There were three: Was a comprehensive change management plan in place? Was the plan articulated clearly to and likewise understood by employees? Was the plan implemented effectively?

A COMPREHENSIVE PLAN

When survivors spoke to us of successful change management, they related experiences in which restructuring, merging, downsizing—whatever the changes—were part of a larger whole. They described these activities not as a series of isolated events but components of an integrated process that provided continuity. Hence, the importance of a *comprehensive* plan.

Survivors' descriptions sounded much like that of one organizational development consultant, reflecting on downsizing she had experienced at a company.

▶ *BEST PRACTICE*

[The] best news about the organizational renewal process was that in the months preceding downsizing, there was a lot of company attention and work on refocus, strategic planning, new direction.... People became increasingly aware that there were new opportunities for the organization and people as [the company] was refocusing. So in that sense downsizing was received as more legitimate, attached to something that made some sense to people. And in that predownsizing phase, themes were established to connect to in post-layoff work around renewal.

Thus, survivors want to know that the plan has not come out of a vacuum and that downsizing is not an isolated event.

▶ *BEST PRACTICE*

One CEO we know repeatedly pointed out to employees—and won high marks for—the five-year efforts of management in preparing for organizational restructuring.

"We have all known it was going to happen and it would impact you, so we have spent a long time looking at options," the CEO told employees.

One part of the restructuring involved moving one division of the business halfway across the country. "Throughout our planning, our focus has been on how we could do it with minimal disruption not only to our customers but to you, our employees," division employees were assured.

Survivors' reports of change management plans were quite positive on several points. Our interviewees generally gave high marks to their organizations for the way downsized employees had been planned for, citing generous severance packages, outplacement services, and counseling programs.

Determining Selection Criteria

Selection of those to go and those to stay—selection was a compelling topic for every interviewee, but one that seldom got praise. The problems survivors described reflected a combination of incomplete planning, poor articulation, and ineffective implementation.

Survivors told us that, in many cases, criteria for selection were missing from the plan. Surprisingly, many of the survivors who told us this were bosses whose departments were impacted and whose direct reports were laid off.

We heard this frequently from survivor managers and employees, and it would seem to be such a glaring gap. How could such a critical element not be included in a change plan?

We also found it disconcerting because we had talked to enough persons integrally involved in the planning to be aware that selection criteria were, in fact, elements of most change plans. So why did survivors believe such criteria were missing in whole or in part?

There were several reasons. For one, some survivors weren't told about the criteria or they didn't understand what was said. We will say more about this when we discuss articulating the plan later in this chapter.

One survivor, a marketing manager, reported to us that on the day of the downsizing,

We were told who was going in our department. Someone said to me, "Here's their names; you need to bring them in one at a time."

Thus, another reason for the survivors' erroneous conclusion was that some survivors in management positions didn't know the criteria because they had been excluded from the planning process.

Imagine what this interviewee would have said had she been a marketing manager in the following organization instead.

▶ **BEST PRACTICE**

When asked about the role of managers in selecting direct reports to go or stay, the director of human resources at a pharmaceutical company reported:

[They were] Totally involved! They were totally responsible for who was on that list. I was just facilitating.

The planning issue here is: Does the plan lay out who will determine the selection criteria and who will apply them? Does it specify how that selection process will work? And, as our HR interviewee demonstrated, whether bosses are the selectors or not, does the plan spell out what role they will have in the selection process?

The situation was somewhat paradoxical: Almost all organizations prepared bosses at length as to how to tell the "selected" the results, but if these bosses were given no specific reasons for the decision, those chosen to be downsized or demoted asked questions managers couldn't answer. Thus, the plan needs to specify not only their role, but how and when bosses will be brought into the selection process.

Excluding the boss from the selection process had unanticipated results for one organization.

All my people kept coming to me, and they were just depressed and they couldn't understand why they weren't taken. Some of them had a very good point. "Why was so-and-so taken? She stinks!" And I said, "I'm sorry; I had nothing to do with it." But, you know, I didn't understand either, so it was very depressing to go into work, very depressing to sit there and listen to these people who had a very valid reason for being depressed.

This survivor, a high-performing manager who was asked to take over two departments, decided to resign after three days of the experience she described.

Internal Relocation

As important as knowing who will be selected for layoff is knowing what is going to happen to those who are not selected—the survivors. What will their life look like after the event?

Frankly, I was thinking seriously of leaving. I liked the company and enjoyed my work, but I really didn't think I wanted to work in another department. But my manager kept telling me how much the company wanted me to stay, and then she got on the phone and really started recruiting. I had two interviews the next day. Since I've moved to the new department, she's called twice to see how I'm doing.

If only this survivor's experience was typical of what we heard. But it was not. Far too many stories were variations of the following:

They told me if I could find an opening in the company, I should apply for it. That, and sending me to a résumé-writing class, was the relocation assistance program.

A "best of luck; you're on your own" philosophy will not work for survivors. For FODs, specifically, it has the effect of pushing them a step closer to the outside. If the organization really wants survivors to relocate internally rather than leave, it needs a well-planned and well-publicized strategy for helping them do so.

One way to retain survivors is to institute an internal job placement program. It may include circulating a list of candidate profiles to other departments or installing an e-mail job line. The implementation plan for this program must enlist managers to work actively as resources and support for their direct reports. Our research showed that managers' attitudes and actions were key to survivors' motivation to put the effort into securing another position in the organization.

The Work

Survivors want to know what is going to happen to them even if the news is not pleasant—even if it will mean relocation, changes in their roles, different responsibilities, or the breakup of a team. So another frustration for interviewees is not having clear ideas about what is expected of them as survivors.

In this regard, a critical element survivors look for in the change plan is an indication of how the work will get done after the downsizing and restructuring. And of more immediate concern is the question of how they will get the work done *during* the change.

What is significant to us is not that these are primary concerns but that they appeared not to have been addressed in much of the change management planning about which we heard.

As Judith Vogel, an organization development consultant, recounted,

> What I've never seen done well anyplace is genuinely to think through carefully and comprehensively enough about what is the work that has to be done after the layoff and what are the structures to do that. As a result, things fall through cracks. . . . [There's a] certain amount of throwing it up and seeing where it all comes down.

The 1993 Wyatt study speaks to this same point in noting that "so few executives reported their companies were able to reduce waste and inefficiency despite their better success rate in reducing expenses. This suggests that work continued to proceed in its normal manner, simply with fewer people performing it. In other words, in many companies, people were taken out of the employment picture while inefficient policies, procedures, and processes remained."

"How will the work get done?" is, indeed, a critical question the plan needs to address. Answering this question via defining the work, clarifying survivors' roles and responsibilities, and putting an organizational structure in place are tasks of the interim organization, a topic addressed in chapter 10.

Planning for Contingencies

Survivors spoke highly of organizations that anticipated problems in implementation and planned for stops and starts, and changes—"what if" situations. When these "what ifs" inevitably happened, management was able to put the contingency plan into operation with minimum disruption or loss of time.

Planning for contingencies as part of the strategic planning process, whether for a major undertaking like a merger or a regular event like a vacation schedule, is not exactly a revolutionary idea, to be sure. Nonetheless, many organizations failed to plan for a wide range of possible outcomes, survivors reported.

We very deliberately chose not to title this section "Contingency Plan" because when we have queried clients about contingency plans in the course of our work, we have sometimes been met with resistance. Some thought we were questioning their planning, as if they were somehow at fault. Others perceived we were suggesting an arduous task, a second plan to be developed separately and at a different time. We were not asking them to undertake the design of Plan B—quite the reverse. Completion of a comprehensive plan means that the contingencies are addressed within Plan A, so there is no need for Plan B.

Survivors' Planning Concerns

Survivor groups differ in the parameters of change management plans that are significant to them.

■ FODs' PLANNING CONCERNS

FODs want the plan to project the global picture. Just as they pose the question "Where am I going?" for themselves, they want to know the same about the organization. For this group, the critical test is not the plan for "getting us through 'this'" but where "this" is leading. Only by providing a clear sense of the future can the company convince FODs that the plan has been well thought out.

I understand that sales needs to be beefed up to get us in the international marketplace, but my concern is, What's going to keep us in the market once we get there, especially if R&D is cut drastically? So how does it all fit together? What is the long-range plan?

For the FODs, it is particularly significant that the plan not limit itself to addressing a singular event—for example, the downsizing—but spell out implementation of a strategy. For FODs especially, the strategy and thus the change management events begin months and months prior to the downsizing and extend well beyond D-day.

■   W&Ss' PLANNING CONCERNS

Though W&Ss are also interested in the future, their more immediate concern lies with the current structure—the policies and procedures that will be applied to guide them through the change.

As one W&S, a sales representative at a retail company, told us:

When we asked about the plans for after the downsizing, they kept saying, "We'll get back to you." Well, the downsizing took place last month, and we're no further ahead with a plan, and we still don't know who we're going to report to. If somebody's sick, they don't even call in anymore; who would they tell?

This statement typifies the W&Ss' concern with the plan's details as opposed to the FODs' focus on the big picture. "When will we move to our new location?" "What are we supposed to tell customers?" "Who do I . . . ?" "How do we . . . ?" are not uncommon W&S questions. Whether asking about a move plan or sequence of events for the downsizing, W&Ss seem insatiable in their quest for information.

But that is not all bad. For this is the survivor group whose discovery of gaps and inconsistencies can help strengthen a plan. And the W&Ss are the ones who, if asked, will suggest the details to fill in the gaps.

Given their concern for fairness, W&Ss focus on such plan issues as, Are the selection criteria fair? Is there an equitable arrangement for accomplishing the work? And, of course, what is the new organizational structure and the W&S's role in it?

■   RIOs' PLANNING CONCERNS

The RIOs do not want reams of information. That might underscore the reality of the changes and thus cause RIOs too much anxiety. At the same time, like the W&Ss, RIOs need the specifics. But they need them for a different reason: as a bridge from the present to the future. Of primary importance to RIOs is the continuity between the before and after—whether the old is being preserved, or at least maintained in some semblance.

Given their loyalties, RIOs need to know how people will be taken care of by the organization. That part of the plan seems as important as— or more important than—either the big picture or details of the new organizational structure.

> *The organization says there will be a good plan for the people who will be laid off. They said there will be generous severance and extras for those who have been here a long time. But they haven't provided any details, and no one's seen a package yet. Everybody's nervous just waiting for the news. I'm not being laid off, but I'm anxious to see a packet, too. Some of these people leaving aren't ready to retire. Will the plan be adequate for them? I don't know what to say to them. I'm probably going to worry until the organization finally gives us the plan.*

What stops organizations from developing comprehensive change management plans, including sure-to-be-needed contingency plans?

B/A/R/R/I/E/R
More Discomfort

The emotional impact of downsizing for the planners (executives) themselves acts as a barrier to adequate planning.

As Vogel points out,

> [T]here's so much anxiety generated by the layoff itself, so much avoidance, so much ambivalence about it, [a] certain amount of holding your nose and jumping in the pool rather than really planning it out at the level I'm talking about.

We found no manager who was comfortable with dismissing people, no matter how much this seemed the necessary course of action. So some leaders concentrated on quantifiable projects, such as counting heads and tallying department statistics; dealing in numbers reduced the human element. "Cut ten percent across the board" may have been a poor decision from a planning perspective, but its impersonal quality was more palatable than an order to "Lay off Tom, John, and Mary."

B/A/R/R/I/E/R
Lack of Experience

Even when outside experts are brought in to help plan the organization's future, leadership's lack of experience with large-scale change remains a barrier to planning. Traveling where the organization has not been before is more hazardous than going along familiar paths.

For some managers, one result of lack of experience seems to be a feeling of not being able to control the change, particularly the "after" part. "So why try to plan?" was a typical response—offered as a conclusion, not as a query.

At the opposite end, another manifestation of inexperience is the belief that change is entirely controllable, given a good plan. We observed several managers who seemed to operate from the fallacious assumption that once the plan was committed to paper, it would go that way. (And if it didn't, the problem was attributable to the execution, hence the execution-ers.) They functioned as if contingency plans were unnecessary, even a sign of flawed initial planning.

"How will the 'what ifs' be dealt with?" we queried one department head who was managing a major restructuring that included a plant reloca-tion. "What if the system's not ready?"

"That won't happen; the schedule is set," was his incredulous response. We had the sense that this individual felt our even raising the issue was insulting his project management skills. Since others on the change project team took their cues from him, their plans, too, lacked backup alternatives. As a result, they were continually coming up with revisions. The fax lines were humming.

For Ozzie Hager, a leader of a human resources consultant team, the response to either type of thinking is understanding the nature of change.

> To me, the dynamics of change break down into two things: things you can control, and things you cannot. The best advice I've seen given to upper management has been, "If you want to come out of this better than you went into it, then focus on the things that you can control."

Thus, although organizations may not be able to control the need for down-sizing, management can control how it is carried out via the plan.

Inexperience also causes others to conclude that "turning on a dime"—reacting quickly—counts more than careful planning that may become moot, given the rapidity of change. This mind-set is problematic for the development of contingency planning.

In some cases, inexperience causes problems even when contingency planning has occurred. As a vice president of operations told us, planning for contingencies is not enough. The restructuring at her company was proceeding right on schedule—for the first six weeks. Then the new computer system developed some glitches that wreaked havoc on the implementation plan. The team responsible for the installation, clearly under pressure, went into what can best be described as a reactive mode. Three alternatives were quickly developed, including one calling for round-the-clock shifts; another started with flying in a consulting group from Japan.

What was amiss? As our interviewee iterated:

> When we encountered our first problem, no one got out the [contingency] plan.

Indeed, the team had carefully considered and planned for a number of "what if" scenarios not dissimilar to what actually happened. Fortunately, this oversight was short-lived, as one experienced person spoke out. The contingency plan was subsequently put into effect.

B/A/R/R/I/E/R
Overlooking Existing Priorities

The organization's failure to reexamine existing priorities in light of the restructuring or downsizing is another barrier to planning.

One health care organization had an ambitious marketing campaign in place when restructuring hit. The accompanying downsizing left the marketing and sales workforces intact but impacted one of the departments that had provided intermittent support to the marketing effort. The campaign went askew when this department did not have the capacity to provide the support needed, and marketing targets were not met. It took negative sales results for the organization to realize how interrelated the downsizing in one department was to the total organization.

When some organizations ended up with multiple or conflicting priorities, they had neither the employees nor the time to address them. Fragmentation of energies for executives as well as line people was the result.

▶ *BEST PRACTICE*

Some organizations did an excellent job of incorporating downsizing activities with reconfigured business plans. A company that had focused heavily on research and development determined that it was time to utilize the results of R&D's efforts. This meant a shift of priority and resources to production and marketing. Downsizing was one component of the change management plan, carefully structured in terms of the organization's new priorities. Rather than directing a blanket ten percent cut across the board or even a ten percent reduction in R&D with a ten percent addition in priority areas, the organization tried wherever possible to shift and utilize existing staff.

▶ *BEST PRACTICE*

One manager at a different company spoke about planning for employee reassignment:

We recognized that by changing the focus of the product line, some of our designers would not want to continue in the department. In the restructuring we planned for that and tried to line up alternative assignments even before we announced the changes.

ARTICULATING THE PLAN

The second major issue survivors raised had to do with whether the plan was clearly articulated to, and understood by, employees. In terms of the organization's communication of the plan, there were two very pronounced concerns that cut across all survivor groups: that they be told of the plan, and that they be informed of the reasons for the organizational change.

Tell Us!

Whether or not they agreed or disagreed with the organization's decisions, FODs, W&Ss, and RIOs alike wanted information—they wanted to know the who, what, when, and where of the plan.

Probably the most frustrated and disillusioned survivors we spoke to were those employees who thought the organization had no plan. They thought so because, among other things, the organization had provided no information about it. "With nothing to go on, a lot of people decided they weren't wanted and should take the money," a survivor leaver told a newspaper reporter, describing what happened when her organization failed to communicate.

▶ **BEST PRACTICE**

The division manager of a company about to downsize described management's approach to informing employees:

We're not going to tap people on the shoulder and say "you're out of here today."... As best we could, we identified people and we gave them advance notice that they were at risk.

We now return to a point made earlier in the chapter: Survivors perceived selection criteria were missing in whole or in part from a plan because they weren't told about the criteria or they didn't understand what was said. In some cases, selection criteria were indeed in the plan, but the organizations failed to articulate that information. The results of this omission were substantial. If, for example, the company was closing a department or division, it was not terminating people for poor performance. But that's what survivors often thought—unless it was publicly stated otherwise.

If there are going to be reductions in numbers of positions, employees want to be told what performance criteria will be applied.

People who were very good and made real contributions survived previous layoffs. But in this round the same type of people who should have been treated well were deadwood. Laid off. It made me realize, You are a disposable commodity. Cogs in the machine. I was a bit naive.

We do not want to suggest that survivors' lacking information was always attributable to management's omissions. There were those survivors who did not want to hear; so no matter how loud the volume, they denied it had been said, or they misunderstood what they had heard.

As one change manager, a survivor, told us:

It takes a lot of effort to pull your thoughts together to prepare to announce the change to your staff. Then, after you do present it, just when you think they're with you, that they understand the changes,

*that they're going with it, you turn around and they're doing the same
old things or they're questioning the plan or they're just not there. You
feel like you're it!*

Surrounded by those concerned with present realities or maintaining the
status quo, change leaders sometimes found themselves leading a party of
one.

Tell Us Why!

The second issue raised by FODs, W&Ss, and RIOs is that survivors
want to know the whys—the reasons for the changes themselves. We have
talked about the need to provide the rationale in chapters 5 and 6, and we
mention it again now because it is a critical element of managing change.

We encountered many survivors who clearly and adroitly articulated
the company's rationale for the reorganization, downsizing, and/or merger.
Those interviewees talked about market share, strategies, decentralization,
and profitability, using facts and figures. And they spoke to the business
realities—lost accounts, fewer job orders, and lowered sales volume—
prompting the changes. These speakers were neither members of upper
management nor company spokespersons; rather, they were most frequently line employees who came from all survivor groups. Indeed, one of the
most impressive presentations was made to us by a RIO customer service
representative. Interviewees' descriptions and answers to questions suggested that their organizations had done a first-rate job of articulating the plan
and the reasons for it.

Moreover, it was apparent that these survivors had accepted the organization's rationale. This brings up another point made by survivors: The
rationale not only has to be articulated by management but has to be convincing. We are not talking about making a good sales pitch but, rather, providing a sound justification for the content of the plan.

As noted earlier, FODs are particularly cognizant of this point.

*I was very skeptical of the organization, because here they are, they've
been the market leaders for twenty-five years, making tons of money,
but yet they need to cut back, to reduce things. And that really struck
me as odd. There's a lot of upper management, a lot of vice presidents,
and now they have to cut costs. And they target areas . . . and I'm
thinking, "Gee, I can't believe that they make so much money, but yet
they're going to reduce the number of staff that they have."*

For this survivor, as for many others, the organization had not even made a convincing case that there was a problem in need of a solution, much less succeeded in persuading him of the wisdom of the proposed plan.

Two situations caused survivors to reject the organization's rationale outright. One was stated by the survivor just quoted: a call for downsizing in the midst of profitability. The other was the combination of downsizing and what one survivor called "overcompensation" for upper management. How could the company justify downsizing while boosting salaries at the top?

They're going to save money by giving the CEO a million dollar raise? Gee, I'll help them save money for a lot less!

As discussed in chapter 5, if survivors believed there was disparity in salaries and/or that management was overpaid, survivors' perceptions that the organization had no justification for its downsizing could not be swayed.

Similarly, providing information about the criteria for selecting those to leave and those to stay is only part of the change management task; the rationale for the selection has to make sense. Survivors' reactions ranged from believing the organization had made reasoned decisions to finding no rationale for the choices or finding what was presented suspect.

Jacqueline McHale, senior consultant, noted:

As the organization downsizes or merges, it's usually for strategic reasons ... and people need to know where they fit into that new organization, that new "thought process and vision of the future." What tends to happen is people get selected or not selected to remain in the organization, and the ones who get selected are considered lucky. Usually there is thought behind it, and very good reasons, but no one tells the individuals why they were selected, and what their real value is to the organization.

Obviously, selection determines those who are staying as well as the people who are going. According to many of our interviewees, however, when they were notified, they were not told the rationale, why they had survived. Hence, they were on their own to try to make sense of the decisions.

Two survivors from one aerospace organization met with us together. These two women had been management peers before the downsizing. The downsizing eliminated their management level; as a result, people at that level were either let go, demoted, or promoted.

For one of our interviewees, demotion occurred.

I got rightsized from the manager of a department of 140 to a supervisor of thirteen. . . . I took the approach of, I don't quite understand this, so let me go ask the people who I work for. . . . The answer to "So what did I do?" was "Nothing.". . . I don't believe there was much in the way of criteria.

When questioned further as to her beliefs about the lack of criteria, she added that she had finally attributed the demotion to "office politics." Clearly, she had to find some rationale; in order to continue working for the company, she had to make sense of the selection process and the outcome for her. Ironically, three months later, still without a rationale from the organization for her demotion, she found herself promoted—again, with no explanation from the company.

The other survivor, who had been promoted, was no more understanding of or comfortable with that decision.

As I walked in, everybody jumps up like they'd handed me a present and said, "Congratulations! You've been promoted!" I stood there—I can't even describe how I felt—it was like, "To what?"

I stood there and I didn't even understand what just happened. I was one of the first, so later people were coming up to me and asking, "What happened?" I said, "Well, I guess I'm promoted to this job. I don't know what it is, what I'm going to be doing." They asked, "How do you feel?" And I was numb. You almost felt like you cheated, getting a promotion. You didn't earn it. You didn't anything. Why me?

When you get promoted, there should be, "Gee, I got promoted!" Some joy. There was none of that.

The second survivor continued:

And as the day went on you were hearing who got moved up [and] who didn't. You didn't understand the rationale behind it on some of the choices, some you could, some not, and all it looked like was there are going to be less people doing more work.

Even when criteria were given, people went back to the organization's history to find a point of reference for evaluating the fairness of the selection process and results.

Some of our interviewees shared with us their opinions about why the organization had not been up front—why it had failed to communicate information fully and/or in a timely manner. Fear of various negative outcomes was a commonly cited explanation.

B/A/R/R/I/E/R
Fears

Survivors' comments supported points we have previously iterated about barriers to management's communicating information to employees: fear that productivity will go down or that the best employees will leave; fear that they (management) don't have all the answers or won't be able to handle employees' responses; and their personal discomfort with delivering bad news.

> *I know he dreads our staff meetings, because eventually someone will ask a question that he can't answer. Or if he does respond, someone won't like the answer, and then he has to deal with that.*

We saw an example of this point with a manager we knew. Her personal discomfort with delivering bad news was magnified by the fact that the "receivers" were direct reports with whom she had built good relationships.

B/A/R/R/I/E/R
Avoidance of Inferred Promises

As Jean Wallace, a director of human resource development, aptly stated:

> There's a reason the company selected those individuals who they're keeping; they [survivors] don't know it. The company needs to tell them. Companies are afraid to do that, because they feel like they are setting expectations for that individual and setting themselves up down the road, but the bottom line is if they don't tell them, they're going to lose them anyway, so what is the risk? And that's what I look at—weigh the risk.

It's a balancing act: How do you make someone feel secure without telling them the job is secure? For, in articulating the rationale for selecting a survivor, companies do need to be aware of the potential risks of inferred promises of long-term or permanent employment. Karen Valentia Clopton, a partner and employment law specialist at Cooper, White and Cooper in San Francisco, cautions,

Given all of the wrongful termination litigation, managers have to be especially careful that they not create any kind of legal or job security. Obviously, telling someone, "Your job is secure," or "Don't worry; you have a job as long as you want"...even something like "We want you to stay" (versus "We want you to be part of the team")—can be an implied contract.

IMPLEMENTING THE PLAN

"So how did people hear about whether they were downsized or not?" we asked our interviewee, a computer programmer at a high-tech company.

Meetings were being scheduled by the new senior VP. People didn't know why they were meeting with him. I thought to myself, Maybe this is just his way of introducing himself. Then I found out only half of the department were scheduled for meetings, and I became concerned.... Wow, we're in this downsizing; why is he meeting with them and not with me? During the meetings, people were told they were out but not to share the information.... So the first couple days, people who had their meetings were really good at keeping their happy faces on.... So I'm alarmed: Why wasn't I chosen? How did this happen? Finally the news leaked out that those people who had meetings weren't the chosen; they were the unchosen.

Whatever the extent of the organization's planning and articulation beforehand, survivors had a lot to say about the issue of implementation, that is, how the changes were carried out.

D-Day!

A major implementation issue is how the actual downsizing, or D-day, as more than one interviewee referenced it, took place.

We found that those survivors who knew the downsizing date were ahead of many of their peers, even if the date was all they knew in advance. Few of those we interviewed knew in advance any of the hows and whats—the details of the upcoming event. As one survivor described it,

At the end of the day you looked around and realized who wasn't at their desk. That's how you found out who had been terminated.

On the other hand, some layoffs were well managed.

▶ **BEST PRACTICE**

One human resources director reported on an implementation process she felt worked well:

Our top executive issued a company-wide communiqué describing what would happen and reiterating that they would take care of those who [were] laid off; the next tier of managers talked to their people as to what was happening and how it would affect their immediate work.

▶ **BEST PRACTICE**

Another HR professional reported:

On the day of the downsizing, each manager met individually with direct reports, both those downsized and those who would be staying.

▶ **BEST PRACTICE**

Another recalled:

Managers and supervisors spoke with survivors as a group, explaining the process and sharing what the plans and next steps for them were.

Some survivors, however, reported instances in which implementation was poorly carried out. One survivor from a high-tech company reported going in to work one morning expecting business as usual only to find that some of his colleagues couldn't sign on to the system. No one seemed to know why some were able to and others not. People watched apprehensively as co-workers—the same people who could not sign on to the system—were called away simultaneously. These people returned, accompanied by "anyone from a manager to a security guard," who stayed with them while they boxed up their belongings and then walked the employees out of the building.

There were no good-byes, no conversations. We were just as afraid, I think, and just as stunned. We just sat there in silence. Even after they were all gone, no one spoke. We were just stunned.

Going through these downsizing events was just too much for some of the survivors—even the high performers. One person we knew said that after experiencing the way the first downsizing was handled, "shrouded in mystery and agonizing suspense," he decided that he didn't want to live through that again. That's when he decided to leave voluntarily. Though he had been a very committed employee, he said that he lost respect for the organization because of the way he felt it had mismanaged the event.

He wasn't unique. We heard his story, or variations on it, from other survivor leavers we interviewed.

Another survivor, a manager at a different organization, was not on the premises when downsizing occurred, again with no advance notice. Indeed, she was across the country leading a training seminar and had no idea D-day was happening until she placed her routine end-of-the-day call to her secretary. Not only could she not learn her fate until she returned two days later, but her employees and colleagues were equally in the dark about her status.

When I got back, the mood in the department was hot. People said to me, "We looked around the room; you weren't there; Steve said you were in Chicago, so we figured, OK, maybe it's not you." A lot of people were agonizing over who was on the list.

Her experience speaks not only to poor implementation generally but, specifically, to the need to deal with employees simultaneously.

What Happened Next

For organizations that had well-conceived plans, careful consideration had been paid to what would happen to people after the downsizing event. As one human resources vice president told us:

So if you came in, and you were going to be laid off, you knew exactly what the short-term plans were for you. "This is what we need you to do; this is how long you're going to stay."

Why aren't we addressing this topic in the planning section of this chapter? Because, in so many situations, "what happened next" appeared almost an afterthought, with not enough attention paid to possible outcomes and impact on survivors.

The survivors and consultants with whom we spoke had varying opinions as to how long the downsized should stay after receiving notification that they would be laid off. Survivors wanted to be assured that these individuals would actually be working, not just occupying desks. Even the RIOs, the survivors most sympathetic to the welfare of colleagues, were concerned about this situation.

The ones let go had to work around us for two weeks. It was upsetting. I felt guilty and angry. I wanted someone who would pull her weight.

Survivors shared examples of organizations that allowed downsized employees to stay on for weeks and even months with laissez-faire supervision. The W&Ss were not the only ones who brought up the inequity of the situation. As another disgruntled RIO told us:

Here they're allowed to be deadwood, while I'm doing their job and mine.

Another survivor expressed fears for the company beyond those of lowered productivity or inequitable work loads:

My personal opinion was that that was a pretty bad mistake, because not only do you have twenty-some people who now have access to all of your files for two months and you have eight competitors within a five-mile radius of you—why are you giving them [downsized employees] that option to pack up their entire office and move someplace else [to a competitor]?

Leadership After Downsizing

For survivors, issues went beyond who was chosen and what happens to them next. Knowing they had not been downsized, they turned their attention to the next implementation issue: Who would lead the survivors?

The three survivor groups applied different criteria in evaluating decisions about who had been selected to lead and manage in the post-downsizing environment.

■ FODs' LEADERSHIP CRITERIA

For FODs, the criterion is, are those selected the best qualified to lead? What roles have they played in the company's history? Are they not only competent as leaders generally but also sufficiently skilled and knowledgeable to lead at this time?

■   W&Ss' LEADERSHIP CRITERIA

For W&Ss, the primary criterion for leadership is fairness. If these survivors perceive someone has been selected because of cronyism or political pull, W&Ss' allegiance to and support of management are diminished.

I can think of half a dozen people who'd be a better choice for the job. The person chosen has connections. The bottom line is politics.

One W&S told us that he kept a running record of promotions. As lists came out, he counted how many of those in new management positions had previously worked with the change manager.

■   RIOs' LEADERSHIP CRITERIA

RIOs' significant criterion for judging managers boils down to whether the individual will be responsive to employees' needs. RIOs fear a leader who in the throes of managing change events will overlook or discount direct reports' concerns.

Survivors' Involvement

We pointed out earlier in the chapter the problems that develop when survivor managers are left out of the selection process. Survivors are equally frustrated when they are not given a role in the implementation.

When upper management takes on all of the implementation, it overlooks an opportunity to gain FODs' buy-in to the change. This survivor group, ready to excel and make a contribution to the organization, may have become vested via involvement; yet many organizations seemingly ignore this vehicle.

▶   *BEST PRACTICE*

A company assigned most of the implementation to an implementation team. The team was composed of managers and employees, many of whom had volunteered for the assignment. According to our interviewee's descriptions, at least half of the team were FODs. Two years and two downsizings later, all of the members, though no longer on the team, were still survivor stayers. Though we would hesitate to point to participation on the team as the determining factor in their willingness to stay, our interviewee would not:

*For me, being on the team made all the difference between my leaving
and staying. I knew I could get another job, but I felt a real commitment to seeing it through. I still feel that way. And when team members see one another, there's that sense of recognition that others feel
the same way.*

As can be surmised from our discussion, there are various barriers to
effective implementation. Sometimes these barriers are specific to individual leaders, whose problematic managerial behaviors seem to be exacerbated by the downsizing.

B/A/R/R/I/E/R
Maintaining Control

One of the personal characteristics of bosses that frustrates survivors has to
do with what survivors perceive as managers' fear of losing control. Our
survivors reported that this concern played itself out in a variety of ways.

In one instance, as part of the restructuring, the manager redesigned
the department, wrote all the new job descriptions, chose employees'
offices, and assigned customer accounts. Although this manager's behavior
was neither new nor unique to this situation, survivors felt particularly dis-
empowered. According to our interviewee, his manager's actions "stripped
away any pretense that anyone else might have any say in the future." For this
FOD, it was the last straw. He resigned. He told us that he felt he could tolerate the manager's control patterns under "normal conditions," but they
were too much to handle along with the added stress.

We talked to another survivor in the same department. A W&S, she
told us,

*Every time I turn around, he's made another decision for me. What if
it conflicts with something else? What if I'd prefer a different assignment? What if I've never done this before? None of those things seem
to matter one bit!*

There were also RIOs in this department. We would have thought the manager would have been more tolerant of and tolerable to this survivor group.
After all, the RIOs are the survivors most often looking for direction, and
they can be counted on to follow the lead with minimal control. However,
in this case, because it appeared to be more difficult for this leader to deal
with the other employees, the manager's reaction was to over-control the

RIOs. Thus, the RIOs paid the price—the recipient of micromanagement and all the assignments at which others balked. The final result? According to a friend, a survivor who gave a later interview, one RIO stopped telling the manager when there was a problem or she couldn't keep up with the work. As the friend revealed, Jane (the RIO)

> *became so stressed she couldn't do it. And then the manager discovered her work wasn't done. So, more control. More stress. And that was the pattern. Finally, Jane had to leave.*

Another scenario, this time in a regional branch of a bank, also centered around the issue of management's desire to maintain control. The boss developed a highly structured implementation schedule that included, in our interviewee's opinion, unrealistic dates, inflexibility, and no backup plans. To paraphrase our narrator, her boss's rigidity prevented him from modifying the plan even when it was off schedule and hadn't worked. Instead of pushing back the schedule to approximate a more realistic time frame or looking at alternative ways to accomplish the same goals, he simply shortened the time to complete tasks.

> *Every time we meet [weekly] he gives us a revised schedule. But you know it's obsolete as you look at it. It makes me question how they came up with the first schedule—and how we'll ever get through this.*

B/A/R/R/I/E/R
No One to Lead

Problems occur when key managerial people start leaving and organizations promote "not ready now" candidates to leadership positions. How does this situation come about? As Pat del Valle, Human Resource Director, Vice President, told us,

> Small to mid-size organizations don't have time anymore for succession planning, for these feedback sessions—all these things that seem to be looked at as nice to have but not necessary anymore. I think that we're finding that some of it is necessary. The longer it takes to integrate, the higher the stress level. Succession planning accelerates successful integration.

The failure of organizations to have good succession plans in place is particularly annoying for FODs, who cite that concern in their assessment of the organization's ability to implement the change successfully. As del Valle suggests, the problem is compounded by the new leaders themselves:

> They don't quite have the skills, but because they're promoted, they have a false sense of their credibility and their knowledge … and situations will come up that they can't handle.

W&Ss' concern is more focused:

> *They chose her, and she better start demonstrating that she can fill Alan's shoes. Right now, I think she's the most inept of all the division heads. It's really unfair that I should have to work for someone like this.*

B/A/R/R/I/E/R
Same Stew

The issue of leadership capability is broader than whether newly promoted managers have the qualifications. Indeed, it is even more virulent when management stays in place. A human relations consultant expressed a survivor's viewpoint:

> [A] lot of times employees don't see any of the senior-level people leaving the organization; instead, they seem to rotate into different senior level roles. In those circumstances, employee trust goes out the window because change at the senior levels looks like "stirring the pot"… you have the same ingredients, and you come out with the same stew.

> It appears that the brunt of the change and loss is felt at the lower to middle levels, while the net change at the top of the house is "slim to none."

CHANGE MANAGEMENT ROLES

What else will help organizations plan, articulate, and implement change in ways that meet survivors' needs and address their concerns?

We recommend that the organization put in place a complement of change leaders, including a change manager, change management team, change coach, and human resources change agent.

Change Manager

The organization needs to designate a change manager, a person who orchestrates the change, facilitates change activities, and serves as a liaison between executive management and a change management team.

The change manager not only acts as one of the planners determining needs, setting direction, and developing change plans but fulfills the role of translator, translating the strategic plan into operational blueprints. With a change management team, the change manager determines the policy and plan for implementation, including communication to employees.

The change manager oversees any task forces and ad hoc committees developed to facilitate the change along with the change management team. The change manager is responsible for managing, hence legitimizing, the transition monitoring team discussed in chapter 8.

When the organization selects the change manager, it needs to consider the person's historical role as well as all of the leadership criteria already discussed. Does the candidate have a reputation for embracing change, or for resisting it? Is the candidate innovative and flexible rather than tied to past practices? A leader rather than a follower? Has this individual been able to take a stand effectively?

In one situation, a W&S had been with the company as long as the change manager, so she had tracked the manager's record. This survivor shared the manager's history as well as her perceptions around the water cooler. When co-workers questioned some of the change manager's actions, wondering if she was on target, the W&S advocated for the leader, citing past experiences. By providing this perspective, the W&S enhanced the change manager's overall credibility with survivors.

Remember the leadership role qualifications vis à vis the survivor groups? For example, FODs will take the selection of a change manager both as foretelling the organization's competence and as indicative of the organization's valuing of this attribute.

Survivors are not the only ones influencing the change manager's credibility.

B/A/R/R/I/E/R
Interference

Interference by executives sometimes has the effect of undermining the change manager's credibility. In one interviewee's experience, upper management challenged and sometimes overrode the change manager's decisions, seeming to delegate control and authority to that person in title only.

B /A/R/R/I/E/R
Inappropriate Selection

The role of the change manager is so critical that the selection requirements cannot be discounted. The change manager role is not one that can be used to help an employee assuage past mistakes. Nor should it be used to provide developmental opportunities for rising stars. There is too much at stake, and employees know it.

Change Management Team

As just stated, the change manager works with a change management team to lead the change effort. The change management team has responsibility for developing the implementation plan and has involvement in the development of the change communication plan as well.

The whos and hows of team membership are critical, since both the team and its work need the buy-in of employees as well as of management. However the change management team is assembled, the members have to have in-depth knowledge of the areas they represent.

Paula Taylor, a San Francisco Bay Area organization consultant, alerts organizations to the pressures inherent in the role:

> Perhaps the most difficult thing that members of the change management team must do is to handle their critical function with the single-minded focus to move the company successfully to the new organization without letting their own potentially uncertain futures interfere.

One survivor, whose company had a change team working on selection and implementation, noted that his trust and loyalty were diminished by his experience with the change team.

> *We were informed they were creating a team to look at the reorganization. The person they elected to represent our division had never done any of the jobs that we did. "You don't know what we do, so how can you represent us?"*

> *They decided to interview every department to see what we do. [An] interview took place, for example, in my department with a person who had been with the company a week. He was supposed to understand what our areas did. He interviewed us in about forty-five*

minutes, and in those forty-five minutes we were supposed to outline everything our department did and everything our people did, and after forty-five minutes he was supposed to understand everything we did. He didn't even understand what the company was, let alone what we did.

Oh, yes. I had a high level of trust, and when I saw how they were coming about making this decision, the forty-five-minute interview, the people they picked on the committee, your trust goes down the drain. You know that these people know nothing about what you do, so what kind of decisions can they make? And the trust and morale in the company went down. It was very hard to get people to work.

Change Coach

Just as messengers need a communications coach, unless the change manager brings substantial experience in managing change and transition to the role, she or he needs a good change coach as well.

Many of the criteria we outlined for communications coaches apply here: Well versed in change and transition, the change coach needs to possess significant understanding of the organization's history, culture, and workforce. The tasks are similar as well.

The human resources professional within the organization may be an ideal candidate to occupy this role.

Human Resources Change Agent

It is important to note that coaching is only one function with which human resources (HR) needs to be concerned. Indeed, HR must be comprehensively involved in the change team, for it is our contention that HR plays a pivotal role as the organization's conscience and as its change agent.

The change manager's coach, the organization's alter ego, a strategic partner at the planning table, and the champion of change—all these roles require HR to be very thoughtful and proactive. HR can't simply wait for an invitation to act. As Wallace, a seasoned HR professional, notes:

The key that HR people have to understand is that they're not going to be given the role; they have to start to go out and take it.

The biggest mistake that HR people make is that they get bogged down in the day-to-day administrivia. It's very easy to do that, because of the nature of HR.

We are far from alone as proponents of human resources taking an active role in the change process. As one manager told us,

Dialoguing with employees, asking what they need, what they want, what they think is going to happen, I go to the premise that we cannot go back to the way we were because the organization is changing.

So [I] look hopefully for a champion, somebody I can get the ear of, somebody who understands the dynamics of the change; when I find that person, I'm going to latch on.

Who better to take on this champion role than the organization's conscience, the human resources professional?

KEY POINTS

Survivors are critically concerned with having a comprehensive change management plan in place—one that is articulated clearly and implemented effectively. The plan needs to address the after-downsizing phase: How will the work get done? What are survivors' roles? Survivors want to know selection criteria, including reasons why they have been chosen to stay.

GROUP ISSUES

FODs   For the FODs, a plan is needed that reflects the change as a part of a total picture and encompasses existing and pending organizational goals. FODs want to be involved in the development as well as the implementation of the plan.

W&Ss   For the W&Ss, the plan needs to provide the structure that will guide them through the process of implementing the plan and clearly set out their roles.

RIOs   For the RIOs, the plan must provide step-by-step guidelines for their day-to-day activities and set out how they and the downsized will be cared for.

STRATEGIES

Develop a comprehensive change management plan that lays out selection criteria and plans for downsized employees, the survivors, and the organization. Involve managers and clarify their change management roles. Designate a change manager, a change management team, and a change coach. Utilize Human Resources actively in all stages of the process.

Given the interconnectedness of change and transition, it is appropriate that we turn to the latter topic next.

8

"The work of transitioning is to build the psychological, emotional, and behavioral *capacity* to reasonably manage continuous ambiguity and uncertainty."

Jeanne Cherbeneau, Ph.D.

Transition

A PSYCHOLOGICAL PASSAGE

A dilemma: how to write about managing transition when our research revealed that it was essentially a management non-issue. Across industries, across the country, inside merged conglomerates and small family businesses, we could find scant evidence of attention to this issue.

At the same time, the consequences for companies of ignoring survivors' transitions were becoming known. You may recall from chapter 1 the responses of executives when asked why their organization had been unsuccessful in achieving its restructuring goals (Wyatt, 1993). Whether the objective was an improved bottom line or increased customer satisfaction, the primary factor that leaders cited was not poor strategic planning or lack of vision. The number one reason for the company's dismal results, in their opinion, was their employees' resistance to change.

The dilemma is further perplexing because transition itself is not an unknown concept. Beginning with Elizabeth Kübler-Ross (1969), the literature is rich with models of and treatises on the psychological processes accompanying death and loss. Indeed, in this country, grieving has become a universally accepted phenomenon of bereavement rituals and customs to facilitate the psychological passage for those who suffered the loss as well as those offering support. What seems ironic is that those same organizational leaders who fail to recognize their employees' losses have undoubtedly participated in those transition events.

Consultants like William Bridges (1988), David Noer (1993), and Cynthia Scott and Dennis Jaffe (1994) have transposed this phenomenon to the organizational arena. Likewise, we talked with organization practitioners from California to Massachusetts who were replete with topical wisdom—

145

but lacked opportunities to apply their expertise because executives saw no need to address survivor's transition.

Yet we could not dismiss the emotions we heard from survivors—the anger, sadness, and denial that were the outward manifestations of a psychological process of grief and loss. The importance of this issue seemed undeniable as survivors spoke of sleepless nights, the inability to focus, and the personal anguish of seeing valued colleagues depart—symptoms and feelings they continued to experience months later.

Nor could we ignore our own understanding of the significance of this issue to these individuals as well as to their organizations.

THE TRANSITION PROCESS

The definition of *transition* bears repeating here. Transition is the psychological process that people experience *in response to* a change. Although transition models vary in the number of stages or phases, their authors seem to divide the transition process into three parts: saying good-bye to the past and embracing the future, separated by some sort of middle state neither attached to the past nor committed to the future. Lewin's "unfreezing, moving, refreezing" (1951) exemplifies this division into three phases.

Where Kübler-Ross describes the first part of the transition journey as movement through the distinct phases of shock, denial, and anger, Bridges speaks more generally of "making an ending," and others talk of the initial shock followed by defensive retreat.

Bridges refers to the middle part as "the neutral zone" and Lewin, "moving." Kübler-Ross' and Fink's "acknowledgment" stages may be that middle state. For all of these models, the last part is more than acknowledgment of the change; it culminates in psychological commitment and/or adaptation to the new situation.

The authors all speak of transition as a process that is not a smooth, linear ride but a route filled with bumps, regressions, and plateaus. Given the continuous and ambiguous nature of change, Cherbeneau notes:

> Transitioning can no longer be viewed as moving from a present/current "state" to a future end/static "state."

Most importantly, the experts conclude that going through all the stages—completing the transition—is necessary for people if they are to accept and embrace a change.

Give-Ups

In our transition workshops we use a variety of methods to help people understand the natural discomfort that change brings. We even use the simple exercise of asking people to cross their arms in their usual way and then without looking down to do the opposite.

As people are bemoaning the difficulty of accomplishing the "unnatural" task and complaining of the resultant discomfort, we display the following definition, from Richard L. Sprague, a "transition consultant" (as quoted in *Training Magazine*, September 1984):

> One of the things we know about transition is that in most cases the experience is one of being forced to give something up and face a change that, under any normal circumstances, one would likely resist.

We then ask, "Why would anyone resist? Why would one try to avoid change? What prompts people to cling to what is familiar, even a job they don't like or a boss they dislike, and do anything—hide files, erase voice-mail messages—to maintain the status quo?"

"Forced to give up." In our interviews as well as in our change workshops, survivors talked of giving up friendships, roles, work that they valued, favorite customers, even a cubicle or desk that had become familiar. And they spoke of the more intangible things they no longer had: security, control, dedication, loyalty. The list of "give-ups" was so consistent that here is where we began to refer to them as the Three C's defined in chapter 1: competence, or know-how, expertise, and the sense of security and control that comes with mastery; connection, meaning friendships, relationships and bonds (with customers, bosses, peers, and the organization), and the sense of belonging and attachment; and commitment, or the sense of dedication and loyalty to the work and the organization. Competence, connection, commitment—their demise is a consequence whether employees are changing the way they cross their arms in a workshop exercise or the way they perform their jobs.

Getting

And giving up is only part of the change experience. Employees are *getting* as well. What are they getting? Survivors talked about increased work loads, unrealistic goals and expectations, and expanded responsibilities, generally accompanied by unfamiliar co-workers, bosses, and/or work units. Internally, they coped with a new set of emotions: feelings of incompetence replacing competence; isolation where connection had been; and a growing sense of "looking out for number one."

> *You know what happened? If I had any loyalty for a company, it got totally erased. I don't feel I have any loyalty for any company. I was loyal, believe me, but now I think if somebody calls me tomorrow and offers me the right job for the right money, I wouldn't even think twice. Because you don't know what's going to happen around the corner.*

Ironically, this interviewee was not speaking to us as a member of a downsized organization. Not only had her company never downsized, but its continued growth made it an industry favorite. But that didn't seem to matter. For she had come to this company as a survivor leaver of another organization, having severed her employment voluntarily after two rounds of downsizing there.

As one participant, who had just completed the arms exercise and reviewed the definition, said in response:

> *No wonder people resist. Who wouldn't?*

What survivors reported as losses occurred not only when changes were negative. One individual described her reaction to being promoted as a result of the restructuring.

> *They said, "You've been promoted. . . . Congratulations, and, oh by the way, we're moving you to a different department. We're moving you back to your old department." And my response: "But I don't want to go back to my old department. This is my department." "That's where you're going. That's it. Congratulations."*

So what people resist is not the change but the transition: the process of giving up and getting incumbent in making an ending and marking a new beginning.

resistance Versus Resistance

Most transition models identify resistance as a natural and expected phase in the transition process; the resulting complaints, errors, and naysaying are all normal reactions during this stage. In that context it's a relatively temporary condition. And it's what we call *resistance* with a small "r." But we found a different type of resistance as well—*Resistance* with a capital "R." This capital "R" Resistance may have shown up initially or been more overt during the natural resistance phase, but it didn't go away. Resistance as a phase became Resistance as a condition. The behaviors continued. Apathy or anger appeared permanent. And they intensified. The impact was different, too. Manifestations included absenteeism, malicious compliance, illness, lowered productivity, resignation, and failure to achieve restructuring goals.

In our opinion, when the Wyatt study ascribed companies' dismal results to "employees' resistance to change," they were referring to Resistance with a capital "R."

MAKING AN ENDING

Saying good-bye and honoring the past ensures that survivors are free to move on, to focus on the future. Effective good-byes move survivors beyond denial and help them to set aside or lighten any emotional baggage they may have.

The importance of individuals making an ending, of completing this first part of transition, came home to us vividly when we were called in to help an organization that had undergone a major reorganization a year before. The company's restructuring had resulted in reconfigurations of roles and responsibilities; functions previously performed by sales representatives were now handled by customer service.

At the office we visited, however, it was still "business as before." Employees were handing out business cards with now-obsolete titles. Sales representatives continued to perform their old functions, as did the other staff members who had been in place prior to the reorganization. Complaints from customers, who might get calls from two employees asking for the same information, increased. The two post-reorganization hires, operating according to the new job descriptions, were confused and frustrated. Management appeared to be in collusion: Though supervisors reiterated corporate headquarters' rhetoric that "everyone is supposed to be operating according to the new system," they continued to tolerate the old ways of working.

What was the problem? In an exhaustive day of transition management work, we learned that these long-term employees were enmeshed in fear and concern about their ability to perform in the new system. In addition, they perceived little reward for learning the new tasks (which would have had to be substantial to compete with the payoffs—the sense of competence and control—for maintaining the old). They were thus stuck in transition, unable to make an ending. They had told none of this to the organization, and the organization had attributed the employees' behavior to their "resistance" period.

Taking the employees through a series of exercises, we ended with a walk outside to a dumpster where people were instructed to throw away what they were ready to let go. This included not only the old roles and responsibilities they had listed but also the payoffs—the psychological rewards for maintaining them that survivors had recorded privately throughout the day. The pull of the past and the power of this experience were astonishing, vividly illustrated by one participant who, having thrown away his pile of notes, paused and then reached into the dumpster to retrieve one piece of paper. "Not yet," he murmured to himself.

Organizational Practices

In our consulting work, "How has the organization helped people to say good-bye?" has always been a useful question, and we have heard about ending events ranging from mock funerals to ice cream socials. At one company, employees held a wake complete with a burial ceremony.

▶ *BEST PRACTICE*

Rose Cohan, a San Francisco Bay Area management consultant, described a transition event she orchestrated:

The company had to lay off about eighteen people in one department, a very central part of the organization. We had everybody in the company who wanted to, come to a luncheon to thank these eighteen for all their work. This provided a formal company-sponsored way to say good-bye.

It's essential that people who are staying have a chance to say good-bye and not feel uncomfortable toward the people who are leaving.

▶ *BEST PRACTICE*

One company developed an interesting way to help employees mark the ending, which included the demolition of a building. Employees used the walls to express their thoughts and feelings about the ending, writing messages, drawing symbols or pictures, and even authoring poetry. One group placed photos of themselves on the wall; individuals then wrote messages under the pictures. Different departments wrote good-byes to each other. Colleagues carried on dialogues about their relationship and what they would miss in no longer working together. These "endings" occurred over a three-week period and thus became an extended process rather than a single event, mirroring the transition itself.

What we found particularly effective in this case was the timing: The organization's beginning this exercise almost a month before the move allowed people to communicate as their transition progressed, so it facilitated as well as documented the working out of feelings.

We ourselves have worked with organizations on their "good-byes." At one company, people brought old files and what would become obsolete forms to a "so long, it's been good to use you" party. Throwing away the materials not only provided a tangible means of making an ending but signaled to employees that they had to move on to new ways of working.

Without good-byes, the consequences to the organization as well as to the individual are significant.

Those two women ate lunch together every day for over a year. We used to joke about it. One of them is leaving. Now they pass each other in the hall and practically don't speak. It's made us all really uncomfortable, but no one talks about it.

With no help, especially from management, these two women were unable to say good-bye, to make an ending with one another. Not only did this damage their relationship, but as this survivor told us, it impaired relationships with and among others in the department. Where there had been camaraderie and shared responsibility, there now were isolationism and a diminishing flow of information as well as conversation. The tension resulted in the department's ceasing to talk about much of anything—including the work. Information needed by survivors about accounts they were acquiring from their departing colleagues was not communicated. And, likewise, survivors didn't ask.

The impact was not temporary. As another survivor told us six months after the departure:

People tend to keep to themselves, during work as well as after. There isn't much collaboration any more, or even talking through problems with customers. It has caused us some problems with several accounts, [with] people giving contradictory information.

Not structuring good-byes impacted more than individual relationships or existing groups. We heard across the board about the need for team building. Upon further exploration, we found that those who had some sort of structured ending with colleagues appeared better positioned to join a new team. Those for whom good-byes were nonexistent or ineffectual seemed to have more difficulty forging new connections. One indicator for us was how much of survivors' conversations focused on their former colleagues rather than new team members.

Not all managers failed to recognize and address employees' needs. We did find examples of survivor bosses who chose different paths.

▶ BEST PRACTICE

A sales manager recognized that her employees were struggling with feelings about the changes. The manager, feeling ill-equipped to deal with survivors' issues and her own transition process, sought help from the outplacement firm that heretofore had been working only with those downsized. At her initiation, a member of the firm facilitated weekly transition sessions as part of her department meetings.

In this case, the manager had the full support of her boss. That approval was critical, serving to legitimize the use of a resource as an appropriate decision rather than a fallback tactic resulting from an inability to deal with a management issue. Indeed, if this individual had called in a financial expert to help with budgeting a project, it is unlikely that it would be perceived as a sign of fiscal incompetence. Similarly, the use of a transition consultant did not signal her abdication of transition management.

Loss of the Three C's

There is a heavy price for going through this ending phase. For in "saying their good-byes" to life as they have known it, survivors are giving up, or reducing, the Three C's—their competence, connection, and commitment to the organization.

Survivors' Reactions

The survivors we interviewed all confirmed the emotional intensity of this phase: FODs, W&Ss, and RIOs alike experienced shock, denial, and anger. The differences were the way they perceived and responded to the change and whether or not and where they got stuck in making an ending.

■ FODs' TRANSITION REACTIONS

FODs' initial responses to change were the most positive of the survivor groups.

> *I have to say that my first hearing about the move was like a shot of adrenaline; I got really excited. Even though I understood the impact of this—or maybe I was just denying it—my first reaction was, " Wow! What a great opportunity!"*

Like other FODs, this survivor had neither bypassed any transition phases nor failed to experience any negative emotions. FODs' generally proactive stance seems to allow them to see opportunities and ways of "making the situation work for me one way or another" rather than get waylaid or derailed by those emotions. And FODs seem to take the least time of any of the survivor groups to come to terms with the change and move through the transition process.

But their skill in this area does not mean that they did not experience the impact. Nor does it signify that they were not cognizant of the effect of the change on their colleagues—and their bosses. As one survivor, knowledgeable in the psychology of transition, described his manager:

> *I feel sorry for him, but he has to get some help so he can deal with the department. I'm annoyed at the organization for not being more observant of his needs. And I'm annoyed with him for not being assertive. . . . I expect him to say "I need help with this transition" and go get it. But I know he's afraid it will affect his image—that the organization will see him as weak. . . . So I find myself managing his transition, not vice versa. And I don't know how long I'll be willing to do that.*

Observing this employee and his boss, we realized that we were seeing an FOD in transition dealing with an RIO manager in transition. We agreed with the employee's assessment that this manager felt it too risky to say, "I'm having problems with my own transition." Given our observations, we thought the manager's fears about management's reaction were not without merit. So this manager, struggling alone and unsuccessfully to manage his own transition, avoided situations that would force him to deal with his people's transition problems.

■ W&Ss' TRANSITION REACTIONS

For the W&Ss, emotions of the first phase of transition were in full view—or to be more accurate, in full volume.

Who planned this thing? You ask a simple question, and they start sputtering. I don't know whether they're stalling, hoping for an answer, or they have the answer and it's so bad they know we'd holler.

The W&Ss we interviewed and observed resembled the FODs in moving fairly rapidly through shock and denial and in recognizing problematic issues and choosing to meet them head-on. But the W&Ss stalled in the anger phase, stopped in part by applying a "what have they done to me?" approach. Some W&Ss appeared to receive the change as a personal affront, each new announcement creating a new sense of personal hurt and assault along with another wave of shock, denial, and anger.

Thus, W&Ss bring two issues to transition: the change itself and the "attack on me" interpretation. It is, therefore, not surprising that they are stopped in anger and stuck in resistance—a state that, for many of them, leads to Resistance with a capital "R." And the resistance is independent of the result for the individual: Promotion, added compensation, and special treatment have little effect on the degree of acceptance or the frequency of outbursts.

Are you asking if the salary increase placated me? Why would it? I deserved it; I've got two departments' work now, not one. And frankly, it was the least they could do.

Unfortunately, management's response to W&Ss was more often than not a shrugged "That's just the way he is" or "That's just the way it is," generated from a reluctance to deal with the W&Ss. Avoiding the W&Ss resulted in management discounting not only the messenger but the message and failing to appreciate the W&Ss' position.

■ RIOs' TRANSITION REACTIONS

To us, the RIOs we encountered just after a change had been announced most resembled the accident victims or disaster survivors seen on six o'clock news reports. This image came across vividly one day when a manager rushed into our training session, apologized for the interruption, and announced a major change to what had been a carefully planned and articulated schedule of events. As the announcement was made, we could literally observe shock on the faces of participants; some, within a few minutes, began asking questions and/or voicing complaints. Others, however, sat silent; their expressions did not change. They did not even appear aware of their colleagues' queries or management's answers. Even when the manager left the room and we resumed the program, these survivors remained detached, shut down intellectually and emotionally by the shock. When we returned to the organization a week later, these individuals appeared numb. One RIO told us,

> I just feel drained. I go home at night and all I want to do is sleep. It's like when I had surgery—I think I'm going to come out of the anesthetic, but I keep going back under. I don't know how I get through each day.

When we asked managers how the group was doing, they shook their heads.

Of the survivor groups, the RIOs appear to get stuck earliest in the transition process—at the stage of denial or even shock. And each new change fuels those emotions all over again.

Unfortunately, the RIOs' silence and tendency to mask emotions act in collusion if management denies that there is a problem, lending weight to management's assumption that everything is OK and thus supporting the notion that transition is a non-issue.

Perhaps due as much to management's preoccupation with W&Ss' demands as to faulty conclusions about the RIOs, management sometimes does not provide the active intervention RIOs need to cut through the denial and continue the process.

Structured Good-Byes

Organizations have to put in place structured events and activities to help people to make an ending, to say good-bye.

There are several levels of good-byes. The company needs to have formalized ways of saying good-bye as a whole organization to the past as well as to the people. There also need to be structured smaller good-bye events within departments or teams—or wherever employees are leaving. This legitimizes interaction between and among survivors as well as between and among those employees leaving the organization and those remaining.

B/A/R/R/I/E/R
Lack of Information

For many organizations, transition management is not something with which management has much experience. The psychological theory and rationale for "making endings" are generally not on management course outlines; nor are they necessarily encountered in the workplace. So it was not surprising when a survivor reported,

> They said, "Relax! You're not being affected at all. Everything's going to be status quo—the same for you." Not affected? Half the department is gone.

Management's Sanction

Top management's sanction of good-bye events and its visible participation and sponsorship are critical for signaling the organization's acknowledgment of the losses and pain and for legitimizing the expression of feelings.

We cannot overemphasize the importance of management's attention to this issue. Management's sanction sets the tenor for the organization's approach to making an ending—the time and attention devoted to the issue, and the legitimization of the events and feelings.

B/A/R/R/I/E/R
Organizational Culture

Survivors were able to articulate to us their feelings about the change and its impact on them. But talking about feelings and sharing emotions in the workplace are not part of most organizational cultures. As organization consultant Betsy Kendall proclaims in change management workshops, "The organizational F word is *feelings*."

The lack of value attached to the expression of feelings is a barrier that cuts across all industries. With neither leadership's sanction nor transition management programs to guide them, most survivors we interviewed were unaware of the acceptable corporate way to express those feelings. So they hid them. As in the case with the two women who ate lunch together and those around them, survivors did not know how to deal with their displaced or downsized co-workers. If they made overtures, would they be perceived as disloyal and wind up next on the list? Thus, their masks came on.

As Houda Samaha, a Massachusetts organization development consultant, added from her experience:

> In many instances, downsized colleagues were asked to leave the organization immediately. There was no opportunity to say good-bye—to say good luck, to express regret—whatever. When survivors complained about this, they were told, basically, to stop whining, to consider themselves lucky to have jobs, to get back to work. Having no outlet to mourn the change and the loss of their colleagues resulted in not only a reduction in productivity and motivation but an increase in health-related problems and medical leave.

MOVING THROUGH THE NEUTRAL ZONE

No matter how difficult the first phase is, the second phase of transition does not spell relief. The "neutral zone," as Bridges (1988) describes it, is a period best described as chaotic and unsettling.

I think I've accepted the department's being downsized. But I can't seem to stay focused—one minute I feel like I have a direction and I'm excited, and the next minute I ask myself, Why am I here, where is this all going? I'm normally a pretty calm person, so this is unsettling for me. And I can't help but think this is apparent to my colleagues and my boss.

In contrast to the inertia and enervation that often accompany the first phase, the neutral zone brings survivors renewed energy and creativity. Given the gamut of emotions that accompany this middle transition state, it is not surprising that survivors experience confusion and loss of control.

Survivors may still have doubts as to their right to be survivors over their downsized colleagues. They may be apprehensive as to the longevity of their new survivor status. And in the neutral zone they are, by definition, in a kind of "never-never land," neither attached to the past nor connected to the future. We frequently use the analogy of travelers on a sea voyage floating somewhere in the middle of the ocean, land no longer visible in either direction, far from both their embarkation and their destination.

Regaining the Three C's

"Will I be able to do the work?" "How will I fit with the new team?" "Can I support the company's new direction?" These are the kinds of questions survivors now ask themselves.

Even survivors who have successfully managed an ending do not likely come to this stage with high levels of self-confidence and self-esteem. How can they, when they feel themselves lacking competence, connection, and commitment?

Regaining Competence

"Will I be able to do the work?" "Can I learn the new equipment?" "Will I meet performance guidelines?" "Will I look foolish?" "Will I sound dumb?" Those are the kinds of competence concerns survivors revealed.

My boss kept talking about the new ways we would be doing the work, the new computer system, the teams and everything, how much more efficient it would be. All I could think about was, Will I be able to do it? Of course, I didn't tell her.

When we talked with survivors about their concerns, we found out that a renewed sense of competence did not remain in abeyance until they finished acquiring the new knowledge and skills. Indeed, one of the survivors who said he no longer worried about whether he could handle his new assignment was only in the first phase of a six-month training program.

Talking to other people who have been working with that system for a while, I just know I can learn how to do it.

For survivors, regaining the confidence that they can master the knowledge and skills results in their regaining a sense of competence. In other words, survivors do not have to do the new work; they just have to believe that they can do it.

Regaining a sense of competence derived as well from having a sense of control over their work environment, a feeling of personal power. Esther Orioli (1992), coauthor of *The Stress Map®* and CEO of Essi Systems, a San

Francisco firm focusing on workplace stress, reported that of all the stress-related factors, one has the greatest impact on an employee's ability to manage work pressures and maintain productivity during change. And that is personal power. It is also the only one, researchers found, that absolutely predicts stress-related illness.

Regaining Connection

Survivors arrived in this neutral phase lacking connection. As Abraham Maslow (1970), a psychologist who identified a hierarchy of human needs, would have described it, they lacked a sense of belonging. Not surprisingly, we found this most true of those RIOs who had fully made their good-byes.

> *I really wondered if I would fit in with the new team. I hardly knew anyone on it. I felt like a kid thinking, "Will they like me? Will I make friends?" Oh, yeah, sure, I didn't forget about the work. . . . Boy, we had had such a smooth operation. . . . Would this group really work that well together?*

Survivors are not only seeking reconnection in the neutral zone but evaluating the cost-benefit, the price of admission, of doing so. Do they want to belong? For some survivors, answering these questions about connection is the most important issue in determining whether they will make an investment in the new role.

Regaining Commitment

Commitment issues for survivors revolve around such questions as "Can I support the organization on this?" "Can I believe in this?" "Do my values and beliefs go along with this?" "Can the organization count on me?"

Regaining commitment is a two-way issue, so it also means the organization's commitment to them. For survivors, that translates to a sense of being valued.

> *Everyone said, "You're lucky to have a job." No one said, "We're lucky to have you."*

Especially in the neutral zone, survivors need to be told they are valued, even if this has been stated to them previously. Survivors want to hear that message from the organization's leadership, and many want to hear it as well from their immediate boss.

Hearing directly from top leadership that they are valued employees seems to carry more credibility for the FODs for several reasons.

My supervisor told me that I was really needed. . . . But she really had no say in the decisions that were made, so I tended to disregard it.

Since what is important is that their contributions, and therefore they, matter to the organization, FODs need to hear from those who are truly in the know about where the organization is headed and how the survivors' work fits in. At the same time, FODs want personal recognition and visibility where it counts—at the top. And they want this on a long-term basis.

When the organization acknowledges the value of their work, FODs rise to the occasion, exercising creativity, taking risks to make things work, and applying their energy to meet the organization's needs. These are important steps in halting their disengagement and gaining their recommitment.

By contrast, the RIOs need to feel valued by their immediate bosses, by those with whom they work day to day. For W&Ss, being valued means valuing W&Ss' questions and respecting what they have to say. And W&Ss need to experience these reactions from someone in a position of power and influence, a leader whom they truly believe speaks for the organization.

Management of the Neutral Zone

What we found from our research was that when this middle phase of the transition process wasn't managed, FODs, W&Ss, and RIOs reacted quite differently. And for organizations, the consequences, though significant, were not always immediately apparent.

■ FODs' REACTIONS

Given their approach to change, FODs react strongly when they encounter an organization's lack of preparedness to meet survivors' needs, whatever their place and pace in the transition process.

One FOD, ready to make a decision about taking a new position within the organization, told us of approaching management with what he considered basic questions about this promotion.

They couldn't answer any of my questions, even the grade level or starting salary. It was clear to me that they didn't really have anything more than a skeleton of a plan. There's no way I'd feel confident making a decision based on poor data.

Management's failure to address a valued employee's questions had ramifications: This survivor moved further through the transition process and then to disengagement.

Some of the FODs in the neutral zone talked of still feeling excited and energetic. Often, however, impatience and frustration accompanied those emotions.

> I've been on this task force working on self-managing teams for ten months. We're working really hard, and some days I can't wait to get to the office. But lately I've begun to have some doubts. Senior management seems less and less interested in the project, even though they picked the group. Will the organization really implement it?

FODs' comparatively calm demeanor may suggest to management that these survivors are at ease with managing transition. In fact, FODs' ease may be attributable to their completion of the transition process and consequent detachment. Their countenance may blind management to the fact that the FODs are actually standing at the door.

> I was comfortable with my decision to leave, but I knew I had to get my people through before I did, that they would need the support to make the move. So I held off giving notice until they were reestablished.

While FODs may be on the verge of leaving, they perform as committed employees—another way in which their intentions are masked.

■ W&Ss' REACTIONS

For many W&Ss, energy and excitement continue to grow—but essentially as a measure of unmitigated fear and anxiety. We think they are as much afraid of their own confusion and limbo as by anything the organization does. The sense of being out of control is most disturbing to this survivor group.

For the W&Ss, anxiety often becomes a desire for justice, a search for fairness that translates into demanding more pay, a promotion, or some other form of recognition.

> I told my boss that they were crazy if they thought I'd take on extra work without a raise. I pushed and pushed—and they came through.

This survivor told us that he wanted, and had gotten, $2,000. It struck us as irrational. How did he come up with this figure, given that he was earning in excess of $60,000 at the time? All the same, he was adamant that his salary needed to be $62,000.

Others opted to reduce their services, cutting back on the quantity or quality of their work or putting in fewer hours.

■   RIOs' REACTIONS

Anxiety for the RIOs appears as a need for security. The result, as discussed in chapter 4, is often cautious, risk-averse behavior. The RIOs, the most elusive survivors, grow even more so in the neutral zone. They look for ways to stay out of sight, disappearing into what appears to be work, work, work—nose to the grindstone, not coming up for air. Work as used by the RIOs in this context is a hideout.

RIOs keep silent, and if they perceive that other employees are too verbal or attracting too much attention, RIOs avoid those individuals.

Now I feel more like a number. In a way I like that—not being noticed.

It is easy for management to be seduced by these conscientious, hardworking survivors, taking the nose to the grindstone at face value—as not only "I'm fine" but "You can count on me"—and responding by piling more work on RIOs' desks.

As one manager found out:

I thought the work was helping her get over this. I had no idea she was so overwhelmed. I was surprised when she said she needed to take a leave.

For many survivors in the neutral zone, the exit looks equally attractive as a way to deal with their discomfort. They are vulnerable from their own as well as from an organizational perspective.

The neutral zone is a dangerous time for a company in terms of survivors leaving; disconnecting, no longer committing, even RIOs become survivor leavers. In the neutral zone, some survivors are particularly vulnerable to a former colleague or boss's "Come and join me at my new company" offer. We've seen numerous examples of managers leaving and being followed by survivors seeking anchors and loyalty once again.

Survivors' Needs in the Neutral Zone

What do survivors need in this midpoint of their transition? What will make them less likely to leave? What can management do that will enable survivors not only to manage the chaos but to utilize their creativity and energy productively, for the benefit of the organization?

For survivors in the neutral zone, organizations have to put three elements in place: structure, norms, and leadership.

Structure

What is the mission? What are the goals? What is the plan? What is my job description? What are my responsibilities? Performance expectations? What will my day-to-day routine be? Who will do what? These are the kinds of survivor questions organizations need to address, not simply with words but by putting actual structures in place: role descriptions, performance expectations, salary schedules, interim policies and procedures, and the new organizational chart, even if it is only "the chart of the week."

Just tell me what I'm supposed to do today and tomorrow, and I'll be real happy. I may not like it, but it will get me through the next few months, and that's all I can focus on right now.

Structure allows people to know how to become competent, how to face in the right direction. In organizations that understand (and meet) this survivor need, there are significant payoffs—especially from W&Ss, who respond to structure by diminishing their queries and turning their energies to problem solving.

Norms

Second, the organization needs to provide the norms, whether or not they are new. No matter how explicit the norms have been in the past, they are of the past. Given all the other changes, survivors assume that the culture has changed and the rules are different. They don't know how or to what extent. Within the context of the neutral zone, they need this knowledge.

Management needs to set out the boundaries, to make explicit the unstated, as well as the stated rules. What is okay or not okay? And are there any got'chas, that is, any taboos that survivors will learn about only when they violate them?

This last question speaks to one rationale for the focus on norms. Norms provide the security that is missing in this middle phase. Putting a set of norms in place enables organizations to create a safe work environment. We're obviously not talking about setting up precautions for operating heavy machinery but creating an environment in which taking risks is encouraged and making mistakes incurs no penalties. Given the uncertainties of organizational life as well as those of the neutral zone, it is legitimate to ask whether there are any got'chas.

Norms also relate to establishing an environment for employee interaction, so the ground rules for connecting and socializing are known. RIOs, particularly, seem to flourish when the norms are made explicit.

Leadership in the Neutral Zone

Third, management needs to provide strong and clear leadership in this transition phase. Survivors look to bosses to lead the way, to provide direction, structure, approval, and acceptance. Management is the "lighthouse in the storm."

> *You know what's really getting me through and making me stay?*
> *No matter how crazy it gets around here, I can count on my boss.*

The tricky part is to provide that leadership in such a way that it encourages autonomy and self-responsibility rather than dependence.

Leadership includes giving and getting feedback, or, as one manager put it, "catching someone doing something right" and praising the employee for it. That is obviously critical in helping survivors to regain competence.

Survivors told us what they often got in contrast to what we have just described:

> *I haven't seen my boss in two weeks. If I go by his office, the door is*
> *always closed.*

We heard about managers' avoidance from persons observing the situation as well as from survivors wanting interaction. As one consultant reported:

> In situation after situation I've had personal experiences with senior-level people hiding out in their offices and cowering. Why don't you come out and walk the floor? Why aren't you with your people?

She paused and then, taking on management's role, answered her own questions:

> Well, I'm cowering in my office because I'm scared that you're going to know that I don't know everything. And meanwhile, the people in the organization know that.

B/A/R/R/I/E/R
Leadership's Inexperience

As several HR professionals iterated, transition management is not something that anyone has much practice at; many companies really haven't had to deal with it.

As Samaha explains:

> No traditional schooling teaches managers how to deal with the complex set of survivor issues and emotions that crop up during these times. Management thinks by being cool in the face of a crisis, by maintaining a stiff upper lip, so to speak, by being analytical and unemotional, that employees will see the decision to downsize as necessary and appropriate. When employees react the opposite of what's expected, management has little or no previous experience for resolving the situation on which to fall back.

B/A/R/R/I/E/R
"For the Good of the Company"

Samaha points out a related barrier:

> When management begins then to see the negative impact of the decision on their employees, for example, lower morale and reduced productivity, they don't understand it. They don't know what to do about it either. They're perplexed because they see themselves as being the saviors of the company. Management's idea is that "we're doing this for the good of the company. We're doing this for the survival of the company. We're doing this so we stay in business, so that those of you who have jobs will continue to have jobs." The expectation is that employees will see their decisions as the right ones and be grateful to them for knowing what to do.

B/A/R/R/I/E/R
Six Steps Ahead

Another barrier is the direct result of management's having lived with the restructuring issues and downsizing decisions and having dealt with their own transition issues. They are six steps ahead psychologically, often moving on to the next series of decisions. So we found in many organizations that it was hard for leaders to step back, to be in synchrony with the survivors' frame of mind. Even when management was sympathetic, it was still hard to muster the patience to lead employees through transition at their pace.

Bridges (1988) speaks to the same barrier when he uses the analogy of the "marathon effect."

ARRIVING AT THE NEW BEGINNING

The survivors who spoke to us of making a new beginning, who had successfully completed the transition process, told us of having regained feelings of confidence about their ability to do the work. They talked of feeling connected with new teams and new structures, and most importantly, they talked of their commitment. As one survivor told us,

I'm committed to where the organization is going, what they're doing. I'm excited about my role, and we've got a really competent team. It's not the same as before, not blind loyalty; it probably never will be.

The Missing C—Commitment

But finding people who were committed in the new beginning was almost impossible, regardless of the amount of time that had passed after the completion of downsizing. Though we did talk with individuals who had regained competence and connection, what they lacked was commitment, as we have defined it.

Commitment goes beyond acceptance and adaptation; it means dedication to the new work and goals of the restructured organization. What we found at best were survivors in an acceptance mode. They'd made adjustments in order to fit in—moving into new offices, adapting to new management, taking on new assignments—but without committing or bonding.

Although I don't know that they will ever commit me again to the organization or to my boss, there are moments when I feel truly committed to my work, because I enjoy it.

TRANSITION MANAGEMENT

There are several additional steps the organization can take to enhance its management of survivors' transition (and the organization's transition as well, the focus of Section III). These actions—developing a transition management plan, creating a transition monitoring team, and providing transition coaching—complement those tasks undertaken in change management.

Transition Management Plan

The change events, from the initial communiqué to the actual D-Day, not only thrust survivors into transition but invite the variety of emotions already outlined. How the organization will orchestrate the actions is spelled out in the change management plan. How the organization will manage the psychological responses embedded in the transition process paralleling the change, is the text of the transition management plan.

Both the tasks of designing the plan and implementing it are complex for the reasons already specified: At any moment in time survivors are in different points and moving at different paces through the transition process. And their reactions to the same change event will be quite different as well. Thus, while an FOD may greet the announcement of D-Day with relief, an RIO or even another FOD may respond to the same message with denial.

The change manager, with the change management and transition monitoring teams, has responsibility for developing the transition management plan.

Transition Monitoring Team

The role of the transition monitoring team, composed of a cross-section of employees experiencing the transition and from all levels of the organization, is to keep abreast of the workforce's transition process and to status the change manager and change management team. For example, has a change event supported or thwarted the transition task of saying goodbye? Has the implementation fostered what people in the neutral zone transition phase need?

As Paula Taylor, organizational consultant, states:

The transition monitoring team is critical to a speedy and successful shift to the new organization. Since the success of this team is dependent on company-wide respect, it should have broad representation, be highly trained and skilled in all phases of the transition process, and be clear as to its role.

The transition monitoring team needs training and ongoing coaching in the transition process.

Transition Coaching

Survivors told us of change and transition workshops sponsored by their companies. While these courses provide an essential grounding in concepts and theory, they appeared insufficient for enabling change leaders to provide transition management. Organizations need to provide ongoing transition coaching to all those whose behavior will influence the transition process: the CEO and executive team, the change manager, the change management and transition monitoring teams, and especially managers and supervisors.

Transition coaching will help bosses be more knowledgeable and comfortable as transition facilitators, so they are more likely to be available to the survivors they manage.

KEY POINTS

Transition by definition involves making endings, saying good-bye. The middle phase of transition, a period of chaos and potential creativity, represents a critical time for survivors. When they successfully complete their transition, survivors enter the new beginning with their Three C's—competence, commitment, and connection—reinstated.

GROUP ISSUES

FODs	FODs tend to move through transition more rapidly than other groups. The problem is that if left to manage their transition on their own, they often transition out the door. FODs need to know that the organization understands, has planned for, and is able to manage survivors' transition.
W&Ss	W&Ss are inclined to resist change. They wrestle with transition; they make endings but often resent the process and, therefore, resist the new. W&Ss frequently get stuck in their anger. W&Ss need structure, a framework, to guide them through their transition.

RIOs   RIOs often find change threatening. They easily become immobilized, detached, and stuck in the early stage of transition, unable to make endings. RIOs need assistance in saying good-bye, particularly to relationships, and in developing skills to foster their reconnection with other employees.

STRATEGIES

Incorporate a transition management plan in the organization's change plan, implement and utilize a transition monitoring team, and develop the organization's and employees' team skills.

KEEPING
THE ORGANIZATION
ON COURSE

———

Our attention has been focused on survivors' needs as they go through the transition triggered by downsizing and restructuring. But the same dynamic affects the organization itself. Is it realistic to expect survivors to go through an indeterminate period of psychological Sturm und Drang while the organization moves as if on cue from its current state to a new one, transforming itself almost overnight? Can the organization itself really be immune to the transition?

The survivors we interviewed provided a chronology of organizational movement: structures and systems dissolving, followed by a period of chaos and confusion, and, finally, in some cases, the emergence of a new configuration. In the midst of these changes some survivors concluded that their company was off course, but it sounded to us as if the organization was going through a natural process, even a welcomed one.

Certainly the concept of an organizational life cycle is not new. What we are suggesting is an extension of that concept: The organization follows a transition process in negotiating the changes brought about by downsizing, restructuring, mergers, and acquisitions. Whether change is confined to one department or encompasses the entire company, the organization as an entity is changing and is in transition.

The organization's fate—whether it succeeds or fails and whether survivors stay or leave—is as much determined by how the organization manages its own transition as by how it addresses survivors' transition. Therefore, even the Wyatt (1993) study's conclusion, that employees' resistance to change is the number one reason for companies' failure to achieve restructuring goals, is cast in a new light. Were the study's respondents pointing to the need to help employees manage transition, or were they misperceiving the cause of poor results?

For employees, managing transition in an organization in transition is difficult at best. But when the organization itself fails to acknowledge or manage its own transition, the task is even more difficult—and more likely to push survivors out the door.

The organization's failure to recognize its transition also deprives management of a key opportunity: to take advantage of the innovative climate that the interim's chaos brings. The organization thus misses the chance to utilize employees' energy and creativity to solve problems, to try out ideas and, ultimately, to transform the organization.

The organization's transition parallels that of the individual: There is an ending of the old, a chaotic middle phase corresponding to people's neutral zone, and a new beginning. We have termed these stages "The Old Organization," "The Interim Organization," and "The New Organization," respectively.

Like individuals, the organization suffers the loss of competence, connection, and commitment as it moves through this transition. To complete the process and to regain the Three Cs, the organization needs to accomplish a set of tasks in each of the transition phases.

In this section we address organizational transition in three chapters, reflecting the organization's three transition stages. In each chapter we describe how that transition stage is experienced by the organization, identify the tasks the organization needs to undertake to complete that phase, and discuss critical barriers that can impede the organization's progress. Throughout the chapter, we examine how these issues affect survivor groups and how they interplay with survivors' transition.

We are not suggesting that employees are unable to complete their transition without the organization's doing so as well. As noted in chapter 8, we met many individuals, particularly FODs, who had managed their transition successfully. But these survivors left the organization because of dissonance between their successful transition and the organization's failure to manage its own. Based on our research, we consider it highly unlikely that a survivor will or can complete the transition process effectively as an employee within an organization that has not managed its own transition.

9

The Old Organization

THE STARTING POINT

Whether they "threw it all up in the air" and let it fall where it might (as Judith Vogel, an organization development consultant, suggested) or engaged in a more planful process of defining the future, for the most part the organizations we heard about seemed to begin, in survivors' perceptions, from a perspective other than the here and now.

Management seemed always to be talking about the vision of where the organization was headed. They never talked about where we were now or where we'd be when we walked in tomorrow.

Other survivors similarly spoke of organizations that failed to begin by taking stock of where they were, by defining the current reality. Why was that stance problematic?

DEFINING THE CURRENT REALITY

The organization of today, the pre-downsizing organization, is, from a transition standpoint, the old organization that is about to change. Without defining the reality of the here and now, how will the organization's leaders know what needs changing, what should stay, or whether the price of change is too high? At the core, is downsizing really necessary—are there alternatives?

175

I feel [that] in times of stress, management falls back on old tried-and-true solutions, things that have worked in the past: "Well, the last time we went through this, we ... and it was fine." ... [It would be] a real paradigm shift for management to sit back and say, "OK, we're in trouble. How can we reduce costs without laying off a single person?" That's a novel way of looking at the problem. But they don't.

We heard survivors and consultants alike report that a downsizing had been shortsighted and based on an insufficient evaluation of the situation.

As one interviewee explained, the issue was not how the organization minus twenty percent of the workforce would address the new mission but whether the downsizing was, in fact, the only or best solution for the current problem or the only option for obtaining the desired future.

They said we had to be a "leaner, meaner organization," so that meant downsizing in every department. Well, people are sure mean, all right, but that was a quick and direct way to gloss over the real problem— which is an antiquated way of providing service, not to mention anti-quated management. I mean, everybody in the industry knows that.

Companies that did a good job of assessing the current reality had several advantages: When survivors believed that the current situation had been thoroughly examined, they were more accepting; as a result those organizations seemed to be on a better footing to orchestrate the change and transition processes. Too, management was clearer about what it need-ed to accomplish with the workforce reduction, which not only directed the downsizing itself—for example, determining where the cuts had to be made—but guided the entire reorganization plan.

So what do organizations have to do to define the current reality, to position themselves for change?

The Three C's

What is relevant to the definition of the organization in the here and now is clarifying its status with respect to the Three C's. As defined in chap-ter 1, an organization's competence is its know-how and expertise, reflect-ed in the company's management, structures and systems, products and services.

Connection refers to the relationships and bonds that the current organization has with its industry, processes, customers, and employees.

Organizational connection is also internal—structures and systems, roles and reward systems, are in alignment with one another. Commitment represents a sense of dedication to the vision and customers as well as loyalty to the workforce and the work that the psychological contract demands.

Baselining and Benchmarking

Determining the company's current levels of competence, connection, and commitment provides a baseline, a marking of the organization's current status with regard to the Three C's. Why is establishing a baseline so important for the old organization? Management will have a clearer understanding of the Three C's for the organization and employees. And, with that understanding, the organization can compare the current reality with industry standards, existing goals and expectations, and the desired future, the vision.

So, management uses the baseline in multiple ways. The organization measures the baseline against what we call Benchmark One: existing industry standards in the areas of, for example, productivity, market share, customer service, or profitability. This comparison tells management how far the old organization is from where it is supposed to be within the industry. At the same time, the organization measures the baseline against current (old organization) goals and expectations—Benchmark Two. Both of these analyses let management know what is required to get up to "par."

The organization also measures the baseline against Benchmark Three: the goals encompassed in the vision for the new organization. This third measure determines the gaps between the company's current levels of competence, connection, and commitment and those which will be required of the organization and employees in the new organization.

While these three measures provide disparate information, the results taken together provide a complete analysis of the work ahead, beginning in the old organization.

For example, if the current organization has a very competent workforce, and those same competencies are requisite in the new organization, getting employees ready will be less difficult. If, however, role expectations in the new organization require problem-solving skills but the assessment reveals that employees lack those skills, the work in developing new organization competency will be extensive.

In addition, the baseline offers a reality check: Do the current organization's Three C's match the organization's perceptions of same? As one manager revealed,

> I think the reason we had so much trouble meeting new goals was a misperception of how far below standards we were when we started.

ASSESSING THE COMPONENTS

How will the organization go about assessing the Three C's, obtaining the baseline, as well as establishing benchmarks for the interim and new organizations? The old organization accomplishes these tasks by assessing the current components—vision, mission, and goals; culture and norms; roles (including leadership); structure/systems; and rewards—which provide the foundation for the Three C's.

Current Vision, Mission, and Goals

The first component that organizations have to assess is the combination of vision, mission, and goals. What are the current vision, mission, and goals? Are they in alignment—with customers' needs, with the industry, and with each other? Do they embody what the organization now wants? Are they not only clear to employees but embraced by the workforce? Will the current vision, mission, and goals support the growth of the organization?

Current Culture and Norms

We are defining organizational culture as the assumptions, beliefs, values, rules and taboos, explicit and implicit, that underlie the organization's actions and direct employees' behavior.

Assessing the current organizational culture is important for the old organization, since the culture's power in shaping organizational transition and its success or failure cannot be underestimated.

We heard over and over about organizations that not only purported to treat employees as valued assets but had a history of doing so. Survivors talked about interesting assignments, supportive bosses, employee sabbaticals, exceptional training, mentoring experiences, and developmental opportunities. Employees felt they were so valued, they were willing to continue working even when the company was sold and their own futures were uncertain.

Conversely, at organizations where individuals already felt they were not valued, the first hint of acquisition or merger motivated them to make plans to leave. Both of these situations speak to the impact that culture and norms can have on reactions to real or even perceived change.

The old organization must undertake activities to evaluate both explict and implicit values and norms. Given that a cultural assessment measures perceptions and beliefs, do those of management and employees match? Will intended change actions support the organization's operating culture and values?

In assessing the status of values, management itself must begin by examining organizational actions. But that isn't enough. Without checking perceptions of employees and customers as well, management may have acted in ways that it believed were congruent with organizational values, and in the best interests of the organization and employees. But employees and customers may have misunderstood those same actions.

Thus the old organization has to assess issues incorporating organizational values like the company/employee relationship, loyalty versus employability, and the employment contract and to do so with an accurate understanding of employees' perceptions.

Current Roles

Assessing organizational roles means comparing written job descriptions with actual practice. While job descriptions are specific in some respects, they are also broad brush and general; in this way they provide latitude for people adapting their roles to get the work done. Too, given the rapidity of organizational and hence role changes, it is unusual to find job descriptions and their practice a match. Therefore, to ensure that it has accurate baseline data, management has to assess current roles and responsibilities as practiced. The company can then with some confidence answer questions like, How similar/different will new roles be?

Assessment of current roles as outlined will reveal any disparities between knowledge and skills currently used and those needed in the future organization. Does the current reality require that employees have not only a high level of technical expertise but an equivalently high level of what has been referred to as "soft knowledge and skills"—that is, skills in problem solving, decision making, conflict resolution, and performance management?

The organization must evaluate leadership roles as well. We are not talking about the capabilities of specific people but the very definition of leadership as enacted in the current/old organization. What kind of authority do first-level supervisors have? Are they in positions where they actively make decisions, or do they manage based on the directives of others?

As Ozzie Hager, a leader of a human resources consultant team, points out:

> You have to define what you want leaders to be. I mean, do you want them to be coaches? Do you want them to be technical experts? Do you want them to be facilitators? How much time do you want them to spend on performance management of their employees? So before we go out and design the [management training] course, we've got to figure out what we want them to be.

Current Structure and Systems

Structure addresses the what as well as the how of the organization. Structure includes the reporting relationships, team configurations, organization structures, and rewards that provide the framework within which employees function. Systems are the methods or processes by which the organization functions; they include communication systems, production systems, and work flow processes.

So the organization must examine what structures and systems are currently in place; for example, how is the company organized to get the work done? What kind of management structure exists? What is the ratio of managers to employees?

Current Rewards

What are the organization's reward structures? What do they support? Risk taking? Following orders? Attendance? Performance? Do they support the stereotypical employment contract—loyalty and hard work in exchange for job security? What is the existing employment contract in this particular organization?

Are reward systems competitive in the marketplace? Do they reflect parity—are they appropriate for the job level and expertise demonstrated by employees? And in employees' perceptions, are they applied fairly?

Alignment of Components

Reward systems, especially, must be assessed not in isolation but in integration with the other components. Do they currently align with and support one another?

Will these norms, roles, and reward structures of the old organization support or thwart the accomplishment of the organization's goals? If the company wants innovation and creativity in work teams but current role definitions and reward structures support hierarchical, top-down management and following orders, what is the likelihood of success?

Assessment Methods

The organization has a variety of tools to use in assessment. There are various surveys to understand organizational culture and climate, assessment centers to evaluate leadership skills, and instruments and programs to analyze work flow processes, structures, and systems. And management can glean a lot of this information through the Credibility Audit described in chapter 5. The guidelines for design, administration, and interpretation of the Audit and the barriers discussed there are applicable here.

We found assessment often done hastily and haphazardly, if at all. This is in large part due to the same barriers to assessment identified in chapter 5, especially the following.

B/A/R/R/I/E/R
Don't See the Need

Probably the most frequently reported barrier to doing assessments was that leadership didn't see the need for it. It was not that leaders doubted the value of assessment, but they appeared to perceive that their own analysis was accurate, their point of view right on target. We do not mean to imply management's arrogance here. Because in most cases management has seen the need for change first and deliberated long and hard, they are already at the solution stage—long past the point of wanting to carry out assessment.

B/A/R/R/I/E/R
"No Time"

Another barrier is the organization's sense that there is "too much to do, too little time." By the time the organization decides to take action, there is the perception that time is compressed. Management's sense of urgency often precludes the kind of detailed analysis we are proposing.

A related barrier arises when an organization approaches change from a crisis stance. If the organization is operating in a reactive mode, leaders may not feel enough in control to be in the frame of mind to do a comprehensive assessment.

B/A/R/R/I/E/R
Insufficient Skill

The organization's current skill level may be insufficient for a careful, thorough analysis—for data gathering, interpretation of results, or both. Management needs to "work the data," evaluating their implications, particularly with regard to the development of a plan. As part of this analysis, management needs to communicate the results, letting employees know how the organization will use the information.

In addition to offering a picture of the current components, the status of the organization's Three C's, and the means to measure the gaps, a comprehensive assessment also provides a cost-benefit analysis and surfaces unfinished business.

Cost-Benefit Analysis

Organizations traditionally do cost-benefit analyses as part of planning a change. These analyses customarily address the more tangible and quantifiable costs in such changes as a move to a new site, the installation of new technology, or the modification of production systems.

For companies involved in downsizing, restructuring, and acquisitions and mergers, a cost-benefit analysis is more challenging because of the intangible, less quantifiable costs—the psychological price of transition, for example. These intangibles are often less well understood and, therefore, harder to measure. Yet completing such an analysis pays off in important ways; it enables the organization to predict what aspects of transition may precipitate what could otherwise be unanticipated dollar costs. For example, if transition leads to diminished connection and low commitment (and these phenomena are unattended), then the company may experience higher than anticipated turnover with its attendant costs.

So the ultimate question the cost-benefit analysis addresses is: Is the organization sound enough to manage these transitions at a reasonable price or will employees' resistance to change be such that the organization does not have the resources to continue?

Unfinished Business

Another benefit of assessment is that it helps the organization to iden-tify unfinished business. Unfinished business falls into two categories: tan-gible and intangible.

Tangible projects are those proposed or already in motion, such as developing a new computer system because the current system has become obsolete. Should the organization let the project die? Or should manage-ment incorporate the unfinished project into the change plan?

We know of a number of organizations in which major change came in the midst of system installation (already in years two or three). In at least one case, instead of letting the project die, paying a penalty for canceling the order, and/or taking a loss for computer systems already installed, the com-pany opted to run dual systems. People were trained on the new system only to go "home" to function on the old. There was no projected date for getting the new computers, and employees agreed that training would need to be repeated as they had no opportunity to apply what they had learned.

▶ *BEST PRACTICE*

One company blended its unfinished system installation project with its change plans by proceeding with a pilot in a specific department and incorporating in the new plan a procedure for bringing other departments on-line over time.

Intangible unfinished business includes the psychological effects—whether of anger, sadness, or fear—left over from the organization's last change. It also encompasses diminished confidence or trust in management based on history. Here is where the Credibility Audit described at length in chapter 5 ties in to the assessment, providing direction vis à vis leftover work to be completed.

Survivors' Perceptions of Assessment

Chapters 5 through 8 spell out how survivor groups assess the issues, so that information does not need to be repeated here. What is important to focus on instead is how the three groups respond to the assessment process itself.

FODs, W&Ss, and RIOs have very different expectations for the assessment process and application of the results as well as reactions to the activity itself.

■ FODs' PERCEPTION OF ASSESSMENT

Generally, the FODs are the most vocal in criticizing the organization's failure to do assessments and/or to interpret them accurately. No matter how elaborate or detailed the plan, no matter the extent of communication, FODs are turned off when they perceive the foundation as faulty.

If the application of results fails, FODs conclude that the organization either didn't know how to work the assessment process or that they were doing the activity for activity's sake only.

■ W&Ss' PERCEPTION OF ASSESSMENT

Both the FODs and W&Ss expect that the organization will apply the assessments. So an organization's seeming to ignore the results, in part or in whole, draws criticism from both groups. Like the FODs, the W&Ss have little forgiveness. Just as they cite history selectively when they want to make a point, the W&Ss will bring up this failure over and over during implementation of a change plan. It is, after all, now a part of history.

■ RIOs' PERCEPTION OF ASSESSMENT

RIOs, so caught up in their denial, may not even recognize the assessment process at first. And when they do, the assessment often seems an intrusion, interfering with the constancy of what they are doing. But their concern goes beyond the notion of the assessment as an intrusion. They worry about what the end result will be. Some RIOs react by avoiding participation in the process, even failing to complete feedback forms.

DEVELOPING THE CHANGE PLAN

Only when management has a clear understanding of where the organization is as well as a clear vision of where it wants to go, only then can the company move forward in its planning—identifying the gaps, determining what needs to be put in place, and developing an operational strategy.

The second task of the old organization is to develop a change plan, as discussed at length in chapter 7. Having ascertained what needed changing and what should stay, the organization's challenge is to determine how to combine the best of the past with new elements.

Through the assessment, management has also ascertained the work that must be accomplished before the final transition phase, the new organization, is reached. The gaps uncovered in baselining and benchmarking have pointed to the nature of the work—for example, how much development employees need just to get up to "par"—and the immediacy of the tasks—that is, what work is urgent and must be begun in the old organization.

This information—the work to be done and the timing for accomplishing the work—provides the foundation for developing the change plan. Management knows what it must plan for in each of the organizational phases.

Survivors' Perspectives

FODs, W&Ss, and RIOs approach change from different perspectives. As a result, they have different priorities for the plan's content, also described in chapter 7. The survivor groups raise issues with regard to how the organization goes about developing the plan, that is, the old organization's planning process.

■ FODs' PERSPECTIVES

Some FODs believed their organizations had engaged in short-sighted planning, focused only on the end result. They predicted that what was ultimately achieved would fall short of the organization's goals. For FODs, the two questions are: Does the organization approach the process in a planful way? And, are those charged with developing the plan the most competent—by virtue not only of their industry or technical expertise but also by their sophistication with regard to change?

■ W&Ss' PERSPECTIVES

Like FODs, the W&Ss are concerned about those doing the planning but from a different perspective. Are these people legitimate stakeholders—as W&Ss define the terms?

Who's going to have to carry out the plan? Who's going to have to contend with all the glitches, the problems? Those are the folks who should be in the room.

For both the FODs and W&Ss, involvement in the process is important. And they want to be involved in a legitimate way; they are quick to
spot "token" attempts on management's part.

> They asked for everyone's input. . . . They had people fill out these
> evaluation forms in the meetings. . . . The feedback forms were given
> to one department, and the department kept them for a month, and
> then they asked our department to look at them and analyze them
> and come up with a summary of what everyone said. And this took
> place three weeks after the department was downsized, so it didn't
> make any sense.

■ RIOs' PERSPECTIVES

RIOs would rather not be involved in any kind of interactive planning. They are concerned that the process may require them to be visible—
to take stands in a meeting or even carry messages that may involve confrontation. This survivor group's concerns about being in the spotlight
manifest in attempts to remove themselves from the planning process,
should they be "volunteered."

The organization must also review the assessment to determine what
training actions it will take to move the organization and survivors forward
in readiness for the new organization. The assessment provides the foundation for the training plan, an important element of the change plan.

PREPARING LEADERSHIP

The old organization focuses on preparing leaders in multiple areas,
including change implementation, transition management, and future
readiness.

> We've taken a fairly young management crew that had never been
> through an event like this in their lives, we've put them through the
> wringer, we've taught them how to lay off people, but what we haven't
> told them is, now what do you do?

Implementing the Change

Organizations generally do a good job of preparing leaders to manage
the change in certain respects. As Right Associates (1992) reported,
"According to the survey, Lessons Learned, most organizations recognize

the importance of training notifiers from sending them out into the field." However, as we pointed out, managers frequently were at a loss to answer employees' questions as to the whys of selection. When queried, managers told us that the training covered how to convey the information but did not give them a lot of the details that downsized employees and survivors wanted to know.

The same Right Associates survey echoed our findings: "The survey did determine, however, that many organizations didn't provide notifiers with enough information about the downsizing to answer the wide variety of questions likely to be asked by employees during the termination interview. . . . How the organization would select employees for separation—a question certain to be asked during most termination interviews—was shared with only sixty percent of notifiers."

The notifier training focused primarily on notification of the downsized employees. Notifier training also needs to include notification of the survivors: how to conduct notification meetings with survivors and respond to their concerns, particularly since survivors are not leaving. They will be back the next day and the next—with more questions and issues for bosses to address.

If employees to be laid off had questions bosses could not answer (for which they had not received training), managers had a fallback sanctioned by the organization: Human resources staff members would answer the questions. But if survivors posed questions for which managers did not have answers, managers were reluctant to utilize the same resource, for several reasons. Some believed that HR had its "hands full" with those to be downsized and should be utilized as a last recourse for survivors. Others worried that sending those not designated to be terminated might be perceived as inability to manage the change. So managers—and survivors—had neither the answers nor an available process for getting them.

Managing Transition

Chapter 8 contains references to the content areas for training in transition management. The points we are making here have to do simply with the importance and timing of such training of leaders.

If employees' resistance to change is the major reason organizations fail to achieve restructuring goals, then their boss's transition management is of critical importance.

Training should begin before change occurs, not only because of the complexity of the subject matter but because later, managers will be in transition themselves, experiencing the same shock, denial, inability to focus, preoccupation, stress, and even resistance as those individuals they are to manage.

Future Readiness

The leadership that will be required in an organization may differ from what has been the predominant style. The organizations our survivors came from were calling for a new breed of employee—empowered, self-managing, prepared to take the initiative, versed in problem solving and decision making, and competent to function as a member of a team.

What does this mean for the organization? Leaders not only have to manage this "new" workforce in new ways but they have to demonstrate the corresponding competencies themselves. They need training in how to perform the skills themselves as models for their employees. And leaders need to be able to train and coach direct reports in these areas as well.

The organization cannot afford to have bosses gaining these skills concurrently with their employees. So training for leaders' future readiness as a task in the old organization is a mandate.

Preparing Others for Leadership Roles

So far, the discussion has focused on the organization's preparing bosses for their ongoing leadership roles. There are two other groups of employees playing leadership roles through the organizational change: the change management team, including the change manager, and the transition monitoring team.

Both of these groups will be integrally involved in carrying out tasks of the old organization. That means that both of these groups will need extensive preparation, including training and coaching in their respective roles and responsibilities. That preparation has to begin as soon as a decision is made that a change will occur.

PREPARING EMPLOYEES

In the old organization management has to complete a skills assessment for each survivor. This assessment is important in several ways. For one, it provides a baseline for the organization to use in determining what training and coaching are needed to bring that employee up to speed as quickly as possible. Too, the skills assessment becomes the foundation for the survivor's job development plan in the next organizational phase. And employees' skills assessments, taken together as a group, provide a measure of the organization's competence vis à vis its workforce.

When the organization changes, the psychological contract, as employees know it, ends. And employees recognize their losses—for example, job security, financial security, sometimes role status—involved in the demise of the contract. So, employee development takes on more significance as a factor in a new psychological agreement.

Preparing employees for the new organization means more than skills training. Most of the changes taking place in organizations today require that employees be able to accomplish ongoing learning. So organizations have to start putting in place the notion of a learning community, learning as an organizational stance. Management has to begin to create that kind of environment in the old organization.

Preparing employees also means involving them in the work of the old organization. For survivors, the psychological payoffs of involvement are as important as the more tangible outcomes of their work.

▶ **BEST PRACTICE**

Hilda Logan, Vice President of Human Resources Operations, GE Spacenet, spoke of mobilizing and empowering the workforce after downsizing.

This process ("Work-Out") gets all the affected employees in the room working on the issues, and it empowers them to find solutions: "Maybe I could take over this"..."Maybe we could standardize that".... The company, using (Jack) Welch's principles, puts employees in situations where they have a direct impact.

This is an important time in the organization's annals. The organization is setting in place an historical marker that will shape employees' response to the next change. And remember, for FODs, involvement could be a make or break, stay or leave factor. The organization's waiting until it is in the interim phase to involve them may be too late.

Finally, as Jacqueline McHale, senior consultant, states:

There is something about giving people some control over their future even though they don't have ultimate control or knowledge of what's going to happen to them. They do need to have a piece of developing what it will be.

▶ **BEST PRACTICE**

McHale described a best practice example.

An organization that I worked with knew for a period of time that they were going to merge with another. What they actually did was use [their time] as an opportunity to take representatives from both organizations, put them on task forces, and jointly determine their products and services for the future and how they were going to organize. It was a tremendously empowering event for both organizations to be able to come together and share their viewpoints before it happened so there wasn't that horrible feeling of helplessness that it's all happening around me and I can't control it. There was actually a way they could build something together—build those relationships, start to get to know each other's issues, and start to jointly prioritize what was really important to the organization and then get a sense of how they fit in.

McHale's description illustrates best practices in a number of areas: employee involvement, how assessment can be carried out when a merger is involved, the benefits of addressing the needs of survivor groups, and giving survivors a sense of control.

When interviewees felt the organization had truly looked at alternatives and they had been involved in the process, and when they concluded that downsizing was in fact a reasoned step, survivors seemed less resistant to moving to the next stage, to saying good-bye, whether to colleagues or systems or roles or any combination of these elements.

MAKING ORGANIZATIONAL ENDINGS

The final task of the old organization is to make endings. The change plan determines what the organization needs to say good-bye to. The organization may be saying good-bye to systems, processes, structures, roles, and even parts of the culture. The organization may be saying good-bye to sites, buildings, and branches as well as to employees. Inherent in the organization's good-byes is loss, to varying degrees, of the Three C's.

Just as organizational transition is separate from individual transition, so organizational good-byes are distinct from individuals making endings. What are some of the ways organizations can make endings?

▶ **BEST PRACTICE**

We participated in one organizational good-bye in which the changes included the company's move to a new building. This move symbolized a major ending in a variety of ways. It was a very visible end, in terms of the company having had a long history at the original site. Some employees had occupied the same desks and workspaces for many years. Figuratively, the move represented a break with the past, since the move brought with it installation of new systems, introduction of new structures and reporting relationships, and a radically different physical work environment. These changes signaled the shift in the corporate focus and direction of the organization.

We worked with the organization on an ending event to mark its good-byes. The event was held in front of the current building, facing the entrance with the address in clear sight. Long-tenured employees spoke of the company's history with the building. As a part of the ceremonial good-bye, employees carried out one of the computer terminals that would become obsolete with the new system's installation; they tossed it into the dumpster after appropriate remarks. The company even said good-bye to the telephone number by releasing helium balloons with numbers on them. These actions were quite powerful in demonstrating the substantiveness of the changes.

Ceremonies, farewells, funerals—we heard about them being used for various employee transition purposes, and we cited some in chapter 8. Similar rituals can be used for a different transition—that of the organization.

Organizational and employee transitions are not unconnected in terms of endings, for the organization's actions in acknowledging losses will model and sanction the process for employees. The organization must publicly acknowledge how the losses impact—that is, decrease—the organization's competence, commitment, and connections. For example, when the organization says good-bye to a skilled staff, the organization loses a level of technical competence. Through this loss of employees, the organization as an entity also loses some of the connections that bound it together.

Why does the organization need to make endings? For one, the process clarifies for the organization what it will and what it won't be. It thus causes the organization to acknowledge that it is in transition; it is engaged in a process rather than a series of events. The organization acknowledges that it must pass through an interim phase, that there will be no catapulting from old to new.

We have observed organizations that have refused or neglected to make endings, hanging onto things and carrying literal as well as figurative baggage into the new situation, just as individuals often do. A prime example is the organization that continues to try to produce the same volume of work using the same structures but with fewer employees. Management refuses to prioritize and eliminate those activities that fall to the bottom of the list, instead continuing to proclaim, "Everything is important." Another is the organization that sets new priorities but keeps the same structures. As one survivor reported:

> We're supposed to be empowered, to think of creative ideas . . . but we have to send those ideas through the same four levels of management hierarchy to get approval. Why bother? Nothing's changed, only the name of the program.

Like the survivor who keeps handing out obsolete business cards, these organizations serve as tangible reminders of the results of failing to make endings and discard baggage.

What are the barriers to the organization making endings?

B/A/R/R/I/E/R
Power Issues

Leadership itself may set up roadblocks, especially if the change means a loss of power and leaders are interested in maintaining the status quo.

B/A/R/R/I/E/R
Lack of Understanding

Management's not knowing about or understanding organizational transition is another barrier to making endings. Even when leaders are cognizant of transition at the personal level, they may be ignorant of transition at the organizational level.

B/A/R/R/I/E/R
Inability to See the Value

Another barrier is that leadership may not see the value in the process, considering the good-bye activities a waste of time.

Happily, in our recent experience we found that companies are increasingly recognizing that a beginning, for example, a move to a new site, means that an ending has taken place and that marking the ending is as important for the organization as kicking off or cutting the ribbon to mark the start of something new. Survivors concurred with our observations, recounting stories of organizations making endings with more and more frequency.

KEY POINTS

The old organization represents the pre-downsizing organization, the here and now for the organization as it contemplates change. This is the time when the organization takes stock of its current organizational components to determine which ones stay, which go, and which are modified as the organization readies for change. This is a period of analysis and planning, of preparing employees and leadership and of defining the current reality.

GROUP ISSUES

FODs   FODs have little tolerance for the organization's failure to analyze and/or its inability to incorporate the analysis into an effective change plan. FODs interpret shortcomings in these areas as indicators of organizational incompetence.

W&Ss   W&Ss tend to see the lack of assessment and planning, or faulty assessment and planning, as signs of arrogance, of intentional neglect.

RIOs   RIOs often find the assessment and planning process intrusive to their present state. What RIOs are most sensitive to is the organization's "good-bye to the past."

STRATEGIES

Assess the current components; incorporate the results in developing a change plan; involve employees in the process of analysis and planning; train leaders for their roles in change and transition; and make endings.

Having assessed the components, developed the change plan, readied leaders and employees, and made their good-byes, the organization and survivors—with lowered competence, connection, and commitment—move into the interim phase.

10

The Interim Organization

CHAOS AND PROGRESS

The organization having completed its good-byes (often paralleling the time of the downsizing event), this ending precipitates a move from business as usual to business as unusual. The organization enters a period of chaos, a time marked by unbridled energy, excitement, creativity, and confusion. Like the neutral zone experienced by individuals (Bridges, 1988), this period is a natural phase of transition for organizations. We call this phase the interim organization.

Why "interim" organization? We considered other terms. We found "transitory" misleading in terms of suggesting a limited time frame that might be controlled and even truncated, when in fact the time frame for the interim period, or any of the organizational transition stages for that matter, cannot be rigidly specified. The interim period represents a passage with fluid time boundaries, with no preset demarcations of beginning and ending.

"Transient" conveys a less than desirable state to be tolerated and endured. "Temporary" implies that at the conclusion, the organization will move into permanency. In our experience these descriptors are equally misrepresentative of this middle state in the organization's transition.

But these definitions are more than misleading. They are problematic, implying that for the company, this organizational state is a throwaway period rather than a critical time—a critical time for the organization's beginning the process of rebuilding its competence, commitment, and connection; a critical time for the work of moving the organization toward the vision, that future state that drove the downsizing; and a critical time for helping those survivors through the transition process that they are experiencing simultaneously. It is also a critical time in which to reengage those survivors with the post-downsizing organization, to rebuild their Three C's, and to redirect, hence retain, them.

A tall order!

The chaos of this period is inherently neither negative nor positive. Whether the outcome for the organization and survivors is successful or unsuccessful is determined by how the energy of this phase is focused and the tension of the period managed.

THE TASKS

The interim organization has a clear set of tasks to be completed in this middle period between the demise of the old organization and the start of the new one. They involve dealing with future readiness, present productivity, survivors' transition, and organizational tension.

Future Readiness

On the one hand, the organization has to be farsighted, focusing on the future, keeping it in clear sight, and determining what the organization needs to do to put in place the vision that has driven the change.

Out of this farsightedness comes one primary task: ensuring future readiness, as shown in figure 4. Readiness for the new organization means clarifying the vision for the future, for the new organization, and refining the values and norms that support that vision. Future readiness also means developing systems, structures, roles, and rewards to ensure that the company is prepared to function as that new organization.

The organization implements this readiness task by putting in place a set of interim components—including systems and structures, role definitions, and rewards—that allow the company to operate while simultaneously providing opportunities to try out and pilot future state options.

The 1995 AMA Survey reported that major workforce reductions are more likely to result in increased profits and productivity if they are followed by incremental adjustments to and fine-tuning of structures and

FIGURE 4 **FUTURE READINESS**

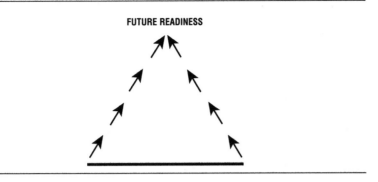

FUTURE READINESS

systems. The AMA study suggests not that fine-tuning means more down-sizing but rather that it means making modifications along the way. The study's findings corroborate our thinking in deliberately putting a set of interim components in place with the understanding that they are temporary and that the task is one of testing and refining them.

No matter how well conceived and well tested new systems and structures are, they will be of little use without a workforce equally prepared to put them into practice. So readiness for the new organization also means development. Besides deciding what new systems and structures to pilot, what else does the organization need to do to regain its competency? And what do employees need? What new competencies do changes in the components mandate, even at the tryout stage? The organization must not only answer these questions but set up these interim components in such a way as to provide opportunities for both employees and the organization to develop the competency, connection, and commitment to engage in the new organization.

Present Productivity

The organization is not going to go on hold while the vision of the new organization is being put in place. So management has to be *now-sighted*, focused on the here and now, maintaining the health of the current organization, as shown in figure 5.

FIGURE 5 **PRESENT PRODUCTIVITY**

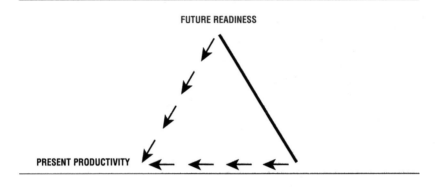

Therefore, another organizational task is determining what kind of temporary components the company needs in order to be productive today. How do the current work flow processes have to be modified if half the workers are gone? What role structures have to be in place to accomplish the work now? What do survivors, calling for structure, norms, and leadership, need in order to cope successfully with their own chaotic neutral state?

Twenty-twenty vision requires a dual focus, with both future readiness and present productivity in clear sight, as figure 6 shows.

FIGURE 6 **DUAL FOCUS: 20/20 VISION**

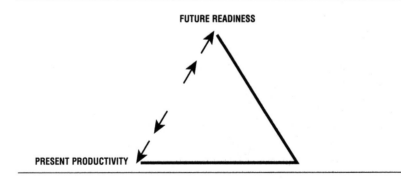

FIGURE 7 **SURVIVORS' TRANSITION**

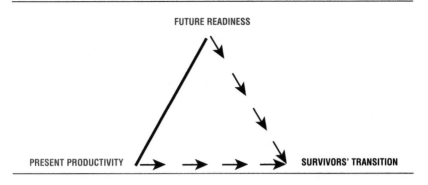

Survivors' Transition

The organization is not the only entity that has this dual focus. As described in chapter 8, survivors are experiencing the confusion and insecurity of their neutral zone simultaneously with the Sturm und Drang of the interim organization. Survivors' transition likewise brings a dual focus that the organization must address. To repeat, survivors need to gain the competence, connection, and commitment to function in the new organization. At the same time, like the organization, survivors have to contend with the now-sighted issue of functioning in the here and now, in the current organization—and, more than ever, functioning means being productive and meeting expectations and performance standards. Hence, managing survivors' transition needs is a third primary organizational task, as shown in figure 7.

Perfect Vision

The interim organization addresses these three tasks simultaneously. So management must maintain its sights on all three points at once. We thus must amend what we said about 20/20 vision. As figure 8 illustrates, perfect vision for the interim organization, with trifocals in place, is 20/20/20.

Tension

The three primary interim tasks, all critical, are not independent but interrelated. At the same time, they represent distinct, separate, competing concerns.

FIGURE 8 **PERFECT FOCUS: 20/20/20 VISION**

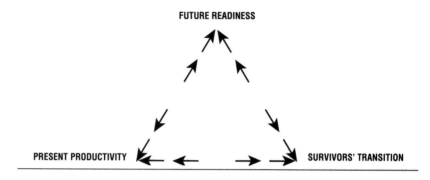

Attending to these competing concerns concurrently creates a pull or tension within the organization, as depicted by the arrows in figure 8. The good news about the tension is that it facilitates keeping the tasks in balance and serves as a check and reminder that the tasks cannot operate in isolation. When management stresses increased productivity, the tension reminds the organization that training and development may be becoming insufficiently attended to. Conversely, if the organization becomes caught up in piloting future systems, the tension will alert management that there is undue stress on present productivity. There may be undue stress coming as well from survivors' unmet transition needs.

Tension acts as a catalyst, fostering creativity and focusing the energy of the interim organization as well as that of survivors. For example, the tension generated by the demands of present productivity gives a sense of urgency to the creation of pilots and the development of readiness. This tension emphasizes that the pilot is not just a simulation; the pilot has to work or be modified to work. The consequences are real, not hypothetical. The tension alerts the organization to the fact that the time available for prototypes is not limitless; if new models of production do not become functional within the allotted time frame, the current production will not be enough to sustain the organization.

Tension can become antithetical to the accomplishment of the tasks. If, for example, the organization simultaneously sets high production goals and superimposes them on new, untested production methods or work flow approaches or roles, then the competing demands may increase the pull, the tension becoming tighter and tighter until there is a snap, resulting in breakdown in one task or the other or both. Production goals will not be met, or people will meet production goals by reverting to old roles and methods and/or forgoing tryout.

If there is a loosening of the tension, a slack, it is an alert to the organization that insufficient attention is being focused on one or more of the concerns. When organizations do not heed that alert and increase the tension by attending to the concern, the consequences may extend beyond those attributed to the unattended concern.

Most frequently, survivors reported conditions in which there was a letdown in the attention paid to their transition needs. The slack between survivors' transition and present productivity translates into unmet goals. How likely is it that survivors with unmet transition needs for leadership and structure, and for clarity around role definitions, will produce at the high levels needed after their peers depart? How likely is it that they will produce even at the same levels as before the change? Failure to meet the needs translates into a diminished ability to generate present productivity.

Inattention to survivors' transition creates a slack between that concern and future readiness as well. How can the organization achieve the goal of establishing that future state if survivors' needs for regaining competence, connection, and commitment are not attended to?

No matter how flexible future assignments or how appropriate current production expectations, the survivors' transition imposes a natural tension between their needs and those of present productivity and future readiness.

Survivors' needs—exacerbated by a diminished focus—are givens and are beyond the organization's control. Therefore, the organization has to balance the tension by providing greater tolerance relative to present productivity and future readiness.

Tension Within Chaos

These competing concerns and the resulting tension do not occur within a vacuum; the organizational tension is superimposed on the chaos and uncertainty of the interim state, as shown in figure 9. The organization must accomplish all these tasks within the context of that interim phase and do so in ways that maximize the creativity, manage the chaos, and focus and harness the energies of the organization and employees.

FIGURE 9 **TENSION WITHIN CHAOS**

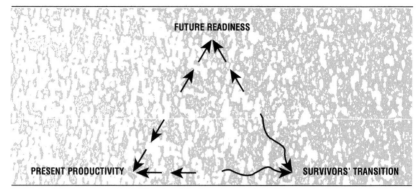

INTERIM COMPONENTS

If the organization has done a good job of saying good-bye, it comes to the interim stage with the components intact to varying degrees.

Whatever their condition upon the start of the interim phase, the components of this middle organization are different than what they have been in the old organization and what they will be in the new organization. They are temporary and they are developmental in nature—and the organization consciously sets them up that way.

There are a myriad of other reasons the interim components are different. In terms of leadership, for example, a hands-off style that may have been very effective in the old organization generally will not work here. The chaos, high energy, and uncertainty demand more presence and direction.

The interim components are the tools the organization uses to accomplish the interim tasks. They include structure and systems, roles, culture and norms, and rewards. Leadership, a part of roles, is considered separately.

Interim Structure and Systems

In creating structure and systems, the interim organization faces a dual challenge: How much structure can be built into this interim organization so it doesn't seem wobbly, without definition—so it actually is an organization? At the same time, how can it be kept flexible enough to function as a tryout ground in which structures do not become ironclad or so embedded that they cannot be changed?

Structure does not negate the idea of fluidity; in fact, just the opposite. Structure is the framework. If the framework is strong, well planned, and well constructed, it fosters and supports movement, just as a well-engineered building sways during an earthquake.

Let's look at the ramifications of one organization's attempts to deal with developing new structures. This company, a pharmaceutical concern in the Midwest, created what appeared to be a very workable solution to the problem of reducing time for responding to customer orders. With a carefully considered focus on the future, the restructuring plan included modified work flow systems, reconstituted teams, and new reporting relationships.

The problem was that the organization did not have a plan to produce in what was now a work environment in transition. It had no systems or structures in place to take into account that a third of the remaining workforce was involved in piloting new systems. How would the work they had left get done? And there were no interim structures to manage those employees not working in the pilots—employees who were themselves in transition, needing extra attention.

As our interviewee described:

Before, they had a very clear structure and they were very specific about following the chain of command.... We're in limbo ... they got rid of so many layers ... [that now] there's a skepticism, "Nobody's in a position to tell me what to do because you're not my supervisor— she's gone, he's gone."

The stage was set for the following scenario: Employees, unable to keep up with production during the regular day, attempted to compensate by working many hours of overtime. In addition, production needs required pulling people away from the pilot program on an irregular basis, thereby skewing the results of the test.

Survivors did provide reports of organizations that had put transitional structures or temporary reporting relationships in place. But as they were described to us, these interim structures seemed transient and illegitimate; they were unanticipated and unplanned, as opposed to the deliberately conceived and defined components of the interim organization.

We were told that the senior vice president would be our supervisor temporarily; however, "You should try to solve your problems on your own without going to him." So he kind of said, "Yes, I'm your boss, but only if you really, really need me."

These characterizations of temporary structures and the assignment of temporary reporting relationships almost bespoke an attitude of laissez faire—that both management and employees could pay minimal attention to these arrangements, since they were somehow less than "the real thing," the envisioned future.

Not only was the structural problem as basic as ill-defined reporting relationships, but survivors described structural gaps extending to production issues. Employees related that they didn't know whom to ask about computer systems problems, interdepartmental issues, and conflicts with co-workers.

It's bad enough our not knowing who to go to, but God forbid a customer should have a complaint and want to talk to a supervisor. We wouldn't have any idea who to refer them to.

We found survivors particularly frustrated when working in organizations that had been very structured and had followed exacting procedures prior to the downsizing. Although some survivors may have felt an initial sense of freedom at the loosened structure, it was short-lived. Even an interviewee's realization, "Can you believe it? Some days we're getting paid for doing nothing," turned to frustration and concern that the organization would never achieve the vision or goals it had announced.

▶ **BEST PRACTICE**

Hilda Logan, GE Spacenet Vice President, describes employees' response to being given responsibility for self-determination.

It's so upbeat. . . . It gets people excited about being able to accomplish things rather than not knowing where the company is going, waiting for someone to tell them what to do. Employees take ownership for making the workplace successful.

Although we heard most about gaps in structure with regard to the here and now—that is, present productivity—some survivors did point out structural problems with regard to future readiness. We talked about this issue with another survivor, a supervisor at a different company. He talked about his assignment to a special task force on work redesign. Initially excited about the possibilities, he said his task force

began to feel like a rudderless ship. We're operating in a vacuum. Are
we creating what the organization wants? We turn in reports, but we
haven't had any feedback in months. And the senior manager who
started this project is gone—took the retirement package.

Coming into the interim period without some structure to guide
them is problematic for FODs, W&Ss, and RIOs from the onset.

■ STRUCTURE NEEDS OF FODs

Of the three survivor groups, FODs appear least dependent on structure. The survivor who spoke of being told to "solve your problems on your
own" could and would do that. In fact, as he told us, he regarded "figuring out
how to operate on our own, how to get work done" as a challenge. At the same
time, he resented how the lack of structure and his "non-boss boss" impacted
his fellow employees who were less comfortable in this environment.

FODs dislike the confusion and drain on energy that a lack of structure generates. They attribute the lack of structure, again, to the organization's inability to lead during this interim state.

■ STRUCTURE NEEDS OF W&Ss

For the W&Ss, lessened or absent structure is more problematic than
that "search for structure" experienced by all survivors in the neutral zone.
For this survivor group, structure represents attachment to the organization. For W&Ss, part of the old employment contract was assurance that the
organization would provide structure and guidance. And, without it, W&Ss'
complaining and blaming covers their sense of abandonment.

Behaviorally, many W&Ss in this situation appear to go in circles,
"chasing their tails." If the structure or management is not there to provide
direction, they turn to their co-workers. Going to colleagues with tales of
the organization's misdeeds and even seeming to champion other employees' causes are, in fact, ways of asking, "Help me to understand what to do."

■ STRUCTURE NEEDS OF RIOs

Lack of a clear interim structure reinforces RIOs' desires to "do it the
old way." Rather than confront the lack of direction, they follow the old
rules, maintain the old methods. Their actions perpetuate systems no
longer necessary—work processes that, in fact, interfere with current systems and slow productivity. The lack of structure also increases their caution and propensity to avoid risks.

Survivors' Reactions to Rigid Structures

Equally problematic for survivors are those organizations that try to maintain rigid or archaic procedures. Trying to get work done, these employees feel they have been put in the untenable position of having to break the rules. Given the combination of a reduced workforce, high productivity expectations, and organizational systems that do not take changes into account, some survivors become impatient with rules that do not work. Faced with the urgency of getting the work done, they become lawless renegades.

If the organization has large components of the workforce breaking the rules, the chaos becomes unmanageable. In the interim organization, where chaos and confusion are already occurring, the organization can cross the line from functional to dysfunctional at any time. The results of the lawless chaos accelerate the process and increase the probability that the chaos will be debilitating to the organization.

The irony, of course, is that the lawless renegades are not out to damage the organization—just the opposite. They break the rules in order to do their jobs, meet performance goals, and keep the organization going.

Unfortunately, the rigid structures that inhibit creativity and flexibility in the here and now have no more chance of working in the future organization, where creativity and flexibility are equally important.

The survivor groups find these inflexible structures equally problematic.

■ FODs' REACTIONS TO RIGID STRUCTURES

Rigid or archaic structures exacerbate FODs' maverick tendencies and minimize their positive contributions. Now the organization has two problems: the rigid structure that does not work and the out-of-control, rebelling survivors. And if these survivors are penalized for breaking the rules, they will leave. Ironically, then, the company is putting a lid on the very thing the interim organization wants: creative solutions. As one FOD said,

They say they want us to be creative problem solvers when they continue to enforce rigid rules and micromanage everything we do.

■ W&Ss' REACTIONS TO RIGID STRUCTURES

Given what we have written about W&Ss' reactions to the absence of structure, one might surmise that interim structures and systems, even rigid ones, are not particularly problematic for this group. In fact, they do pose problems. W&Ss pointed out the absurdity of simultaneously following the rigid procedures and doing creative problem solving.

If I have to get permission from six layers of management every time I want to try something, that does not allow me to creatively solve problems very well, does it?

While the FODs sometimes break the rules, W&Ss seldom do. W&Ss adhere to the structure but express their continued frustration, challenging management to address the situation.

■ RIOs' REACTIONS TO RIGID STRUCTURES

RIOs, of course, are the least resistant to rigid structures. They can enmesh themselves in tight systems and processes with ease, particularly if they are old, familiar systems. This collusion only provides the illusion of skills competence and the rationale for postponing their readiness. And the archaic systems support their contention that the status quo will win out.

Interim Roles

Closely connected to structure is the component of role. Why are role definition and role clarity so vital for survivors coming into the interim organization? People in transition, whether reacting to downsizing or another change, have an abbreviated ability to focus and/or function in a nondirective environment. Many survivors are simultaneously in the middle phase of their own transition, contending with the uncertainty and confusion of the neutral zone. They look to management to meet their needs for structure, norms, and leadership, as described in chapter 8. So these survivors welcome structured role definitions that are specific and explicitly lay out role responsibilities. It would not be an exaggeration to say that survivors often seek role definitions as basic as "Here are the eight things you are responsible for." Or as we heard,

Just tell me to put the rock in the hole, and I'll be really happy. It will get me through the next couple months, and that's all I can focus on.

Our interviewees were people in transition reacting to a very specific change; their concerns for role clarity were exacerbated by the insecurity resulting from the downsizing. Role definitions, set in place, provide a kind of safety net, diminishing the risk of doing the work wrong, making a mistake, and suffering what many perceive as the automatic consequences—termination.

Contrast survivors' needs for stability and structure with the behaviors and attitudes that organizations simultaneously want from them. Management wants survivors, in their roles as developers of the future, to be creative; to deal with ambiguity; to be flexible, adapting and turning on a dime; to be open and take risks; and to be willing to make mistakes and report on how they fared. No wonder the results are less than stellar!

The tension between the needs of survivors and those of the organization vis à vis the future is not the only stress.

Citing an earlier Wyatt study, Right Associates (1992) reported: "Sixty-seven percent of the study's participants said it took more than six months for survivors of a major corporate restructuring to fully recover from the experience and get on with the work of the newly defined enterprise. Thirty percent said the recovery time took a year or more."

Self-absorbed, caught in their own transition states, some survivors can barely perform at normal work levels, even given realistic interim production goals. So imagine their reactions to increased or unrealistic production goals!

Role clarity in the interim phase can be very empowering for some survivors. Conveying to them what they are to do and how they are to do it—that the organization has a plan—provides a sense of personal power, a sense of control over one's environment rather than vice versa. For employees, a sense of personal power translates into their ability to manage work pressures and maintain productivity during change. It also brings a sense of competence.

The payoffs are significant for the organization as well. And from the organization's perspective there is yet another reason to make survivors' roles clear. As Ozzie Hager, Human Resources Team Leader, points out:

Tell me what my role is and what the expectations are. Make them clear. Employees might not necessarily like them, but at least you can say, "It's clear, we communicated it, we're reinforcing it; now you make the decision whether you want to live here with them or not."

Providing specific role definitions and explicit expectations does not mean developing a pseudo or throwaway set of tasks. Role responsibilities have to be based on the real needs of present productivity and future readiness.

If you have been tracking the personae of the survivor groups through the book, then you have already identified why role clarity is important for each of the groups: It provides stability for the RIOs, offers W&Ss a place within the structure, and establishes personal parameters and career challenges for the FODs.

The issue of interim roles for W&Ss is somewhat complicated. On the one hand, the organization must legitimize the immediate (interim) role in terms of expectations, performance, and fit within the interim plan. At the same time, because these survivors are interested in hierarchy and structure, they may react negatively when hearing it is not "permanent"; they may begin to discount the role, interpreting it as inconsequential the minute they hear the word "interim."

Without role structure, W&Ss are not willing to risk making mistakes. So they avoid taking risks and do the minimum—for many of them, quite a contrast to their previous high productivity.

Interim Culture and Norms

A part of the old organization's effectively making an ending was clarifying which norms were no longer viewed as valuable or congruent with the vision for the future organization, which ones were desirable, and what norms needed to be added.

Culture in the interim organization is in a mid-phase of development, characterized as a moving away from what norms were and a moving toward what the organization ultimately wants them to be. Anna Ewins, Ph.D., an organization consultant, suggests:

> While learning new behaviors can ultimately be clarified through experimentation and practice, what can be made clear is that the new culture is not expected to materialize overnight. The experimentation and, therefore, errors or lapses are recognized and accepted as part of the learning process.

Survivors want clarity about norms especially. Dealing with their own transition, they are already concerned about rules, as described in chapter 8. Yet coming into the interim organization itself is problematic for most employees, whether they are survivors or new hires. They are unsettled by the atmosphere of chaos and confusion permeating the work environment. They wonder, What are the norms for operating in this chaos, for interacting with bosses and co-workers right now? They want to know which rules are different, which the same, from starting times to grievance procedures.

Many employees in the interim organization worry about their fate in the event of another downsizing; they believe that following current rules and meeting expectations are critical to their survival. They are even more anxious when they don't know what to expect.

We felt like we were walking on eggshells for the first months. You didn't know what the rules were. So you were cautious as hell, trying not to step over any line—even if you didn't know where it ended.

Even when the old organization's culture held values that still appeal to survivors and that the company intends to continue, survivors do not necessarily know these norms are in place—unless the interim organization explicitly says so.

Survivors watch closely to determine if there is congruity between what management espouses about culture and what management demonstrates through behavior. Sometimes the interim measures required for immediate survival seem counter to the collectively desired norms. We heard from many survivors about "the new rules for work"—mandatory overtime and cancellation of vacation schedules—in companies that professed values about quality of life and balance. When this conflict occurs, management has to be honest and direct, communicating the rationale behind the rules. Companies that acknowledged the apparent conflicts, that explained the need for short-term survival tactics in order to have long-term company health, received high marks from survivors—*if* those companies had a track record of telling the truth.

No matter how frank and complete the explanation, some survivors still do not believe management. What counts for these survivors is whether the organization attempts to balance the current and future needs of the organization with those of employees. For example, how can the organization go about getting the work done in a way that does not become punitive or undermine the desired culture?

Whenever possible, management needs to engage employees in the resolution of these issues. Engaging the workforce in resolution of these problems reinforces the desired norms of participation and empowerment.

A major culture change—for example, a move from a culture of hierarchical decision making to one of delegated accountability—requires more time. Without constant reinforcement, new norms may give way to old habits. As Ewins notes,

The process of establishing new norms tends to be awkward, involving the prescribed use of new norms coupled with frequent lapses to old, undesirable behaviors. It often feels like taking one step forward and one step back, or worse, that no progress is being made. Only with consistent diligence on everyone's part to reshaping old behaviors over time can the new norms be integrated into everyday life, and the espoused culture become the enacted one.

▶ BEST PRACTICE

Logan relates:

I was with an organization that was acquired. After the change, the company that acquired us held an orientation. We had twelve hours on the values and principles of the new organization. . . . We were encouraged to buy-in. Those sessions, held right at the beginning, got employees set to relate to the new culture.

The orientation that Logan discusses can be utilized in developing an "Interim Organization Orientation." The Orientation takes place at the beginning of the interim organization, an appropriate time in the transition process because it follows the organization's making endings.

Organizations regularly hold programs to orient new employees. However, when the organization is "new," as is the case of the interim organization, even existing employees need to be reoriented. The Interim Organization Orientation makes the interim components explicit and encourages that same buy-in from survivors that Logan describes.

Interim Rewards

During the interim stage the level of energy required of employees to focus on tasks is greater than in any other period. Paradoxically, survivors have many concerns distracting them during this time. Their personal transition, especially if they are in the neutral zone, consumes lots of their energy. Redefined reward structures help employees identify those areas of performance they must focus on now.

An interim reward system needs to be two-pronged: First, it needs to address the more standard practice of rewarding employees' job performance. At the same time, the structure needs to reward development of skills and behaviors needed for the new organization.

To ensure the latter, not surprisingly, many organizations need to reward different kinds of behaviors, those that reflect, for example, adaptability, initiative, and risk taking. As the Wyatt study (1993) suggests, "Rewards and recognition systems [need] to support the value of and accomplishment of learning. . . . This step ensures that people are indeed motivated to embrace the desired behaviors."

How to apportion rewards between the two points is the challenge. There are a number of considerations in designing an interim reward structure, particularly with regard to development. For one, the interim organization needs to focus rewards on employees' display of effort and/or their early successes. Particularly for the RIOs, rewarding approximations to goals shows that success is possible.

The organization needs to pace interim rewards. Just as the production bar or performance expectations can be raised higher during the interim period, so the reward structure needs to realign with changes. It needs, therefore, to be flexible. Rewards also need to be appropriate to the level of success.

As for timing of rewards: As stated in chapter 5, management should reward immediately rather than delaying recompense. Survivors, questioning their long-term prospects with the organization, need more immediate gratification. And promises of future rewards, no matter how large or how well intended, carry even less weight now when the likelihood of the "rewarder" remaining at the organization to fulfill that promise at "reward time" may be in doubt.

Last, but perhaps first, the organization must remember that its objectives in developing an interim reward system are not only to compensate people but to retain survivors. Retaining high performers has become a major challenge in post-downsizing organizations.

As Jean Wallace, a director of human resource development, stated:

In retaining employees, a company **must must must** look at being more competitive compensation-wise and go past that to developing alternative reward systems for these individuals.

Work motivates high performers, but they have to know there's something else in it for them, the opportunity to have a promotion that's different or outside the normal track . . .a weekend away that the company pays for . . . some type of recognition program in front of their entire organization . . . the company purchasing a computer for someone to have at home as well as at work.

The key is, you can't just have programs that are across the board. People have to identify what's important to them and you have to motivate toward that. But your system has to have the flexibility in its reward system to provide that.

How do you put such a reward system in place when it may be so new and different for the company? According to Wallace,

The executive team is generally not going to buy it without proof—particularly when there's so much change going on in the company . . . to add another piece . . . and especially [on] the compensation side. . . . So you have to find an area in the company that is interested in doing something. [Perhaps an area experiencing] high turnover or where they're trying to turn their organization around.

A caution: Don't splurge on extravaganzas. Rewards can't be so big or costly that employees wonder why, if the company had the money for parties and recognition events, the downsizing was necessary.

In addition, an interim reward system needs to reflect the desired norms the organization is working toward. As one executive told us:

If you want people to take personal accountability for their performance, but you're still rewarding following orders or how many widgets they make, how likely is it that your organization is really going to be any different?

B/A/R/R/I/E/R
Nonalignment

The barrier we encountered over and over again from survivors and in our own work was that of nonalignment of components. Frequently this nonalignment is the result of putting a mixture of old and new components in place in the interim organization. For example, we heard often about organizations changing expectations and norms but maintaining basically the same reward structure as in the old organization. Thus, they rewarded employees for old behaviors—hardly surprising, then, that employees continued to perform in old ways or their performance dropped as they became immobilized with mixed messages.

They said they wanted us to reengineer the sales function. They approved the idea of account teams. But when we got to the issue of compensation, they said rewarding the team would never fly past

management—maybe twenty percent—but the rest had to go to the salesperson who "sold" the account.

In a similar situation, the organization put out a new vision for customer service, which included developing service teams and expanding employees' authority to solve customers' problems. Role assignments were completed and team-building sessions held. It was not until "ribbon-cutting" time that the manager released performance standards. Examining the detailed system for measuring employee performance, we were struck by the fact that almost all expectations were based on individual performance (for example, the number of accounts an employee handled and the number of customer complaints he or she received) and, as before, speed was an important criterion. Nowhere were there rewards for working collaboratively or problem solving. What had changed?

INTERIM LEADERSHIP

Survivors' needs for clarity around roles and norms in the interim lead us to our next focus: leadership in the middle phase. Survivors need to know who will guide them through the chaotic period, who will manage performance, and who will direct their development.

Leadership is at the crux of successful transition. We have written in previous chapters about the leadership attributes required during change and transition if survivors are to stay. A number of them are shown in figure 10, taken from the Wyatt study.

As the Wyatt report clarifies, "The desired managerial behaviors listed above are arguably helpful at any point in time. They are particularly necessary during restructuring to help keep employees productive and to ensure that the process of restructuring moves as smoothly as possible."

In the organizations we looked at, we found that interim leadership needed to be flexible and adaptable, moving as the organization moved. Interim leaders needed to be open to new ideas. They couldn't succumb to, "Well, we tried that before and it didn't work."

Leading in the face of the unknown also forces managers to deal with constraints and barriers they may not have encountered before. And, most important, leaders need to provide all this direction in ways that do not foster dependency.

FIGURE 10 **MANAGERIAL EFFECTIVENESS DURING RESTRUCTURING**

SHOWING PERSONAL INITIATIVE — 31%
SUPPORTING THE EXECUTIVE MANAGEMENT VISION THROUGH THEIR ACTIONS — 30%
INCREASING COMMUNICATIONS WITH EMPLOYEES — 30%
FOCUSING ON NEAR-TERM TASK ACCOMPLISHMENT — 30%
GIVING RECOGNITION TO EMPLOYEES — 28%
KEEPING A POSITIVE ATTITUDE — 28%
ENTHUSIASTICALLY IMPLEMENTING NEW APPROACHES TO WORK (E.G., TQM) — 20%
CELEBRATING SMALL ACHIEVEMENTS — 18%
DEVELOPING A MORE PARTICIPATORY STYLE — 17%
ADDRESSING THE NEEDS OF SURVIVORS — 13%
DEALING OPENLY WITH RESISTANCE TO CHANGE — 11%

Ratings of Managerial Effectiveness: The bar graph and numbers represent the percentage of respondents who say their average manager exhibits these behaviors. Respondents: Senior executives of 531 organizations. *Best Practices in Corporate Restructuring: Wyatt's 1993 Survey of Corporate Restructuring.* Used by permission.

Survivors' reports and our own observations revealed that such leadership is often in short supply. That leadership void is costly—payoffs from appropriate leadership have proven to be one of the most underrealized gains for the interim organization.

As the Wyatt study points out, "It is easy to acknowledge that the typical manager also experiences stress in times of change. However, these behaviors (figure 10) are, in a sense, a test of leadership in organizations. Just as we found in our 1991 study on corporate restructuring, the typical manager in companies came up short on leadership during restructuring."

While our research concurs with the Wyatt study's findings, we think it is illuminating to understand the context in which those desired managerial behaviors come into play. Managers, going through their own transition, have to manage their own stress and skills development with respect to both currency and readiness. At the same time, they must meet heightened production goals and performance expectations with some combination of depleted staff, diminished budget, and broader span of responsibilities.

Said one consultant, "It's no surprise that they go into their offices, close the doors, and do the work themselves."

As management consultant Rose Cohan suggests:

A company has to take care of the manager. Oftentimes, when downsizing is done, the manager is given a lot more work with fewer resources and more expectations. That in itself is difficult. The organization needs to really assess what kind of transition is necessary in terms of work load and other things. The organization must give the manager support, training, and resources to get the larger job done.

What are the barriers preventing this type of leadership?

B/A/R/R/I/E/R
Off with His Head!

One barrier comes from employees' expectations that leadership has the ability either to avoid problems or, when that is not possible, to have the answers to resolve them. These expectations are often compounded when they mirror those that executives hold for themselves.

As a result, a CEO is trapped. According to Lebby,

Nobody ever thanked a CEO for throwing them into chaos.

A CEO is very rarely likely to get up and say, "You know, the next three to five years are going to be hell. Many of you are going to be wounded. We have no idea of what the organization is going to look like at the end of this because we're entering into a transformational change process. We have no answers. The only way we can produce answers is for all of us to struggle together to get us through this."

A CEO believes that if she/he were to say that, people would say, "What!! He's supposed to know how to do this. Off with his head!"

B/A/R/R/I/E/R
The Old Rules

Some survivors reported that managers responded to the interim chaos and discomfort it brought either by reverting to old ways, becoming more directive, or taking the opposite approach, seeming to abdicate even the presumption of control ("Let's see where it falls. . .").

Hager offered a partial explanation:

I'm forty years old; I've been in industry since I was twenty-one. I was educated; I learned all the great business things; I went to my production management class and learned, "You as a manager will need to plan, organize, direct, and control." That was reinforced many, many times.

Leaders of organizations today came up in a very similar environment.... Now we have people who are steeped in this practice, reinforced by their education and training. We had the best business schools in the world teaching this. And now we've changed the rules for the first time in postwar America. But the people who are having to make the change were trained under the old rules.

INTERIM FOCUS

The interim organization directs its attention to two issues—production goals and development—thus illustrating the competing demands of present productivity and future readiness during this mid-transition phase.

Production Goals

We repeat: The interim organization is not without production goals. But we believe that they cannot be as ambitious as they ultimately will be in the new organization, if the organization wants to retain its workforce and achieve the goals for which it downsized and restructured in the first place.

I find myself resisting even small projects. If you're working sixty-hour weeks, one more hour is a big deal.

This is the time to encourage managers to weed out extraneous job tasks and duplication of effort.

▶ BEST PRACTICE

Discussing the need to prioritize and decrease the amount of work, Logan noted that,

"Work-out" started as "Let's get rid of the work. We know we can't do the same amount of work with a smaller group, and we have to get rid of anything that is unnecessary." And you would be amazed what can be accomplished when you turn employees loose!

Many of the survivors complained that the organization seemed oblivious to the amount of work now expected—and to the consequences.

Our productivity is still up, but I know it's only temporary. No one can keep up this pace forever. Half of our group has been out sick the last month.

We stand behind the notion of modified production goals in the interim organization for several reasons: First, employees in transition cannot produce at the same levels as they did prior to transition, no matter what incentives or sanctions leaders put in place; survivors' performance ebbs and flows. Even those who manage transition successfully and emerge at the other end still lack the new skills and knowledge needed to produce at top speeds.

Nonetheless, we heard about organizations that referred to the interim state as a downtime, a brief period of diminished productivity followed by a resumption of performance. At issue is the inappropriate use of initial productivity as a benchmark for determining that the organization and employees are back on track. According to a study by Lee Hecht Harrison (1994), an initial increase in productivity did not necessarily signal that the organization had completed the transition process: "[T]eamwork and productivity are often sustained or even rise in the first few weeks following a downsizing regardless of any organizational effort. No matter why . . . it is important to recognize that these are short-term reactions."

We heard exactly that from survivors.

When the announcement was first made, my initial reaction was, "Well, let me put on the afterburners here, really put in the extra effort to be noticed . . . let me really show them what I can do!" And there were a lot of extra hours put in, a lot of extra effort. And as the time grew closer and closer, a lot of the people in the area—at least in the part of the organization affected—had the mind-set that "Well, it's not going to matter what I do; it's just going to happen, so why am I killing myself?"

We interviewed one manager whose department experienced a rise in productivity exactly as the study reported. The manager concluded that the brief downtime was done; the department was now in the new organization. He started treating employees as if they should be up to speed, raising the bar of production standards to what he had planned for the restructured organization. The manager's change in expectations coincided with the beginning of the natural drop in production cited in several studies.

The manager's response? He concluded that the new ideas and structures—for example, cross-functional teams, changes in individual role responsibilities—wouldn't work. So he began to treat the post-downsizing department as a now-dysfunctional organization and set about determinedly to bring back the previous structures despite their acknowledged long-term inefficiencies.

Another reason for modified production goals is that the organization itself while in transition doesn't have the competency to produce in new ways and at the new standards immediately. Remember that the organization said good-bye to the Three C's of the old organization.

A final reason: The interim organization, as we define it, is the period for trying out, piloting, and experimenting with new components—new roles, structures, and systems.

In our judgment, management experiences additional costs for tension unaddressed. Those organizations that try to focus on ambitious production goals—and even those that initially achieve them—do so at the expense of attending to survivors' transition issues and future readiness tasks. If the organization sets such high production goals while people need to reposition themselves and develop new skills, many survivors turn back to old ways of working. By doing so they may achieve high productivity, but only temporarily. Something has to give: acquisition of new skills, development of new behaviors like risk taking, or implementation of new systems.

The ultimate consequence of setting unrealistic production goals is that an organization finds itself back where it started, looking and acting just like it did before. Or the organization becomes a new organization that is a shadow of the old with only limited improvements. Or the organization goes out of business. Thus, the organization needs to set incremental production goals to facilitate future readiness.

Survivors and the organization will demonstrate readiness through increased productivity, providing, of course, that other components are in place and aligned. So the organization must be alert to changes in the tension that will serve as cues and clues that it is appropriate to put more stress on present productivity, hence raising production goals. Figure 11 illustrates how the organization shifts its focus on development and productivity as the interim period progresses in contrast to what was often the case— organizations' focus on productivity high from the start with lesser attention paid to development all along.

FIGURE 11 **INTERIM FOCUS**

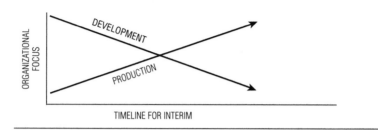

The organization's goals and expectations for employees are fluid, not bound or rigid, calling for flexibility on the part of the organization—especially its leadership. This may involve a new way of thinking, specifically within the context of production.

If you're an organizational leader reading this and convinced you cannot modify production goals, then you need to consider how the organization can set up alternative production systems. One alternative is to engage temporary employees to do the work using the old organization's processes while training survivors on future systems.

A second alternative is to take those selected for downsizing and provide incentives for them to remain with the organization for a period of time, again maintaining present productivity while survivors are developed. However, explicit performance expectations are just as important as incentives, as survivors want to be assured that these individuals (downsized employees) will actually be working, not just occupying desks, as noted in chapter 7.

Another alternative is to outsource the work. But respondents participating in the Wyatt study reported that they had better results from eliminating tasks than from outsourcing work.

Eliminating work was only part of the issue in organizations we observed. As Joe Willmore, a Virginia consultant, told us,

> What is immobilizing people in the post-downsizing organization is
> not necessarily the quantity of work, although they are labeling it that.
> It's that nobody is setting priorities, giving direction, being explicit
> around it. So employees sit with the work in front of them not knowing
> what to do first, what to let go.

Finally, interim production needs to integrate quality standards with quantity goals. Many survivors across all survivor groups perceived that quantity was now what mattered.

I feel like the only goal now is to pump out the work. No one seems to care anymore about the finished product.

Ironically, this survivor came from an organization in contention for the Malcolm Baldrige National Quality Award. Survivors, especially the high performers, found this focus on quantity, not quality, very frustrating.

Development: Training

As the acquisition of the Three C's is a mandate for the new organization's success, we cannot overstate the importance of training and coaching as developmental functions in the interim organization. According to the 1995 AMA survey, "There is a remarkably strong correlation between increased training budgets and increased profits and productivity following workforce reductions. Long term, firms that increased their training budgets after workforce reductions were twice as likely to show increased profits and productivity than firms that cut their training expenses."

If leadership is serious about creating a new organization and helping people develop new skills, then the organization cannot afford to delay training for future readiness. At the same time, survivors cannot provide present productivity without training.

Moreover, management cannot reassess the components if survivors are not using them. Survivors cannot pilot programs according to design if they are not trained. If a system being piloted is not giving the desired results, the organization is hard pressed to know if the problem is a faulty system, poorly designed pilot, or a lack of skills among employees. Development as an interim goal is not limited to increasing competency; it must also establish connection and rebuild commitment.

People are now pushed into jobs they don't have the skills for, so they're not performing very well. If there's another downsizing, what will happen to them?

Our research suggests that what survivors need in the interim organization is what we are calling a job development plan. Note that we did not say career development plan, which is appropriately addressed in the new organization. Based on what work needs to be done to meet the interim goals, the job development plan integrates those needs with the results of the skills assessment done in the old organization, creating a training plan to address the gaps. Because a job development plan relies on a department work plan, it will be faulty if the work has not been defined and prioritized as suggested earlier.

The content of training is prescribed by what survivors need to know and be able to do both to make an effective transition and to be productive in the interim organization. Content is also based on the skills and knowledge survivors will need in order to be successful in the future organization.

Obviously, the "hard skills"—the technical knowledge that is part of the training content—are very specific to the industry and organization and cannot be generalized. What we did hear across the board was the need for training to address what have commonly been referred to as "soft skills": problem solving, decision making, and critical thinking. Many of the studies also confirmed the consequences of the organization's overlooking these skill areas. Why were they overlooked?

As organization consultant Mardy Wheeler notes:

> I think the answer is when people start talking to us about "Well, this is a soft skill and this is a hard skill," and I say, "The reason you're calling it a soft skill is because it's much more difficult to describe; you can't touch it," and so these soft skills are really many more times more difficult to deal with.

If the company's preoccupation is with present productivity, the tendency is to focus training on technical skills that can be applied to immediate production. As a result, the soft skills that need to be rehearsed and practiced fall by the wayside, ultimately reducing people's readiness to perform in the new organization.

We continue to find organizations in which the technical expertise of employees has risen dramatically in recent years. At the same time, search consultants corroborate that those employees most sought after by companies not only possess sound technical skills but also the much-prized skills of decision making and problem solving. Vying to pull in people who have these so-called soft skills, organizations are, in fact, wooing away each other's high performers.

Many of the skills we are talking about cannot be mastered in a one-time workshop, no matter its length. The learning challenge posed by ongoing change requires that the acquisition of knowledge and skills be positioned as an ongoing process for organizations and employees.

The content will impact the training approach, whether a one-on-one coaching session or group seminar, whether a classroom workshop, a self-study course, or computer-based training. The approach needs to be responsive to the challenges posed by learners who are in transition, in this case survivors.

As one respondent in the Lee Hecht Harrison study pointed out: "Right after the layoffs, people were in a state of shock and were nursing their emotional wounds. But now they're experiencing a lot of stress, so there's tremendous resistance to this change. And not only are they upset about being responsible for extra work, they have a lot of anxiety about whether they will be able to perform their new functions well enough to keep their jobs."

Whether seasoned managers in a leadership class or newer employees in systems training, survivors in the interim organization come into this middle time not only with gaps in the competencies required in their new roles but with acute awareness of this chasm. For survivors, this situation poses a serious dilemma: On the one hand, survivors need to gain knowledge and skills in order to perform, to feel competent again; on the other hand, they fear that in going through the process of gaining that competence, they will not look capable or, even worse, will fail. "Who will evaluate me?" "How will I be judged?" "Will I be downsized if I fail the training?" are common worries. Survivors' general perception of a high-risk environment all around them extends, then, to perceiving training as fraught with danger.

We found that learners' fears were compounded when survivors knew they were not first choice for a position and imagined there was someone else in the wings waiting to take over. Some were told that they would be replaced "if you can't cut it."

While training (and learning) in the interim organization are not without challenge, there are payoffs for the survivor groups as well as the organization.

■ PAYOFFS OF TRAINING FOR FODs

FODs are probably the most realistic about the demise of the employment contract, long-term security, and continued employment. FODs recognize "employment at will" as the organization's "will" as well. What the organization does offer them through training is a path to interesting work, their career focus. This survivor group's concern in restructuring is that the work they did, and by association they themselves, are no longer valued. Training in new competencies, in new responsibilities, sends the message that "the work you will be doing is valuable" and reinforces their value as the producers of the work.

■   PAYOFFS OF TRAINING FOR W&Ss

The job development and training plans signify the organization's commitment to W&Ss. W&Ss want to know especially about their personal training plan and how it fits into the overall restructuring plan. Their training plan provides a structured way to assure them that they will be ready for new roles and new expectations.

■   PAYOFFS OF TRAINING FOR RIOs

The organization's approach to training as well as its provision of opportunities to practice skills will do much to assuage RIOs' fears of being unable to master the requisite competencies. This survivor group's desire for high performance will resurface. RIOs want to perform; they just do not want to take the chance of failing.

For RIOs, context and process combine to meet their connection needs. Relationships are the key and the path to commitment as well as to connection.

Each of the survivor groups present a special training challenge above and beyond issues expressed by survivors generally.

As long as RIOs are anxious, fearful, and in denial, they will be unable to learn. For W&Ss, the issue is more content-oriented; they need to know that the training is purposeful, that it has a payoff for them. Thus, training has to be job related, linking the job to the future vision. For FODs, the content has to be of value to the organization, clearly part of a plan as well as challenging in itself.

The same guideline we offered for communicating with people in transition—turn up the volume—applies to training these survivors. Survivors can't hear and they can't remember. So repeat not only the instruction and directions but the application of training on the job, that is, the practice. Learning has to take place beyond the classroom.

Immediate application of training on the job means learners are less likely to forget and coaching is more likely to stick. Likewise, managers can do immediate correction. On the other hand, practicing on the job can lead to employees feeling the "make it or break it" pressure at a time when their skills are not up to speed. "Not getting it" is readily apparent to bosses and perceived consequences—termination—heighten pressures to perform.

It is critical during this period that trainers and learners' managers function as a team, to ensure that the training is supported by appropriate coaching back on the job and by the creation of a safe environment to try out the skills.

Trainers and bosses can create that safe environment in a number of ways. For example, assigning a complex spreadsheet to a survivor beginning to learn a new computer program would hardly dissipate fears. Instead, the boss needs to provide a low-risk assignment that almost guarantees success. At the same time, low-risk assignments need to relate to the job and production.

Based on our interviews with survivors, we also recommend training in small groups. We see this training method as particularly significant for RIOs, who are especially concerned about competency. If skills training is geared to small groups rather than one-on-one sessions, many RIOs feel less threatened, less on the spot to perform. And if a trainee has difficulties, reliance on other learners can take place.

There are two primary organizational barriers to training.

B/A/R/R/I/E/R

Inconsistencies

Many survivors told us of inconsistencies between what organizations said and what they did. Proclaiming the importance of a highly trained workforce in the new organization, management set immediate production expectations requiring employees to get up to speed quickly. Management then shortened training time, applying the rationale that "we can't have employees away from the job that long."

Sometimes a well-intentioned manager, trying to reassure survivors, instead adds to their fears by suggesting that "you've done this kind of thing before; it should come quickly." True, survivors may have "done this kind of thing before," but they have not done it within this chaotic environment and perhaps not for the same intended outcome.

Even when companies provided the workshops and bosses sanctioned their direct reports' attendance, corporate trainers told us of participants calling in sick the first day of the course so they could "postpone" their workshop attendance. The next day they were back on the job.

B/A/R/R/I/E/R
Training As "Dessert"

A survivor recounted another mixed message from the organization's management:

"Yes, you can go to that outside training course next month, as long as your work is current."

Survivors translated the message as: "We are going to give you development to show that we value you—but you'd better produce, produce, produce first." In other words, "I've made this lovely dessert, but you have to eat all your food (including two servings of broccoli) before you can have it." The appetite for dessert, understandably, diminishes, when diners are too stuffed by what was on their plates.

Some candid survivors stated to trainers directly, "I don't have the time to be here because I have so much work to do." Other survivors signaled their frustration by arriving late and leaving early, by not completing assignments, or by appearing preoccupied and unprepared during the session. It was not uncommon for trainers to report survivors' bringing work into the workshop and attempting to complete it during class time.

Once again, the tension brought about by a disproportionate emphasis on present production had consequences. Future readiness suffered. At the same time, survivors' needs to regain the competence, connection, and commitment to progress through transition were equally stifled.

As Linda Squires Grohe, Coordinator of Contract Education at City College of San Francisco, reflected:

Companies are clearly reducing management workshops, both in number and in length.

Across the country, organization consultant Betsy Kendall, concurred:

Fewer and fewer people seem to be able to do a three-day workshop. Getting away from the office for three days is a luxury.

Focusing on present productivity at the expense of future readiness, canceling workshops and training events, can have an even greater consequence for the organization. To reiterate what was said in chapter 9, initial training focuses on preparing leaders to manage change and transition as well as to start their readiness for managing in the future organization.

If training has not been done in quantity or in depth in the old organization, then the company finds itself in the interim phase trying to play catch-up. The organization is caught in a bind: Leaders do not have the skills to do what the organization needs them to do and the organization frequently believes it cannot afford the "luxury" of letting managers go to training. The managers themselves are in a similar bind, increasingly aware that they are having trouble managing situations but afraid to leave for fear the situations will get worse while they are away, or that they will get further behind in meeting the now-increased production goals.

How to manage this tension? To us, the answer is again to take a balanced approach. On the one hand, there is no way to truncate development. It does take time. On the other hand, training does not have to be an isolated activity, requiring extended periods away. Rather, training activities need to be integrated into the individual's work schedule and practiced and applied on the job.

As the organization cannot do business as usual, training must likewise adapt to the changes. Training and human resources departments are asked to do training more quickly and to do more with less. Wheeler, who has worked with a number of training departments, expresses the challenge:

> Is there another way we can deliver this? Is there another medium? Is there another time frame to consider? Is there another way of funding this? Training departments have to be creative, to look at any and all options.

We have already talked about how effective training rebuilds competence and connection. Training, if done properly, can address commitment as well. As Cohan relates:

> People develop loyalty when you invest in their skills, when you invest in them growing with the company. I think people are looking for that. It doesn't guarantee anyone's going to be loyal, but it certainly is something that people look for and appreciate.

Development: Team Building

Many of the survivors we talked to spoke of new team assignments and new team configurations—such as self-managed teams and cross-functional teams—figuring predominantly in the new organization. Many began such assignments following the downsizing.

Whether or not survivors are working in defined teams in the interim organization, organizations cannot delay team building. There are several reasons for this. First, survivors bring into the training room their concerns about connection ("Will I belong?"). Their concerns are immediate. A side benefit of group training is that it will facilitate team development, but it is not enough. Team building is needed to create this connection.

As one survivor said,

> *You need to do something with the new teams that are formed to make them feel like a cohesive group, whether it's doing something like teamwork in action or a class . . . so these people who are kind of like, "All my friends are gone . . . now I'm all by myself." Many survivors don't feel they will make new friends and new connections. . . . There has been team building, but they need to do it more quickly afterward.*

The second reason to expedite team building is that employees cannot wait to begin to acquire team skills, particularly if teams will become the modus operandi for accomplishing work.

If work teams were new, reconfigured from former teams, or formed as the results of a merger, we heard a lot about "them versus us." This is not surprising, given the varied profiles, agendas, and concerns of survivors. This is a third reason that team building needs to start right away.

Connection is a concern for all survivor groups; hence, team building and teamwork have payoffs for FODs and W&Ss as well as RIOs. Bosses can further support development of team behaviors via teamwork: assigning tasks to teams.

■ PAYOFFS OF TEAMWORK FOR FODs

If the organization's future vision involves team structures or teamwork, and if FODs embrace that vision, then this survivor group eagerly looks for opportunities to develop and explore teamwork. The organization's structuring the team building or teamwork as well as FODs' participation speaks to FODs of the organization's viability.

> *I really like being able to design how I feel the teams should be working. This experience has made me understand the company's direction, and I agree it's the way to go. The work is really interesting, and that's a big reason I decided to take my chances and stay.*

■   PAYOFFS OF TEAMWORK FOR W&Ss

Very basically, putting W&Ss in teams provides their pathway for success. It gives them a role.

■   PAYOFFS OF TEAMWORK FOR RIOs

For RIOs, team building and teamwork offer a number of benefits: support, a sense of affinity, a safe way to explore the other skills the organization may require, and a chance to try their fledgling wings. As we said, RIOs in particular perceive training in a team format as less threatening.

Curiously, few survivors described organizational attention to team building. Why? What got in the way?

B/A/R/R/I/E/R
False Indicators

One of the most common barriers to initiating team building stems from the misreading of survivors' behaviors in relation to one another immediately after downsizing.

As one vice president told us:

> What do you mean, team building? Everyone is really working closely together now.

The Lee Hecht Harrison study appears to corroborate our interviewee's observation. Two-thirds of the respondents reported that teamwork stayed the same or increased after downsizing. But we suggest the importance of understanding the context in which those results occurred. "Several HR professionals noted that in the immediate wake of a downsizing, remaining employees tend to naturally band together for emotional and work-related support. The idea that 'we're all in this together' or that 'we're the lucky ones' are common reactions—short term." If only our interviewee had finished the survey's statement: As with productivity, "[teamwork] normally declines as time goes by unless specific steps are taken."

PROBLEMATIC THINKING

While we have examined a range of issues facing the interim organization, the most compelling concern expressed by survivors had to do with organizational misperceptions of the interim organization and the specific barriers that caused these misperceptions. Although we are looking at "problematic thinking" last, it may be the first issue that needs to be addressed.

False Perceptions

According to our survivors, some of their organizations appeared not to recognize the interim period at all. Management seemed to think it would be business as usual, that the organization could move from the old to the new with a news release, the cutting of a ribbon, or the installation of a new system. These were frequently the same organizations that did not recognize the transition process for either the organization or its employees.

If leaders do not understand this mid-transition state, they may perceive the chaotic interim environment as indicative of a faulty new organization. As a result, they conclude that "the plan doesn't work" or "productivity is not where it should be." In many cases, their misperception of the interim phase as the new organization gone awry and their resulting skepticism prompt them to institute another round of downsizing as a "solution."

Assigning Blame

We heard about executives of other organizations holding the same misperception but concluding, "The organization is problematic because these employees aren't cutting it; they're botching it up," thus ascribing the blame to the workforce. The result: Survivors reported assignments of weekly instead of monthly reports, diminished bonuses, and increases in the numbers of people having to approve requests and authorize expenditures. This meant more control, more sanctions—and more "out the door."

Discounting the Impact

Yet other companies recognized the organization's interim status but they discount the impact, downplaying and minimizing what the organization is experiencing as if this phase can be glossed over. They put off issues, dismissing them as unimportant or suggesting that they will resolve themselves on their own in the future.

Also discounting the impact are those organizations that view transition as a one-time event. "We won't do it again," is a company's reprise, despite the growing evidence that organizations today continue to engage in a renewal process, that change is ongoing and essential, and thus, that it is likely the organization will engage in transition again. Nevertheless, this "one time only" stance may serve as part of the rationale for assessing the interim phase as not requiring much attention.

Command and Control

Organizations that embrace a command and control management style tend to believe that period can be controlled and even truncated. When the situation becomes chaotic, leaders try harder to impose control, most often using methods and tools they know best, such as revising the project schedule, tightening policies and procedures, or imposing new rules and strictures for behaviors. As Houda Samaha, an organization development consultant, states,

> When a company's survival is at stake, one of the greatest challenges management has is to mobilize the workforce to focus on turning the company around. At a time when they most need to involve the people impacted by decisions, they fall back on the old command and control style of managing. Instead of asking for the input of those doing the work and making the changes, managers tell people what to do and what not to do, what to say and what not to say. Their bias is that the sense of urgency is so great, they need to take control of the situation as quickly as possible—to do otherwise is too time consuming. When employees don't respond as expected, controls are tightened further.

Faulty Benchmarks

Other companies conclude erroneously that they have achieved their goals and arrived in the new organization, basing their conclusion on faulty benchmarks such as a new system in place, completion of employee relocation, or the departure of the downsized employees.

Misplaced Justification

Even when organizations seem to appreciate the significance of organizational transition, problems may occur. A manager from still another organization recognized the chaotic state of his company but justified the organization's downplaying transition, stating that explaining the interim organization to employees would add to their insecurity and discomfort and, therefore, impact productivity negatively.

As an organization development consultant at the same company noted:

Unfortunately, that doesn't make employees feel very secure, because they'll say, "Why are they doing this [downsizing] if they don't know what they want?"

We suspect withholding information was due to management's discomfort as well.

The concern this manager cited—employees' discomfort—is the very reason management needs to tell survivors of the company's transitional state. Whether organizations reveal it or not, the interim environment with its chaos and uncertainty will come to be. How much more will survivors' discomfort rise if they don't have a way to make sense of what they are experiencing? Telling employees enables them to begin to work within the constructs of the chaos.

Fear of Prompting Employee Departures

One consultant noted that management may not acknowledge the interim organization because it fears good employees will leave if they hear all is not settled.

Aren't they more likely to exit, we queried, if management paints a scenario of stability ("Welcome to the new organization") while a different one, fraught with confusion and chaos, unfolds around them—or if management claims to have the answers but does not?

And rather than inviting those high performers to participate in the renewal, to become involved in determining the organization's future, the organization's announcing the arrival of the new organization invites employees to conclude, "You have bypassed me, my opinions, and my expertise, and denied my opportunity to contribute and have some voice." That stance is exactly the opposite of what survivor groups, particularly FODs, want and need in order to reengage.

Survivors' Reactions to the Organization's Misperceptions

When organizations acted on these misperceptions, survivors had strong reactions. Some survivors reported being furious that the organization "did not recognize what's going on," while other interviewees' stories suggested survivors' collusion with the organization's denial. Still others confessed to feeling something was wrong with them: "Why can't I keep up?" "Why can't I handle the turbulence?"

LEGITIMIZING THE INTERIM ORGANIZATION

For all of these reasons, we believe that the interim organization has to be legitimized. Legitimizing and naming the interim organization normalizes this phase and helps survivors make sense of what is going on. Legitimizing the interim organization prevents short-circuiting or dismissing the critical processes. Representing the interim organization as equal in status to the old and the new organizations also calls the interim organization to task.

When the organization legitimizes the interim phase, it sends a message—that this period requires very specific leadership and certain role behaviors and that different components and different ways of producing work need to be put in place. It is a call to action to management and survivors: "This is what needs to be done."

Legitimizing the interim organization acts as a reaffirmation and reassurance to survivors that the organization is in charge. It is an affirmation as well that what employees are doing is of value.

Impact on the Survivor Groups

What effect does legitimizing the interim phase have on the survivor groups?

■   EFFECT ON FODs

If the organization legitimizes the interim state, FODs conclude that management understands where it is going and what is involved in getting there. FODs perceive that the organization is actively engaged in determining its future, that this chaotic period is not a surprise to the company, and that any temporary structures are a part of a long-term plan.

■   EFFECT ON W&Ss

The organization's legitimizing this period makes it more likely that the management team will not only pay attention to issues and problems but try to resolve them without delay. This organization's stance is critical to W&Ss, who need answers, structure, and clearly defined roles right now.

At the same time, legitimizing and defining the interim phase indicates that it is acceptable, even expected, that management will not have all the answers. Legitimizing the organization frees management from engaging in fruitless debate with W&Ss. Legitimizing the organization encourages W&Ss to be part of finding the answers, thus providing them with a legitimate role. By taking this approach, management succeeds in answering W&Ss' real question "Where do I fit in?" by giving W&Ss a place in the interim organization.

■ EFFECT ON RIOs

For the RIOs, legitimizing the chaotic period they are experiencing provides a breather, takes the pressure off, and offers a safety net.

Legitimizing this phase indicates management's recognition that the organization and employees need time to get up to speed and to try out skills (versus have them in place). Legitimizing the interim period sends the message, "It's OK to come out of hiding, to ask for help." The organization's acknowledging that this is a chaotic time for people makes it easier for RIOs to interact by suggesting both that it is safe to be seen making mistakes and that the chaos is normal.

> The CEO has been visiting different plants, and he's been real clear that we are in for a rough time. We have lots of changes to make, a lot of learning to do. Some of what we'll be doing may work, and some things we may need to fix. And that's OK. We just have to do them. And he probably said about six times, we have to get through it as a team.

Benefit to the Organization

Legitimizing the interim period benefits the organization in very specific ways. It provides the impetus to meet the challenges posed by survivor groups.

■ MEETING FODs' CHALLENGE

Legitimizing the interim stage provides the organization a reengagement opportunity with the FODs, a last chance to "hook'em in"—to capture FODs' attention. Because chaos is a catalyst for creativity, it often tends to entice FODs into transition roles anyway. If channeled, FODs' creative energy can keep them on the road to recommitment and simultaneously fuel their ability to do the critical work of the interim organization. FODs' natural energy can then become a positive part of the chaos. Of all the survivor groups, FODs tend to perceive the chaos in the most positive light, which becomes synergistic for other survivor groups.

■ MEETING W&Ss' CHALLENGE

While the FODs may be the creators and the designers, the W&Ss are the analysts, the assessors. If the organization wants to find out how temporary structures or roles are working, what's going well, and what needs changing, W&Ss will provide detailed responses. As suggested in chapter 3, W&Ss are already engaged in a kind of quality control, so the issue is how to harness their analysis and turn it into a proactive rather than reactive activity. As long as the organization provides structured avenues for assessments and gives W&Ss a role, W&Ss will act as "depth sounders," keeping management apprised of what is working and what is not as well as the dangers ahead and where adjustments to the plan are needed.

■ MEETING RIOs' CHALLENGE

Of all of the survivor groups we interviewed, the RIOs demonstrated their loyalty and commitment most consistently. How does this tie in to legitimizing the interim organization? If management tells RIOs what they need to do, what is critical at this phase, they will do it for the organization over and over. They can, in other words, be counted on to keep the business going. While FODs may engage in planning the future and carrying out pilots, the RIOs are more likely to be in the present. The organization can thereby realize immediate payoffs in terms of productivity. As we have cautioned already, RIOs will produce as long as conditions are set for their safe participation. They will tolerate the chaos if there is order imposed on it, even if that order is part of a transition state.

KEY POINTS

The interim organization represents a transition state equivalent to the individual's neutral zone. In this interim period the company, through the modification and refinement of the organization's components, reestablishes its own as well as survivors' competence, connection, and commitment. Management has to meet the competing demands of developing organizational and employee readiness for the future state (the new organization), maintaining current productivity, and responding to survivors' transition needs.

GROUP ISSUES

FODs   FODs want to be actively involved in the developmental aspects of the interim organization. They are distressed if the organization loses its readiness focus or is unable to manage survivors' transition needs during the chaotic period.

W&Ss   W&Ss want the organization to establish interim structures and roles to guide their progress through this period. They are frustrated if management gives conflicting or contradictory messages about the interim organization's goals.

RIOs   RIOs want to continue to be as productive and feel as competent as they did in the old organization. They need a safe environment in which to master new skills and regain connections.

STRATEGIES

Legitimize the interim organization; modify components to facilitate managing future readiness, present productivity, and survivors' transition; provide training and development to enable survivors to regain their diminished Three C's.

Having completed the tasks of the interim phase, the organization is now in a position to complete its transition by moving into the new organization.

11

The New Organization

ARRIVING

Webster's Dictionary defines *new* in part as "taking the place of one that came before; refreshed, regenerated." We think this definition apt for several reasons: If the organization has successfully completed the interim phase, it is a revitalized organization, regenerated, transformed. While Drew Lebby, organizational consultant, spoke of transformation in terms of the chaos of the interim organization, consultant Anna Ewins presents another perspective on transformation.

> Transformation is far more than a change in organizational form. Transformation is based on systemic change, changing not only each part of the organization but [the part's]relationships to one another and to the whole. Transformation speaks to fundamental changes—changes in the underlying assumptions in these relationships, changes in the psychological contract.

Hence, the new organization—this renewed entity—is fundamentally different, more than an improved version of what came before. Indeed, if the "new" organization is really the old organization in new packaging, then it is not a new organization at all.

A task of the old organization as discussed in chapter 9 is to define the vision of the new organization. That vision clarifies not only where the organization is headed but sets out the benchmarks to measure achievement of the new organizational state. Those benchmarks relate to the Three C's for the organization and the employees.

237

Competence

Competence for the new organization means that it has a sense of control and mastery; competent management to lead the organization; structures, products, and services to achieve its new goals. And part of the organization's competence is having systems in place to ensure the competence of survivors.

Organizational competence implies that the company's resources and systems are functioning at an optimal performance level. For example, the new computer system is not only installed but operational throughout the designated work areas; not just operating but functioning at the requisite level. As stated in chapter 10, hitting production targets or cutting costs for the third quarter does not equate to competence; rather, sustaining performance at a predetermined standard, inclusive of quality as well as quantity, is a more reliable indicator of the organization's competence.

A popular school of thought holds that a company's strength derives from its ability to identify its core competencies (what it is "good at") and build the organization around them. Testing, tryout, and piloting in the interim organization provide a more precise understanding of those core competencies.

Connection

Connection refers to the company's relationships and bonds with its industry, customers, processes, and people as a whole. As we are defining it, the achievement of organizational connection in the new organization means several things. Ewins addresses connection at a primary level.

> Relationships are based on shared meaning, values, and purpose. It is the role of leadership to provide the forum for discovering the common ground that will help align each of the organization's members to its purpose and goals. It is the discovery of this common ground that will form the basis of the new psychological contract.

Connection also means that the components are in alignment with one another—for example, that the reward structure supports the organization's new role configurations. A survivor manager we met in one of our workshops offered an example from his organization. The company established self-managed teams but was still developing a compensation system to support the new roles. So structure and role and reward systems were not connected; the organization had not yet completed its interim tasks.

Last, organizational connection means that from a systems perspective, the organization is functioning as a whole; all parts are linked and synchronized. To continue with the self-managed team example: In the actual case, the self-managed work teams were confined to one division. Whether self-managed teams become the modus operandi in other divisions is not germane to the definition of connection. As the survivor involved in the pilot stated:

> What concerns me is not how other divisions in the company operate, but how are we going to work with them? There has to be a mechanism to link us, and we haven't established that yet.

What is critical for connection is whether the self-managed work teams in one part of the organization are communicating effectively with the other organizational entities, the departments and divisions.

Commitment

Commitment is in place when the organization and employees are pulling together to carry out a common vision. As Ewins points out, commitment is evident when "values and beliefs are manifested in the actions of the organization and its employees." Do the organization's actions demonstrate commitment to espoused values and beliefs as well as to vision and goals?

This perspective goes beyond the organization's having a narrowly defined commitment to a single goal. For example, if the company's sole commitment is to increasing profits or protecting management or growing the company, then it is not even in the commitment game.

The Survivors' Three C's

Organizations cannot achieve highs level of the three C's without a competent, connected, and committed workforce. The survivors we interviewed had not regained the Three C's. There are several explanations.

Survivors' movement through transition often does not parallel that of the organization. Some survivors are in the neutral zone while the organization is "ahead" in its transition process. Even those survivors who have completed the neutral zone and entered the new beginning may not have the Three C's in place. As discussed in chapter 8, these survivors may have regained competence and connection, but commitment is still missing.

In the new organization, the organization's competence, connection, and commitment continue to strengthen, although they may never reach

100 percent. However, the more closely the Three 3 C's approach this target, the greater the likelihood that survivor trust is reestablished. What the organization tells survivors by having the Three C's in place is that it is acting in good faith; it can be trusted to act on its vision and values and follow through on its commitments.

Survivors' Perspectives

What is the payoff for the organization's achieving the Three C's from the survivors' points of view?

■   KEY C's FOR FODs

Attaining organizational competence speaks most to the concerns of the FODs: Does the organization have a future? Can it carry out the plan? Will there be an entity with which to engage?

■   KEY C's FOR W&Ss

An organization committed to the future meets the "where are we going?" concerns of the W&Ss. The organization demonstrates that commitment through meeting the future readiness needs as well as defining the structure and providing role clarity.

■   KEY C's FOR RIOs

The organization's reestablishing connection by helping employees develop team skills meets the needs of the RIOs. They can now safely disconnect from the past because they have not only new connections and new teams but the ability to establish new connections on their own.

As in the old and the interim phases, the new organization has specific tasks. The primary tasks of the new organization are to reassess the components (and the change process), codify the new organizational components, celebrate the achievement, and provide employee development.

REASSESSING THE COMPONENTS

There are several reasons the organization needs to engage in reassessment: to evaluate the original change plan; to carry out the other tasks of this phase; and to determine whether another change program is called for. Reassessment consists of looking at not only the end results but also why and how the results were obtained.

Reassessment entails examining new components individually and in combination. What new reward systems and role configuration have resulted from tryout, piloting, refinement, and modification in the interim organization? Are components in alignment and in support of one another? Reassessment means evaluating components not just against those goals and benchmarks established in the original change plan but also against the revised benchmarks and goals of the interim period.

New Vision, Mission, and Goals

The reassessment answers such questions as, Does the original mission statement (in the change plan) hold? Is that vision possible? Is it realistic? Were the goals realistic and appropriate to support that vision? Were they on target?

▶ BEST PRACTICE

We worked with one organization whose vision included an empowered workforce. The company defined an empowered workforce as one in which employees took broader responsibility for solving problems, making decisions, and trying out new ideas. We worked with management to define the kind of environment and norms that would support the vision. As a part of assessing the results a year later, we suggested that the organization remeasure employees' perceptions of risk taking, this time couching the questions in the context of the current environment. When the results suggested that employees perceived inconsistent organizational support for the vision, management went another step: The president convened a special task force to focus on the issue.

New Culture and Norms

The reassessment clarifies whether the new organization's environment fosters the desired norms and values. This means checking to see whether current actions are explicitly and implicitly congruent with the vision and mission for the change. If the mission and vision have been changed during the interim organization, the prevailing culture and norms should reflect and support those changes.

The reassessment also determines to what degree survivors demonstrate the desired culture and norms, examining the progress made in the interim phase and the success of reinforcement efforts.

New Roles

As the organization goes through the interim phase, it has redefined and refined roles and responsibilities. Roles, like norms, are an evolving component, achieving certain levels of maturity as the organization's transition continues. In most cases roles expand as people take on tasks and responsibilities unanticipated in the change plan. Reassessment has to delineate current tasks and responsibilities because the results are the foundation of new job descriptions.

As Rose Cohan, management consultant, points out:

> The job description provides a framework the survivor can now make a commitment to. When employees know what is expected, they set goals and objectives to implement their responsibilities. People begin to show more commitment and enthusiasm towards their work as they now have something more tangible to focus their efforts on. A job description provides a tangible indication that the new responsibilities have some stability to them. It reassures employees and helps them move forward.

New Rewards

The new reward systems need to be aligned with the new roles, new expectations, and new levels of performance. As one survivor told us,

> *They've asked me to extend my customer service into selling as well. I've had to learn new skills to do this, and it adds to the time I need to talk to a customer. It's also increased the documentation—all in all . . . it's almost doubled my workload even though the number of customers I talk to each day is not really much different.*

This survivor's role responsibilities changed quantitatively (more time required to do additional tasks) and qualitatively (new job attributes requiring a greater skills repertoire). Reassessing rewards evaluates whether current reward systems reflect these role changes. All too often, survivors told us that rewards had stayed the same or were not adequate for their expanded responsibilities and performance expectations.

The Results

The base level of the reassessment enables management to answer the question, Compared to what we envisioned in the change plan, did we get what we wanted? Less than we wanted? More than we wanted?

A higher level of analysis examines not only how management planned and achieved the change but also why. The organization begins by going back to the change plan created in the old organization: Was the original vision realistic? Did the plan support the vision? Reflect the assessment results? Set realistic time frames? Were production goals achievable? Did the organization plan for future readiness? Present productivity? Survivors' transition needs?

The organization also examines how the plan was implemented: Did the organization follow the plan? Modify it? Involve employees? Provide necessary resources? Do appropriate testing, tryout, and piloting? Manage survivors' transition?

Survivors' Assessment

Survivors themselves evaluate both the components and the organization's reassessment procedures and conclusions. Once again, survivors' perceptions are important to the organization. Management must know whether new components meet survivors' needs—according to survivors. If FODs, W&Ss, and RIOs perceive that new components do not address their needs, the organization will likely meet with employees' initial resistance. And, on a long-term basis, survivors are unlikely to demonstrate commitment to new components.

Survivors' assessments are influenced by their own transition state, their historical perspective, and their survivor group.

■ FODs' ASSESSMENT

For FODs, evaluation and reassessment are integral parts of the change process. If the organization is competent and wants to move forward, as one FOD put it, "It only makes sense that management is going to do an analysis." FODs are measuring management's competence in the assessment process it uses and its interpretation of the results as well in the results themselves.

■   W&Ss' ASSESSMENT

W&Ss are the survivor group that challenges the organization, seeking the rationale and justification for management's actions. So for W&Ss, the organization's assessment of the components is the logical way to get the answers in this organizational phase. Reassessment as a process appeals to W&Ss because it provides a structured methodology for addressing issues and questions and obtaining results.

■   RIOs' ASSESSMENT

For RIOs, reassessment by the organization is necessary to address their underlying concerns: Are we done? Are there going to be more changes? Am I going to have to go through disruption and disconnection again? RIOs want to know, Does the reassessment confirm that we've arrived? The information from the reassessment confirms whether they can anchor themselves and begin the recommitment process. The organization's reassessment serves to jump-start the RIOs' reengagement and movement in their own transition.

Reassessment Methods

Organizations can undertake reassessment using the procedures and mechanisms such as surveys and focus groups suggested in chapters 5 and 6. Whatever methods are selected, they need to be ones with which employees are familiar. From a historical perspective, these mechanisms need to have a good track record. In this way survivors will perceive the reassessment as less threatening and have more trust and confidence in the results.

B/A/R/R/I/E/R
Don't See the Need and Insufficient Time

The assessment barriers "Don't See the Need" and "Insufficient Time" described in chapter 9 apply here. There are additional barriers.

B/A/R/R/I/E/R
Survivors' Readiness

Survivors still in the neutral zone are looking for more clarity and may not feel ready to assess the components. For them, the reassessment process is premature; they are not prepared to explore what has happened, much less to finalize their position or make any commitment.

Other survivors who are further along in transition are more open to reassessment. For them, the organization's reassessment represents a vital step to mark their movement in transition. These survivors perceive reassessment as a step in defining the new organization, stabilizing the environment, and putting an end to the interim chaos and uncertainty.

B/A/R/R/I/E/R
Survivors' Responses

Some survivors, depending on their transition state, are not well positioned psychologically to provide feedback for the reassessment. As noted, those in the neutral zone may not want to give input, or if they do, they may answer some questions with "Not sure" or "No opinion."

If management understands the effects of survivors' transition, it is more likely to interpret responses accurately rather than discounting or exaggerating their importance.

CODIFYING THE COMPONENTS

The reassessment may reveal that the components and procedures are appropriate as they now exist and that no immediate changes are necessary. Alternatively, the reassessment may suggest that change is needed, either because the components are incomplete, the cost-benefit analysis renders them unachievable, changes in core competencies or the external environment make them no longer desirable, or the organization has achieved more than it expected and wants to capitalize on the success.

Whether or not immediate change to the components is necessary or planned, the organization needs to codify the components. Codification, possibly the most critical task of the new organization, documents the components, including the procedures and methods that are a part of them.

The issue is not whether to codify the components but why. If the organization does not propose immediate changes, codification formalizes components and processes. The codified components now become part of the fabric of the organization; they act as historical markers, defining who "we" (the organization) are now. For example, codification serves to finalize human resources issues. Codification signals an end state. It does not mean there will be no more refinement, even sweeping changes at some point in the future, but not as a part of the original mandate.

Even if planning for another change has begun, the codified entities provide stability for the organization and employees functioning day-to-day. The codification process makes job descriptions, performance standards, salary ranges, and grievance procedures concrete. These codified components enable survivors and the organization to get their bearings, to steel themselves for the next series of changes. And there is no guarantee that the estimated time frame for the new organization will not change, the duration of operating in this state lengthening.

If the organization has identified a need for more change but has not yet begun planning, codification again establishes current benchmarks. The codified components and processes become the current components, that is, the components of the old organization that management will analyze as a step in the change plan.

CELEBRATING

Celebrating the new, celebrating the achievement—we are talking about celebration beyond a ribbon-cutting event; celebration at a more profound level in a way that provides grounding for survivors.

▶ *BEST PRACTICE*

One East Coast company completed a systems change after eight years of starts and stops. This was almost six years—and several restructurings—after management thought it would be done. Despite the lag time, this organization did remember to mark the achievement. The company held a closure event for all those who had been a part of the work, including those who were no longer employed. To provide closure, the MIS engineers who had managed the change signed off on the project, followed by everyone else.

At the risk of being trite, we remind readers that success breeds success—recognizing survivors for successfully completing a change and the accompanying transition greatly enhances the likelihood that they can successfully conclude future ones.

▶ **BEST PRACTICE**

Another company completed changes in mid-April, and, although the organization began working on a small project, it took the summer to evaluate the organization's change experience. At the end of the year, some eight months after the organizations's transition ended and as a part of the end-of-year "wrap up," management celebrated the completion. Like codification, celebration provides an historical marker.

Many of the survivors we interviewed told stories of their organizations having "kickoff" or ground-breaking ceremonies to launch a major change or start a new project. Few of them, however, could provide examples of their organization's having acknowledged or celebrated the successful completion of those same activities.

As one survivor recounted,

We had the press and local dignitaries out for the groundbreaking. Twenty-four months later when they opened the doors of the new building to the public, the company had an open house, and, yes, the press and dignitaries were on hand again. No one said anything, I'm sure, about the fact that half of the systems still weren't in place, and we were a skeleton staff because a good number of transferring employees hadn't arrived. It was a good four years before the operation was functioning as it was supposed to, but when that time finally arrived, it was somehow overshadowed by the next project. It was hard to get any, you know, sense of "Wow, we did it!" or even a "Thank God it's done," though it had been really tough at times.

This survivor's experience illustrates one barrier to the new organization's completing this task of celebration.

B/A/R/R/I/E/R
Losing Track

Because change and hence transition do not happen overnight or generally even within a few weeks or months, organizations can get so involved in daily operations that they do not always recognize when the end has come. They are not aware that they have arrived. As another survivor noted:

It seems like there is always some kind of change going on. If you're not actually implementing one, you're involved in planning the next one.

So organizations lose track of completion of the last change.

We are not proposing that organizations call a halt to future changes or plans until the last one is done; rather, we are suggesting that companies build in closure for employees as well as for the organization itself and, though the date for completion may not be known, that this task be at least recorded in the change management plan.

Remember the change management and transition monitoring teams? They function as well in the new organization. "Celebration" falls within the purview of their work. These are the ideal groups to take charge of monitoring the progress of changes and ultimately orchestrate the celebratory events.

DEVELOPMENT

In the old and interim organizations, development of survivors focused on meeting the demands of present productivity and future readiness dictated by the change. Consequently, development was driven primarily by the organization's needs. In the new organization, development is both a continuation of the activities of early phases and a shift in perspective.

Employee Development

Development in the new organization is more directly concerned with meeting employees' needs. If the organization has been successful in meeting goals and orchestrating the change, it is in a better position to turn its attention to these needs. Survivors, if successfully managing their transition, are more in control, less confused about what they want. For both the organization and employees, the new organization phase brings another moment of truth as survivors again evaluate current conditions and decide whether to stay or to leave. The result: Development becomes more employee-driven.

The organization continues to be responsible for creating a learning environment and for providing training, team building, and other skills-enhancing opportunities. Additionally, according to many of our interviewees, management has an ethical responsibility to employees. As Ozzie Hager, a human resources team leader, states,

> We can't guarantee you lifetime employment. What we are going to do for you is provide a continuous learning environment and resources, the tools for you to build your skill levels and manage your career development and employability. The organization has the responsibility to define and communicate the skills people are going to need in the future to grow and partner with the business.

Hager's statement serves as the basis of the new employment contract the organization needs to put in place.

Career Development

With rounds of downsizing becoming an organizational norm and with the acknowledged demise of the psychological contract and promises of lifetime employment, how can we propose career development as a task? Hasn't the concept itself become an anomaly?

Hager, for one, believes career development is viable and valuable as he has redefined it.

Director of Human Resource Development, Jean Wallace, agrees that career development is important, adding,

> You have to be able to show them [employees] that there are opportunities within this company and that the company recognizes their value.

We believe that career development as our interviewees describe it is an important tool in retaining survivors.

Downsizing and restructuring result in new challenges. For many organizations with flatter structures and the elimination of layers of management, there are fewer promotional opportunities. Indeed, some human resources executives no longer refer to career development as a ladder to be climbed but rather a lattice to be worked through.

Having fewer promotional opportunities does not mean elimination of the acquisition of new skills and competencies. Gaining new skills and competencies may be more vital than ever, as pointed out in the discussion of succession planning in chapter 7. But they may have to be acquired in new ways, through lateral moves.

A human resources executive in the Lee Hecht Harrison (1994) study stated, "We recognize we can't give people the same promotions and financial incentives we used to, but we can make their jobs more interesting and reward hard work with new opportunities and modest pay increases."

▶ **BEST PRACTICE**

One organization appeared to be doing all this with one FOD we interviewed. Management had selected this high performer for a cross-functional team charged with developing a plan for a new self-managed team structure.

Talking about his outside networking and interviewing forays and the subsequent offers he had received, this survivor couched each description with rejoinders:

But I really like what I'm doing right now. I'm excited about this project and the challenge we have.

His eyes flashed and his voice got louder. We could hear excitement and energy as he talked.

B/A/R/R/I/E/R
Letting Go

Patricia Fritts, Ph.D., an organizational consultant, identifies a potential barrier that may inhibit this FOD's experience from being replicated in other organizations. She also notes what companies need to do.

I think on the organizational side, what happens is the human resource systems, the career management systems, the reward systems or whatever have not been aligned with the rhetoric around free agentry and [taking] charge of your career. People hear, "I can go out and, if I can, find an opportunity in another division where I think I can make a real contribution."

That's easier said than done. Bosses aren't going to want to let them go—the chances are they're probably doing five people's work anyway now, and it's going to be hard for them to spot those opportunities.

So somehow with those high-performing types, we have to give them the tools they need to go through that—"How can I make a contribution, How can I take charge of my career?" But then if you do it, you figure out in the organization how you're going to make that happen.

What I've seen is the last part doesn't get done. They talk about it in career management, but then the opportunities aren't there. The system is still operating the old way.

LEADERSHIP IN THE NEW ORGANIZATION

Management is responsible for continuing the synergy generated in the interim organization, continuing to have responsibility for monitoring survivors' performance as well as their development. Indeed, managers need to be much more active in leading their direct reports. If survivors become the independent, empowered, self-managing employees that many organizations aspire to create, these "renaissance" survivors have little tolerance for what they perceive as passive leadership. Closed door, nonresponsive, reactive, absentee, or distant leadership does not pass muster and can actually maneuver the survivors who have come so far to move once again toward the door.

And this is only part of the leadership task in the new organization. Harkening back to what we wrote in the preface, we alerted readers that organizations would be faced with managing survivors not only of their own creation but survivor leavers from other organizations. So leaders have to actively manage this group of new employees as well. Assimilating these new employees requires the continued application of all the skills that leaders have to use in managing, motivating, and retaining their own survivors.

KEY POINTS

The new organization represents the organization that has attained its vision. This is the organization that has successfully regained its Three C's and is positioned for its next challenge.

GROUP ISSUES

FODs	FODs need to know the organization has a future. They want the new organization to include ongoing career development and job challenges. They are particularly frustrated if the organization loses its energy or reverts to a status quo posture.
W&Ss	W&Ss need to feel that the organization is also committed to their needs. They want a career plan that provides specific career options within the organization. They find the organization's failure to codify components off-putting.

RIOs

RIOs need new relationships as well as the skills to develop further connections. They want the organization to acknowledge the efforts of survivors in regaining their Three C's. They are most concerned if new employees entering the organization are not effectively assimilated into work groups.

STRATEGIES

Reassess and codify the components of the new organization; celebrate, acknowledge the successful attainment of the vision; and establish career development plans for employees.

REFERENCES

American Management Association (AMA). 1995. *AMA Survey: Corporate Downsizing, Job Elimination, and Job Creation (Summary of Key Findings)*. New York: American Management Association.

Bridges, W. 1988. *Surviving Corporate Transition*. Mill Valley, CA: William Bridges & Associates.

Bridges, W. 1991. *Managing Transitions*. Reading, MA: Addison-Wesley.

Bridges, W. 1994. *JobShift*. Reading, MA: Addison-Wesley.

DeMarco, T. 1996. Human Capital, Unmasked. *New York Times,* 14 April, F 13.

Handy, C. 1992. *The Age of Unreason*. Cambridge: Harvard Business School Press.

Hammer, M., and J. Champy. 1993. *Reengineering the Corporation*. New York: HarperCollins.

Jaffe, D. T., C. D. Scott, and G. R. Tobe. 1989. *Managing Change at Work*. San Francisco: Crisp Publications.

Kübler-Ross, E. 1969. *On Death and Dying*. New York: Macmillan.

Lee Hecht Harrison. 1994. *After the Downsizing: Getting Your Employees Back to Work*. New York: Lee Hecht Harrison.

Lewin, K. 1951. *Field Theory in Social Science*. New York: Harper & Row.

Lohr, S. 1994. For Big Blue, the Ones Who Got Away. *New York Times,* 9 January, G1.

Marbler, K. 1994. Change Management: Still a Scary Prospect. *CMA Magazine,* (February): 27.

Maslow, A. H. 1970. *Motivation and Personality*. New York: Harper & Row.

Noer, D. 1993. *Healing the Wounds*. San Francisco: Jossey-Bass.

Orioli, E. M. 1992. The Key to Controlling Your Stress Claim. Part two of a three-part series, Why Stress Programs Won't Work. *Personnel News,* (May): reprint.

Quint, M. 1995. Company's Buyout: Was It That Good? *New York Times,* 15 December, C 1.

Rice, D., and C. Dreilinger. 1991. After the Downsizing. *Training & Development* 45, no. 5 (May): 41–44.

Right Associates. 1992. *Lessons Learned: Dispelling the Myths of Downsizing*. 2nd ed. Philadelphia: Right Associates.

Tichy, N. M., and S. Sherman. 1993. *Control Your Destiny or Someone Else Will*. New York: Doubleday.

Tomasco, R. M. 1987. *Downsizing*. New York: American Management Association.

Uchitelle, L., and N. R. Kleinfeld; Kleinfeld, N. R.; Bragg, R.; Rimer, S.; Johnson, K.; Kolbett, E.; and A. Claymer; Sanger, D. C., and S. Loher. 1996. The Downsizing of America. Seven-part series. *New York Times,* 3–9 March, A1.

Work Week: Reich Redefines . . . 1996. *The Wall Street Journal,* 13 February, A1.

The Wyatt Company. 1991. *Restructuring—Cure or Cosmetic Surgery: Wyatt's 1991 Study on Corporate Restructuring*. Chicago: The Wyatt Company.

The Wyatt Company. 1993. *Best Practices in Corporate Restructuring: Wyatt's 1993 Survey of Corporate Restructuring*. Chicago: The Wyatt Company.

FURTHER READING

Adams, M. 1992. Helping the Survivors. *Successful Meetings* 41, no.3 (March): 48–49.

Baker, R. 1996. The Market God. *New York Times,* 23 March, Y 17.

Baker, W E. 1995. How to Survive Downsizing. *USA Today,* 23 March, 74–76.

Barnes, B. K. 1992. *The Mastery of Change: Thriving in Uncertain Times (Workshop workbook).* Berkeley, CA: Barnes and Conti Associates, Inc.

Boroson, W., and L. Burgess. 1992. Survivors' Syndrome. *Across the Board* 29, no. 11 (November): 41–45.

Bridges, W. 1992. *The Character of Organizations.* Palo Alto, CA: Davies-Black.

Brockner, J. 1992. Managing the Effects of Layoffs on Survivors. *California Management Review* (Winter): 9–28.

Cameron, K. S. 1994. Guest Editor's Note: Investigating Organizational Downsizing—Fundamental Issues. *Human Resources Management* 33, no. 2 (Summer): 183–188.

Cameron, K. S. 1994. Strategies for Successful Organizational Downsizing. *Human Resources Management* 33, no. 2 (Summer): 188–209.

Cascio, W. F. 1993. Downsizing: What Do We Know? What Have We Learned? *Academy of Management Executives* 7, no. 1: 95–104.

Challenger Employment Report. Challenger, Gray & Christmas, Inc. (Monthly).

Doe, P. J. 1994. Creating a Resilient Organization. *Canadian Business Review* 21, no. 2 (Summer): 22–25.

Downsizing and Its Discounts. 1996. *New York Times,* 10 March, E 14.

Dunlap, J. C. 1994. Surviving Layoffs: A Qualitative Study of Factors Affecting Retained Employees After Downsizing. *Performance Improvement Quarterly 7,* no. 4: 89–113.

Duran, S. 1993. *The Reality of Downsizing: What Are the Productivity Outcomes?* (Unpublished doctoral dissertation.) San Francisco: Golden Gate University.

Feldman, L. 1989 Duracell's First Aid for Downsizing Survivors. *Personnel Journal 68,* no. 8 (August): 94–94.

Feldman, D. C., and C. R. Leana. 1994. Better Practices in Managing Layoffs. *Human Resources Management 33,* no. 2 (Summer): 239–260.

Gault, S. 1992. Leaders of Corporate Change. *Fortune 126,* no. 13 (December): 104–114.

Grensing, L. 1993. Downsizing: How to do it Right. *Office Systems 10,* no. 5 (May): 62–65.

Gutknecht, J. E., and J. B. Keys. 1993. Mergers, Acquisitions and Takeovers: Maintaining Morale of Survivors and Protecting Employees. *Academy of Management Executive 4,* no. 3 (August): 26–35.

Huey, J. 1994. The New Post-Heroic Leadership. *Fortune* 129, no. 4 (February): 42–50.

Isabella, L. A. 1989. Downsizing: Survivors' Assessments. *Business Horizons* 32, no. 3 (May-June): 35–41.

Kendall, B., and M. Wheeler. 1994. Managing the Recovery. *Society of Insurance Trainers and Educators Journal* (Spring): 16–18.

Knowdell, R. L., E. Branstead, and M. Moravec. 1994. *From Downsizing to Recovery.* Palo Alto, CA: Davies-Black.

Kochanski, J., and P. M. Randall. 1994. Rearchitecting the Human Resources Function at Northern Telecom. *Human Resources Management* 33, no. 2 (Summer): 299–315.

Kouzes, J., and B. Posner. 1995. *Credibility.* San Francisco: Jossey-Bass.

Lee, C. 1992. After the Cuts. *Training* 32, no. 7 (July): 17–23.

Marks, M. L. 1992. *Managing the Merger.* New York: Prentice Hall.

Marks, M. L., and P. H. Mirvis. 1992. Rebuilding after the Merger: Dealing with "Survivor Sickness." *Organizational Dynamics 21,* no. 2: 18–32.

Mishra, A. K., and K. E. Mishra. 1994. The Role of Mutual Trust in Effective Downsizing Strategies. *Human Resources Management* 33, no. 2 (Summer): 261–279.

Mone, M. A. 1994. Relationships between Self-Concepts, Aspirations, Emotional Responses, and Intent to Leave a Downsizing Organization. *Human Resources Management* 33, no. 2 (Summer): 281–298.

Moskal, B. 1992. Managing Survivors. *Industry Week* 241, no. 15 (August): 14–22.

Myers, J. E. 1993. Downsizing Blues: How to Keep Up Morale. *Management Review* 82, no. 4 (April): 28–31.

Noble, B. P. 1995. The Bottom Line on People's Issues. *New York Times,* 19 February, F 23.

Ryan, G. R. 1989. Dealing with Survivors of a Reorganization. *Research Technology Management 32,* no. 2 (March-April): 30–42.

Samaha, H. E. 1993. Helping Survivors Stay on Track. *The Human Resources Professional* 5, no. 4 (Spring): 12–14.

Teese, M. 1995. *Impact of Management Reorganization Practices on Survivor Trust.* (Unpublished master thesis.) Belmont, CA: College of Notre Dame.

Uchitelle, L. 1996. A Top Economist Switches His View on Productivity. *New York Times,* 8 May, C 18.

Weinstein, H. P., and M. S. Leibman. 1991. Corporate Scale Down, What Comes Next? *HR Magazine* 36, no. 8 (August): 33–37.

Wilde, C. Downward Spiral. 1994. *Computerworld* 26, no. 22 (May): 81–86.

Zemke, R. 1990. The Ups and Downs of Downsizing. *Training* (November): 27–34.

ABOUT THE AUTHORS

Gayle Caplan, MSW, is a management consultant specializing in productivity, leadership, and change. She brings broad experience in the start-up of strategic business units and in change management. As Director of National Training for Consulting Psychologists Press, Caplan created a program of public and on-site workshops attended by more than 3,000 professionals. Previously, she was a chairperson and faculty member at Columbus State Community College, where she developed a nationally acclaimed curriculum for mental health professionals and received a Faculty Award of Merit.

Mary Teese, MA, consults extensively on work redesign, productivity enhancement, and performance management issues associated with change. She has presented hundreds of workshops for executives, managers, and line and staff employees. As Training Director for Fireman's Fund, Teese taught and coached management teams to develop productivity programs nationwide. She was one of the first female casualty field adjusters in the insurance industry. Teese is a Training Service Manager at California Casualty Management Company.

The authors began collaborating as management consultants in Caplan/Teese, a joint venture, in 1986. The firm's projects range from the design of a new operational system to the presentation of a training workshop or team building session. Clients include Pacific Gas & Electric Company, Internal Dispute Resolutions, Ltd., San Francisco International Airport, Yuskewich CPA Group, and Sun Microsystems.

The authors can be reached via fax (415) 788-7762 or by e-mail, gayle _caplan@bmug.org

INDEX